T0185099

Communications in Computer and Information Science 1389

More information about this series at http://www.springer.com/series/7899

Božo Bekavac · Kristina Kocijan ·
Max Silberztein · Krešimir Šojat (Eds.)

Formalising Natural Languages: Applications to Natural Language Processing and Digital Humanities

14th International Conference, NooJ 2020
Zagreb, Croatia, June 5–7, 2020
Revised Selected Papers

 Springer

Editors
Božo Bekavac
University of Zagreb
Zagreb, Croatia

Kristina Kocijan
University of Zagreb
Zagreb, Croatia

Max Silberztein ⓘ
Université de Franche-Comté
Besançon, France

Krešimir Šojat
University of Zagreb
Zagreb, Croatia

ISSN 1865-0929 ISSN 1865-0937 (electronic)
Communications in Computer and Information Science
ISBN 978-3-030-70628-9 ISBN 978-3-030-70629-6 (eBook)
https://doi.org/10.1007/978-3-030-70629-6

This Springer imprint is published by the registered company Springer Nature Switzerland AG
The registered company address is: Gewerbestrasse 11, 6330 Cham, Switzerland

Preface

NooJ is a linguistic development environment that provides tools for linguists to construct linguistic resources that formalize a wide range of linguistic phenomena: typography; orthography; lexicons of simple words, multiword units, and discontinuous expressions; inflectional, derivational, and agglutinative morphology; local, phrase-structure, and dependency grammars; as well as transformational and semantic grammars. For each linguistic phenomenon to be described, NooJ proposes a set of computational formalisms, the power of which ranges from very efficient finite-state automata (that process regular grammars) to very powerful Turing machines (that process unrestricted grammars). NooJ also contains a rich toolbox that allows linguists to construct, maintain, test, debug, accumulate, and share linguistic resources. This makes NooJ's approach different from most other computational linguistic tools that typically offer a unique formalism to their users and are not compatible with each other.

NooJ provides parsers that can apply any set of linguistic resources to any corpus of texts, to extract examples or counter-examples, annotate matching sequences, perform statistical analyses, and so on. Because NooJ's linguistic resources are neutral, they can also be used by NooJ to generate texts automatically. By combining NooJ's parsers and generators, one can construct sophisticated NLP (Natural Language Processing) applications.

Since its first release in 2002, several private companies have used NooJ's linguistic engine to construct business applications in several domains, from Business Intelligence to Opinion Analysis. To date, there are NooJ modules available for over 50 languages, and more than 140,000 copies of NooJ have been downloaded. In 2013, an open-source version of NooJ was released, based on the JAVA technology and available to all a GPL project and supporte and distributed by the European Metashare platform.

NooJ has recently been enhanced with new features to respond to the needs of researchers who analyze texts in various domains of Human and Social Sciences (history, literature and political studies, psychology, sociology, etc.), and more generally to those of all professionals who need to explore their own corpus of texts.

This volume contains 20 articles selected from the papers and posters presented at the International NooJ 2020 conference organized in Zagreb, Croatia. Because of the COVID pandemic, the conference was organized virtually as a video conference. However, this hindered neither the quality of the presentations nor the conference's success, as over 70 participants were able to attend and participate in the ten thematic sessions.

The following articles are organized into three parts: LINGUISTIC FORMALIZATION, containing eight articles; DIGITAL HUMANITIES AND TEACHING, containing six articles; and NATURAL LANGUAGE PROCESSING APPLICATIONS, containing six articles.

The articles in Part I involve the construction of electronic dictionaries and grammars to formalize various linguistic phenomena in several languages:

- In their article "A Morphological Grammar for Modern Greek: State of the Art, Evaluation and Upgrade," Lena Papadopoulou and Elina Chatjipapa show how they tested and updated the Greek NooJ module using six texts compiled from the resources available at the Centre for the Greek Language.
- In "The Lexical Complexity and Basic Vocabulary of the Italian Language,", Annibale Elia, Alessandro Maisto, Lorenza Melillo, and Serena Pelosi show how they designed and implemented the New Basic Vocabulary of the Italian Language (NVdB) dictionary, evaluate it by applying it to six classic texts of fiction for children aged between 8 and 10, and discuss how this type of text analysis can benefit language education.
- In "Formalizing the Latin Language on the Example of Medieval Latin Wills," Linda Mijić and Anita Bartulović describe a new NooJ set of linguistic resources created to formalize medieval Latin lexicon and morphology, and then test the description by processing a corpus of 337 wills written in the Zadar commune between 1209 and 1409.
- In "The Morphological Annotation of Reduplication–Circumfix Intersection in Indonesian," Prihantoro describes the phenomenon of Indonesian reduplication and proposes a set of NooJ morphological and syntactic grammars to handle the various types of reduplication.
- In "Multiword Expressions in the Medical Domain: Who Carries the Domain-Specific Meaning?," Kristina Kocijan, Krešimir Šojat, and Silvia Kurolt present a set of linguistic resources giving NooJ the capability of automatically detecting and annotating all multiword expressions in a Croatian medical corpus.
- In "Transformations and Paraphrases for Quechua Sentiment Predicates," Maximiliano Duran presents a set of grammars that represent sentiment predicates, a set of grammars that represent elementary transformations (e.g., passivation), and applies them with NooJ to perform an automatic paraphrase generation, as well as produce the translation of the corresponding predicates from French.
- In "Arabic Psychological Verb recognition through NooJ transformational grammars," Asmaa Amzali, Mohammed Mourchid, Abdelaaziz Mouloudi, and Samir Mbarki present a set of transformational grammars that recognizes sentences that contain a psychological verb, even when they are transformed (e.g., in passive, negative, or nominative form).
- Finally, in "Grammatical Modeling of a Nominal-Ellipsis Grammar for Spanish," Walter Koza and Hazel Barahona formalize two types of Spanish ellipsis (ellipsis of a noun phrase, and the ellipsis of its head) and proceed to implement a set of grammars that recognize ellipsis in sentences and produce an explicit (non-elliptic) paraphrase.

The articles in the second part, DIGITAL HUMANITIES AND TEACHING, show how NooJ linguistic resources can be implemented to help analyze corpora in various applications in the social sciences (gender studies, literature, and pedagogy):

- In "Where the Dickens are Melville's Phrasal Verbs?" Peter Machonis designs a set of linguistic resources to compare the corpus of the complete works of the nineteenth-century British author Charles Dickens (4 million words) and that of his American counterpart Herman Melville (1.3 million words) and shows that, contrary to common language, the extensive use of Phrasal Verbs was not a characteristic feature of early American English.
- In "Depictions of Women in 'Duga' and 'Tena': A Computational Analysis," Lorena Kasunić and Gordana Kiseljak analyze the depiction of women in two particular short stories written in Croatian: "Tena" by Josip Kozarac and "Duga" by Dinko Simunović. Their goal is to build a model with NooJ for the quantitative analysis of female characters, by using methods borrowed from both quantitative and qualitative approaches.
- In "The Use of Figurative Language in an Italian Dream-Description Corpus: Exploiting NooJ for Stylometric Purposes," Raffaele Manna, Antonio Pascucci, Maria Pia Di Buono, and Johanna Monti present research that exploits NooJ and its linguistic resources to identify metaphors, oxymorons, and similes in a corpus of Italian dream descriptions built by collecting dream descriptions from several blog users. They are then able to implement a set of NooJ linguistic resources that can be used to automatically recognize, extract, and tag these figures of speech.
- In "Paraphrasing Emotions in Portuguese," Diana Santos, Cristina Mota, and Anabela Barreiro show how they used the NooJ-based eSPERTo paraphrasing system in conjunction with five annotated parallel texts in European and Brazilian Portuguese to develop formalization strategies for analyzing the paraphrasing of emotions.
- In "Preparing the NooJ German Module for the Analysis of a Learner Spoken Corpus," Mirela Landsman Vinković and Kristina Kocijan describe a system capable of detecting and annotating errors found in the spoken discourse of Croatian learners of German as a foreign language, using a corpus of five different classroom interactions. The system is capable of evaluating students' competence based on various criteria encompassing general linguistics, vocabulary, vocabulary control, grammatical accuracy, coherence, and pragmatic appropriateness.
- In "Automatic Treatment of Causal, Consecutive, and Counterargumentative Discourse Connectors in Spanish: A Pedagogical Application of NooJ," Andrea Rodrigo, Silvia Reyes, and Maria Andrea Fernández Gallino present a pedagogical application capable of recognizing causal, consecutive, and counterargumentative discourse connectors in Spanish. This system is used to help students with enormous deficiencies by having them understand and manipulate dictionaries and grammars formalized with NooJ.

The third and final part, dedicated to the presentation of NATURAL LANGUAGE PROCESSING APPLICATIONS, contains the following articles:

- In "NooJ for Artificial Intelligence: An Anthropic Approach," Mario Monteleone describes the state of the art of the works in Artificial Intelligence as well as its challenges and deficiencies. He shows how NooJ local grammars can be used to enhance Question-Answering systems based on AI Fuzzy Logic.

- In "Answering Arabic complex questions," Sondes Dardour, Héla Fehri, and Kais Haddar present a system, constructed with NooJ, that is capable of answering why-questions in medical texts in Arabic, using both Natural Language Processing and Information Retrieval techniques.
- In "The Optimization of Portuguese Named-Entity Recognition and Classification by Combining Local Grammars and Conditional Random Fields Trained with a Parsed Corpus," Diego Alves, Božo Bekavac, and Marko Tadić present the results of a study concerning named-entity recognition and classification for Portuguese. They show how they were able to enhance the Conditional Random Fields (CRF) probabilistic method by adding to the system a NooJ local grammar that recognizes Time entities.
- In "The Automatic Recognition and Translation of Tunisian Dialect Named Entities into Modern Standard Arabic," Roua Torjmen and Kais Haddar have build a set of bilingual (Tunisian dialect/Standard Arabic) resources that can be added to an Arabic named-entity recognizer in order to automatically recognize named entities in texts written in the Tunisian dialect.
- In "A Legal-Question Answering Ontology-based System," Ismahane Kourtin, Samir Mbarki, and Abdelaaziz Mouloudi describe a new method of developing a question-answering system for legal texts in Morocco written in French, Arabic, and English. The system consists of three processes: building an ontology of the legal domain, extracting the RDF triplets from the user's question, and reformulating the question as a SPARQL query applied to the ontology, thus retrieving the appropriate answer.
- In "A Legal-Question Answering Ontology-based System," Ismahane Kourtin, Samir Mbarki, and Abdelaaziz Mouloudi describe a new method of developing a question-answering system for legal texts in Morocco written in French, Arabic, and English. The system consists of three processes: building an ontology of the legal domain, extracting the RDF triplets from the user's question, and reformulating the question as a SPARQL query applied to the ontology, thus retrieving the appropriate answer.
- In "A Bottom-Up Approach for Moroccan Legal Ontology Learning from Arabic Texts," Kaoutar Belhoucine, Mohammed Mourchid, Samir Mbarki, and Abdelaziz Mouloudi present a system capable of constructing a legal domain-specific ontology from unstructured texts and propose a bottom-up approach based on Natural Language Processing (NLP) techniques that includes three main tasks: corpus study, term acquisition, and conceptualization. The results, reviewed by a legal expert, constitute the ontology used by the Moroccan Legal Information Retrieval System (LIRS).

This volume should be of interest to all users of NooJ software because it presents the latest development of its linguistic resources, as well as a large variety of applications, both in the Digital Humanities and in Natural Language Processing software.

Linguists as well as Computational Linguists who work on Arabic, Croatian, English, German, Greek, Indonesian, Italian, Medieval Latin, Portuguese, Quechua, and Spanish will find advanced, up-to-the-minute linguistic studies for these languages.

We think that the reader will appreciate the importance of this volume, both for the intrinsic value of each linguistic formalization and for the underlying methodology, as well as for the potential for developing NLP applications along with linguistic-based corpus processors in the social sciences.

Božo Bekavac
Kristina Kocijan
Max Silberztein
Krešimir Sojat

Contents

Natural Language Processing Applications

Contributors

Diego Alves Faculty of Humanities and Social Sciences, University of Zagreb, Zagreb, Croatia

Asmaa Amzali MISC Laboratory, Faculty of Science, Ibn Tofail University, Kénitra, Morocco

Hazel Barahona Pontificia Universidad Católica de Valparaíso-Project FONDECyT, Valparaíso, Chile

Anabela Barreiro INESC-ID, Lisbon, Portugal; Linguateca, Aveiro, Portugal

Anita Bartulović Department of Classical Philology, University of Zadar, Zadar, Croatia

Božo Bekavac Faculty of Humanities and Social Sciences, University of Zagreb, Zagreb, Croatia

Kaoutar Belhoucine Faculty of Science, MISC Laboratory, Ibn Tofail University, Kénitra, Morocco

Elina Chadjipapa Democritus University of Thrace, Alexandroupolis, Greece

Sondes Dardour MIRACL Laboratory, University of Sfax, Sfax, Tunisia

Maria Pia di Buono UniOR NLP Research Group, "L' Orientale" University of Naples, Naples, Italy

Maximiliano Duran Université de Franche-Comté, Besançon, France; LIG, UGA, Grenoble, France

Annibale Elia University of Salerno, Fisciano, SA, Italy

Héla Fehri MIRACL Laboratory, University of Sfax, Sfax, Tunisia

María Andrea Fernández Gallino Facultad Regional Rosario, Universidad Tecnológica Nacional, Rosario, Argentina

Kais Haddar Faculty of Sciences of Sfax, Miracl Laboratory, University of Sfax, Sfax, Tunisia

Lorena Kasunić Faculty of Humanities and Social Sciences Zagreb, University of Zagreb, Zagreb, Croatia

Gordana Kiseljak Faculty of Humanities and Social Sciences Zagreb, University of Zagreb, Zagreb, Croatia

Kristina Kocijan Department of Information and Communication Sciences, Faculty of Humanities and Social Sciences, University of Zagreb, Zagreb, Croatia

Ismahane Kourtin ELLIADD Laboratory, Bourgogne-Franche-Comté University, Besançon, France; MISC Laboratory, Faculty of Science, Ibn Tofail University, Kenitra, Morocco

Walter Koza Pontificia Universidad Católica de Valparaíso-Project FONDECyT, Valparaíso, Chile

Silvia Kurolt Department of Information and Communication Sciences, Faculty of Humanities and Social Sciences, University of Zagreb, Zagreb, Croatia

Mirela Landsman Vinković Department of German Language and Literature, Faculty of Humanities and Social Sciences, University of Zagreb, Zagreb, Croatia

Peter A. Machonis Florida International University, Miami, USA

Alessandro Maisto University of Salerno, Fisciano, SA, Italy

Raffaele Manna UniOR NLP Research Group, "L' Orientale" University of Naples, Naples, Italy

Samir Mbarki Faculty of Science, MISC Laboratory, Ibn Tofail University, Kénitra, Morocco

Lorenza Melillo University of Salerno, Fisciano, SA, Italy

Linda Mijić Department of Classical Philology, University of Zadar, Zadar, Croatia

Mario Monteleone Dipartimento di Scienze Politiche e della Comunicazione, Università degli Studi di Salerno, Fisciano, Italy

Johanna Monti UniOR NLP Research Group, "L' Orientale" University of Naples, Naples, Italy

Cristina Mota INESC-ID, Lisbon, Portugal; Linguateca, Aveiro, Portugal

Abdelaaziz Mouloudi Faculty of Science, MISC Laboratory, Ibn Tofail University, Kénitra, Morocco

Mohammed Mourchid Faculty of Science, MISC Laboratory, Ibn Tofail University, Kénitra, Morocco

Lena Papadopoulou Hellenic Open University, Patra, Greece

Antonio Pascucci UniOR NLP Research Group, "L' Orientale" University of Naples, Naples, Italy

Serena Pelosi University of Salerno, Fisciano, SA, Italy

Prihantoro Lancaster University, Lancaster, UK; Universitas Diponegoro, Semarang, Indonesia

Silvia Reyes Facultad de Humanidades y Artes, Universidad Nacional de Rosario, Rosario, Argentina

Andrea Rodrigo Facultad de Humanidades y Artes, Universidad Nacional de Rosario, Rosario, Argentina

Marko Tadić Faculty of Humanities and Social Sciences, University of Zagreb, Zagreb, Croatia

Roua Torjmen Faculty of Economic Sciences and Management of Sfax, Miracl Laboratory, University of Sfax, Sfax, Tunisia

Diana Santos ILOS-UiO, Oslo, Norway; Linguateca, Aveiro, Portugal

Krešimir Šojat Department of Linguistics, Faculty of Humanities and Social Sciences, University of Zagreb, Zagreb, Croatia

Linguistic Formalization

A Morphological Grammar for Modern Greek: State of the Art, Evaluation and Upgrade

Lena Papadopoulou[1](✉) and Elina Chadjipapa[2](✉)

[1] Hellenic Open University, Patra, Greece
papadopoulou.lena@gmail.com
[2] Democritus University of Thrace, Alexandroupolis, Greece
elinaxp@hotmail.com

Abstract. The objective of this paper is six-fold. First, a brief review of the state of the art of the Greek NooJ Module is outlined, in which the need for specific primary lexicographical resources is pointed out. Second, a corpus compilation using the entire text databank of the Centre for the Greek Language is described. Third, a dictionary of simple nouns and an integrated inflectional grammar, which are the outcome of the linguistic analysis of the new Greek NooJ corpus, are presented, with an emphasis on the full alignment of the latter with the inflectional codification of the Dictionary of Standard Modern Greek. Fourth, the compilation of a manual comprising guidelines for inflectional grammar editors is presented. Fifth, the validity of the aforementioned work has been tested through the processing of unknown word forms from the corpus. Sixth, future work is proposed in terms of the educational employment of the Greek NooJ Module and its implementation.

Keywords: Modern Greek · Corpus · Inflection · Lexicography · Simple nouns

1 Introduction

The first steps of the Modern Greek NooJ Module were made in 2007 [1] with the compilation of a dictionary of simple words and a corresponding inflectional grammar, which constituted the basis of the present work. Since then, lexicographical data as well as morphological and syntactic grammars have been imported in order to improve the results of Greek language automatic processing.

Among others, local grammars for the automatic recognition of proper nouns have been compiled [2]. A Greek-Spanish NooJ module has been created [3], where the equivalence between these two languages is studied for educational purposes. Enriched versions of the Greek NooJ module have been developed, such as in the case of the lexicographical elaboration of simple and multiword adverbs, acronyms, and borrowed words written using the Latin alphabet [4]; in addition, formalized methods have been proposed for data enrichment, such as for adjectives [5]. Lexicographical data compilation has been conducted on specific classes of objects, such as professional nouns [6] and <material> predicative adjectives [7]. The compounding and derivation of specific categories – such as neoclassical compounds [8], numeral-noun/adjective construction

© Springer Nature Switzerland AG 2021
B. Bekavac et al. (Eds.): NooJ 2020, CCIS 1389, pp. 3–13, 2021.
https://doi.org/10.1007/978-3-030-70629-6_1

[9], and the derivation of multiply complex negative adjectives from verbal stems [10] – have been studied. Furthermore, phraseological units, such as frozen expressions [11] and pragmatemes [12], have been processed.

Although, so far, rich lexicographical data have been produced and a series of linguistic phenomena have been studied, the accomplished work has mainly been based on secondary lexicographical resources. As a consequence, a dedicated corpus was required: a corpus that would meet the quality requirements of our project, a corpus that would comprise representative authentic texts and would be easy to handle as far as size and representativity are concerned. Such requirements seemed to be fulfilled by the text databank of the Centre for the Greek Language.

Therefore, in the present work, first, both primary and secondary lexicographical resources are defined. Afterwards, the procedure that has been followed for the retrieval and processing of simple nouns, as far as their dictionary compilation and inflectional properties attribution are concerned, is described. In addition, the manual for inflectional grammar editing is outlined. Finally, the results of our work plans for future work are presented.

2 Lexicographical Resources

The lexicographical resources that have been defined for our project are primary and secondary. On one hand, the entire text databank of the Centre for the Greek Language was designated as the primary lexicographical resource. On the other hand, a series of previous Greek NooJ data and the Dictionary of Standard Modern Greek [13] were chosen as secondary lexicographical resources.

2.1 Primary Lexicographical Resources

The entire text databank of the Centre for the Greek Language has served as the primary lexicographical resource for our corpus compilation. This choice was dictated by the quality requirements that our project set for itself, and it can be justified based on four main criteria: (a) resource reliability, (b) material purposes, (c) text representability, and (d) corpus size.

First, as far as the resources are concerned, they have been retrieved as educational material for the teaching of Modern Greek as a foreign/second language by the Support and Promotion of the Greek Language research division of the Centre for the Greek Language [14]. The Centre for the Greek Language[1] acts as a cooperating, advisory and planning body of the Ministry of Education on matters of language policy. It is an academic institution dedicated to the description and documentation of trends in the Modern Greek language, and therefore, it follows strictly scholarly methods. Consequently, the text databank is considered reliable with respect to its methods of text compilation.

Second, the text databank in use has been compiled for educational purposes, such as to assist students who take an exam for the Certification of Attainment in Greek. Thus, it is in accordance with the aims of the Greek NooJ module, given that the main

---

[1] https://greeklanguage.gr/en/.

perspective of the latter is to use the NooJ environment as a tool for Greek language learning and teaching.

Third, the text databank is a compilation of originally written and spoken texts from a wide range of sources including different genres and text types. Consequently, the representability criterion is completely fulfilled. This is considered a feature of great importance in view of the beneficial impact of students' exposure to diverse authentic texts [14].

Fourth, the text databank of the Centre for the Greek Language fulfills the size criterion, given that it is feasible to deal with total data volume, considering the above-mentioned qualitative features.

In total, the corpus includes six (6) text files, one for each level according to the Common European Framework of Reference for Languages: Learning, Teaching, Assessment (CEFR) [15], comprising a total of 336 text units and 117,892 word forms (Fig. 1):

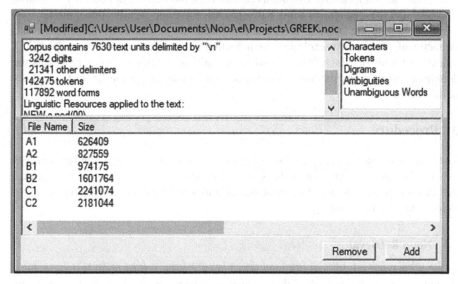

Fig. 1. The GREEK.noc corpus

Table 1 presents thorough information regarding corpus structure, providing information about the number of texts and word forms that each text file comprises.

2.2 Secondary Lexicographical Resources

A series of previous Greek NooJ data, as well as the Dictionary of Standard Modern Greek [13] (hereinafter DSMG), are defined as secondary lexicographical resources for our project.

The DSMG is a monolingual comprehensive definitional, orthographic, and etymological dictionary of Modern Greek published by the Institute of Modern Greek Studies at the Artistotle University of Thessaloniki in both paper and digitalized format. The

Table 1. Corpus data

CEFR level	Number of texts	Number of word forms
A1	78	9,059
A2	77	11,273
B1	45	12,229
B2	45	21,828
C1	49	32,494
C2	42	31,009
TOTAL	336	117,892

DSMG has been selected for two main reasons: (a) it provides an opportunity for online research[2] and (b) it annotates a link between each entry and its inflectional model.

In addition to the DSMG, the Greek NooJ dictionary, from which all semantic and syntactic information was excluded; the inflectional grammar, comprising a total of 757 inflectional rules of which 266 refer to nouns; and the grammar, which processes the double accent in proparoxytones, were applied as resources for the linguistic analysis of the corpus.

3 Procedure

The procedure that has been followed consists of two major stages. The first consists of the retrieval of nouns, while the second consists of the parallel compilation of a dictionary of nouns and an inflectional grammar as well as the redaction of a manual for inflectional grammar editing.

3.1 Noun Retrieval

In the noun retrieval process, through which a validation test of noun lexicographical data was carried out in parallel, three major steps were involved: (a) corpus linguistic analysis within NooJ, (b) noun extraction, and (c) database compilation.

Within the first step, the Greek NooJ dictionary (GLE), the inflectional grammar, and the grammar that processes the double accent in proparoxytones were applied as resources for the linguistic analysis of the corpus (Fig. 2).

The results that the linguistic analysis produced are considered quite satisfactory. They conclude that there were only 2,660 unknowns, that is, out of the total number of 117,892 word forms encountered in the corpus, 2.25% were unknown.

In the second step, nouns were extracted in a semiautomatic way with the aid of ambiguities and unambiguous word annotations. Once we got the output of the annotations of the ambiguous and unambiguous words, the information regarding the lemma, the grammatical category, and the corresponding inflectional paradigm was filtered out.

---

[2] At   https://www.greek-language.gr/greekLang/modern_greek/tools/lexica/triantafyllides/search.html?lq=.

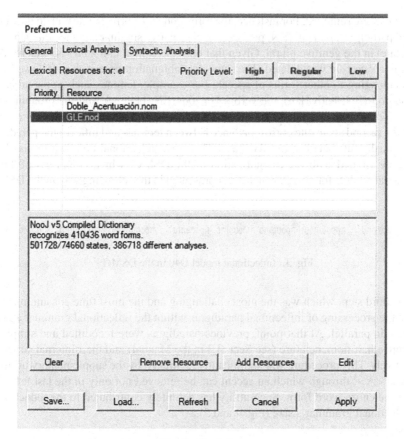

Fig. 2. NooJ data

Subsequently, 3,464 lemmas were annotated as nouns along with their corresponding inflectional property codification. These lemmas consisted of the base on which the manual validation process was grounded.

3.2 Nouns Dictionary and Inflectional Grammar Processing

Once the database was set up, a four-step procedure was followed, comprising (a) the exclusion of word forms, (b) the correspondence of inflectional codes, (c) the simplification of inflectional rules, and (d) the elimination of non-active paradigms.

Firstly, a series of word forms was excluded. On one hand, these word forms included nominal word forms located exclusively within multiword units. This elimination is due to our particular focus on simple nouns. Within this framework, for example, the nomineme[3] *Αγία Σοφία* (EN: Hagia Sophia) was deleted. On the other hand, ambiguous word forms regarding lexical units and part-of-speech properties that are not used in

---

[3] See Mel'čuk [16] for more information on lexical phraseme classification.

the corpus were removed. For instance, the form $\kappa\rho\alpha\tau\acute{\omega}\nu$ corresponds both to the nominalized participle $\kappa\rho\alpha\tau\acute{\omega}\nu$ (EN: prisoner) in nominative singular and the noun $\kappa\rho\acute{\alpha}\tau o\varsigma$ (EN: state) in the genitive plural. Given that only the lexical unit $\kappa\rho\acute{\alpha}\tau o\varsigma$ was located, the lemma $\kappa\rho\alpha\tau\acute{\omega}\nu$ was deleted. The same disambiguation process was followed with forms belonging to other forms of speech. For example, lemmas such as the adjective $\beta\acute{\alpha}\rho\beta\alpha\rho o\varsigma$ (EN: barbarian), the verb $\pi\iota\sigma\tau\epsilon\acute{\upsilon}\omega$ (EN: believe), and the pronoun $\epsilon\gamma\acute{\omega}$ (EN: I) were eliminated given that their form belongs to a non-noun form in our corpus.

In the second stage, the correspondence between lemmas and inflectional paradigms was manually attributed in our database. This way, inflectional codification has been absolutely aligned with the categorization of the DSMG, which comprises 68 broad inflectional models for nouns, which are represented in the following way in the DSMG:

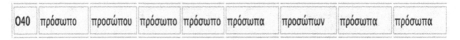

| 040 | πρόσωπο | προσώπου | πρόσωπο | πρόσωπο | πρόσωπα | προσώπων | πρόσωπα | πρόσωπα |

Fig. 3. Inflectional model O40 in the DSMG

The third step, which was the most challenging and the most time consuming, concerned the processing of inflectional paradigms within the inflectional grammar and the database in parallel. At that point, previous paradigms were recodified and simplified as regards their nomenclature (see Sect. 3.3 in the Manual) and their internal structure, respectively. This procedure was significantly facilitated by the supplementary utility of operator <A>, through which an accent can be removed not only in the last letter but also in the entire word form. Such utility has definitely contributed to the reduction of the inflectional grammar's size (Fig. 4 and 5).

```
#φύλακας#
N5 = <E>/nom+m+s + <B>/gen+m+s + <B>/acc+m+s + <B>/voc+m+s +
       <B2>ες/nom+m+p + <L5><A><R2><Á><RW><B2>ων/gen+m+p + <B2>ες/acc+m+p + <B2>ες/voc+m+p;
#μεσαίωνας#
N5_a = <E>/nom+m+s + <B>/gen+m+s + <B>/acc+m+s + <B>/voc+m+s +
       <B2>ες/nom+m+p + <L4><A><R><Á><RW><B2>ων/gen+m+p + <B2>ες/acc+m+p + <B2>ες/voc+m+p;
#ήρωας#
N5_b = <E>/nom+m+s + <B>/gen+m+s + <B>/acc+m+s + <B>/voc+m+s +
       <B2>ες/nom+m+p + <L4><A><R2><Á><RW><B2>ων/gen+m+p + <B2>ες/acc+m+p + <B2>ες/voc+m+p;
#Ελληνας#
N5_c = <E>/nom+m+s + <B>/gen+m+s + <B>/acc+m+s + <B>/voc+m+s +
       <B2>ες/nom+m+p + <L6><A><R3><Á><RW><B2>ων/gen+m+p + <B2>ες/acc+m+p + <B2>ες/voc+m+p;
#ελέφαντας#
N5_d = <E>/nom+m+s + <B>/gen+m+s + <B>/acc+m+s + <B>/voc+m+s +
       <B2>ες/nom+m+p + <L6><A><R2><Á><RW><B2>ων/gen+m+p + <B2>ες/acc+m+p + <B2>ες/voc+m+p;
#υδατάνθρακας#
N5_e = <E>/nom+m+s + <B>/gen+m+s + <B>/acc+m+s + <B>/voc+m+s +
       <B2>ες/nom+m+p + <L7><A><R4><Á><RW><B2>ων/gen+m+p + <B2>ες/acc+m+p + <B2>ες/voc+m+p;
```

Fig. 4. Operator <A> removing an accent in the last letter in paradigm N5

#φύλακας#
N5 = <E>/nom+m+s + <B>/gen+m+s + <B>/acc+m+s + <B>/voc+m+s +
    <B2>ες/nom+m+p + <B2><A>ων<L2><Á>/gen+m+p + <B2>ες/acc+m+p + <B2>ες/voc+m+p;
#ελέφαντας#
N5a = <E>/nom+m+s + <L2><B3>/nom+m+s + <B>/gen+m+s + <B4>/gen+m+s + <B>/acc+m+s
+ <B4>/acc+m+s + <B>/voc+m+s + <B4>/voc+m+s +
    <B2>ες/nom+m+p + <B2><A>ων<L2><Á>/gen+m+p + <B2>ες/acc+m+p + <B2>ες/voc+m+p;

Fig. 5. Operator <A> removing an accent from an entire word form in paradigm N5

Given that Greek is a heavily inflected language – for example, the inflection of nouns includes four cases (nominative, genitive, accusative, and vocative) and two numbers (singular and plural) within the declension many times the accent is being both removed and moved and there are nouns that have double inflectional forms – high precision is required in inflectional rule editing. Such precision results in the generation of more inflectional paradigms than the DSMG provides. Consequently, the proportion between the DSMG's inflectional paradigms and ours is in total 68 to 122, almost 1 to 2. For example, the inflectional model O40 in the DSMG corresponds to 6 different inflectional paradigms in the NooJ inflectional grammar (Fig. 3 and 6).

#πρόσωπο#
N40 = <E>/nom+n+s + <A><L2><Á><RW>u/gen+n+s + <E>/acc+n+s + <E>/voc+n+s +
    <B>α/nom+n+p + <A><L2><Á><RW><B>ων/gen+n+p + <B>α/acc+n+p + <B>α/voc+n+p;
#γυμναστήριο#
N40_a = <E>/nom+n+s + <A><L><Á><RW>u/gen+n+s + <E>/acc+n+s + <E>/voc+n+s +
    <B>α/nom+n+p + <A><L><Á><RW><B>ων/gen+n+p + <B>α/acc+n+p + <B>α/voc+n+p;
#ένοτικτο#
N40_b = <E>/nom+n+s + <A><L3><Á><RW>u/gen+n+s + <E>/acc+n+s + <E>/voc+n+s +
    <B>α/nom+n+p + <A><L3><Á><RW><B>ων/gen+n+p + <B>α/acc+n+p + <B>α/voc+n+p;
#περίχωρα#
N40-s = <E>/nom+n+p + <A><L2><Á><RW><B>ων/gen+n+p + <E>/acc+n+p + <E>/voc+n+p;
#Χριστούγεννα#
N40-s_a = <E>/nom+n+p + <A><L3><Á><RW><B>ων/gen+n+p + <E>/acc+n+p + <E>/voc+n+p;
#γενέθλια#
N40-s_b = <E>/nom+n+p + <A><L><Á><RW><B>ων/gen+n+p + <E>/acc+n+p + <E>/voc+n+p;

Fig. 6. Paradigm N40 in the NooJ inflectional grammar

Finally, the fourth step consisted of deleting non-active paradigms, given that they are not related to any lemma of the noun dictionary in use (Table 2).

Table 2. Structure of inflectional grammar

Type	Number of paradigms	Codes in grammar
Masculine	34	*N1-N22*
Feminine	30	*N23-37*
Neutral	42	*N38-N53-s*
Non-inflected	3	*N_INDECm- N_INDECn*
Irregular nouns	3	*NIRRn1-NIRRn3*
Nominalized adjectives	9	*NA1m-NA17f*
Nominalized past perfect participles	1	*NPARPPmm*

In conclusion, a dynamic morphological grammar for simple nouns based both on primary and secondary lexicographic resources has been completed. Such a dynamic applies both to the Greek inflectional grammar as well as to the Greek NooJ dictionary, given that the introduction of new lemmas and their inflectional paradigms correspondence have been performed smoothly in the case of the 1,101 word forms of 947 new nouns.

3.3 Manual

Our aim to align the codification of paradigms with those of DSMG seemed doomed to failure in case of lemmas that either the DSMG does not comprise at all, such as proper names and gentilics, or does not provide them with an inflectional paradigm, such as nominalized words. Such a failure has been avoided by the development of a redaction manual. The manual aims to serve as a guideline for the inflectional grammar compilation for present and future versions by old and new users.

On one hand, useful information about the nomenclature of paradigm is provided. The first number of each paradigm name corresponds to DSMG codification. Meanwhile, information following an underscore (_) refers to accentuation variants and inflectional particularities, while information introduced by a hyphen (-) indicates the exclusion of grammatical categories (Table 3).

For example, the code NA5n-s indicates that the paradigm refers to a nominalized noun (N) which is inflected via adjective inflectional model "1" (A1) according to the DSMG and it does not have any singular forms (-s).

On the other hand, a series of conventions has been created in order to formalize lemmas that are not included in the DSMG. Such standardization has been followed mainly for proper nouns and gentilics that the DSMG generally does not include. For example, the codes N25a and N35 are proposed for feminine proper names ending in -ία and -ος, respectively.

Table 3. Indicators in paradigm nomenclature

Indicator	
_a, b, c…	*subclass of paradigm because of accent movement*
-	*exclusion*
A1, 2, 3…	*adjective inflectional model*
ac	*accent*
f	*feminine*
g	*genitive*
INDEC	*non-inflected*
irr	*including an irregular form*
IRR	*irregular inflection overall*
m	*masculine*
n	*neutral*
p	*plural*
PARPP	*past perfect participle*
s	*singular*

4   Results

Once the dictionary and the inflectional grammar of simple nouns were compiled, we proceeded to the processing of unknown forms, which were extracted from the database.

Due to the high number of typographical errors, which concerned mainly the interference of similar Latin characters (Fig. 6) in Greek words, a new file was introduced in order for linguistic analysis results to be optimized. This file has in view the aforementioned interference, by providing the Greek-Latin correspondence of similar characters, so that such word forms will henceforth be recognized, thus reducing the total number of unknown word forms (Fig. 7).

The database of the unknowns comprised 2,660 word forms in total, which were manually analyzed. The total number of noun word forms amounts to 1,101, which corresponds to 947 entries. It has to be pointed out that only simple nouns have been considered, while noun word forms that appear solely in multiword units were excluded.

Through this process our main aim, which is the aim of a dynamic morphological grammar for simple nouns based both on primary and secondary lexicographic resources, has been achieved. Such a dynamic applies both to the Greek inflectional grammar as well as to the Greek NooJ dictionary. The introduction of new lemmas and their corresponding inflectional paradigms has been performed in a systematic and lower time-consuming way.

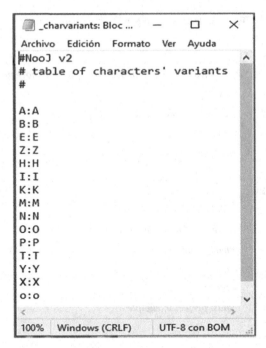

Fig. 7. Variants: Greek - Latin characters

5 Future Work

Within the present work a series of resources has been developed: (a) the compilation of a corpus for educational purposes, (b) a dictionary of simple nouns based on corpus resources, (c) an integrated inflectional grammar for simple nouns, and (d) a manual for inflectional grammar editing.

Undoubtedly, the present work will be the engine for future work on the educational purposes of the Greek NooJ Module. In view of its implementation, the linguistic analysis of the corpus has to be improved. First, the same procedure has to be followed for all parts of speech and for multiword units. This will smoothen the way to proceeding to the syntactic and semantic processing of our corpus in order to reach our ultimate aim: for each lemma of our dictionary to correspond to a lexical unit. Subsequently, lexical richness and core vocabulary could be studied in the future.

References

1. Gavriilidou, Z., Chadjipapa, E., Papadopoulou, E., Giannakopoulou, A.: The New Greek NooJ Module: morphosemantic issues. In: Blanco, X., Silberztein, M. (eds.) Proceedings of the 2007 NooJ International Conference, pp. 96–103. Cambridge Scholars Publishing, Cambridge (2008)

2. Gavriilidou, Z., Papadopoulou, E., Chadjipapa, E.: New data in the Greek NooJ module: a local grammar of proper nouns. In: Silberztein, M., Varadi, T. (eds.) Proceedings of the 2008 International Conference (Budapest), pp. 93–100. Cambridge Scholars Publishing, Cambridge (2010)

3. Papadopoulou, E., Gavriilidou, Z.: Towards a Greek-Spanish NooJ module. In: Hamadou, A., Mesfar, S., Silberztein, M. (eds.) Finite State Language Engineering: NooJ 2009 International Conference and Workshop (Touzeur), pp. 301–315. Centre de Publication Universitaire (2010)

4. Papadopoulou, E., Chadjipapa, E.: Version 4 Greek NooJ Module: adverbs, acronyms and words with Latin characters. In: Gavriilidou, Z., Chadjipapa, E., Papadopoulou, L., Silberztein, M. (eds.) Proceedings of the NooJ 2010 International Conference and Workshop, pp. 95–101. Komotini (2011)

5. Papadopoulou, E., Anagnostopoulos, G.: Enrichment of the Greek NooJ module: morphological properties and translation equivalence of Greek adjectives. In: Silberztein, M., Donabédian, A., Khurshudian, V. (eds.) Formalising Natural Languages with NooJ, pp. 182–193. Cambridge Scholars Publishing (2013)

6. Chadjipapa, E., Papadopoulou, L.: Greek professional nouns processed with NooJ. In: Gavriilidou, Z., Chatzipapa, E., Papadopoulou, L., Silberztein, M. (eds.) Proceedings of the NooJ 2010 International Conference and Workshop, pp. 183–191. Komotini (2011)

7. Gavriilidou, Z., Papadopoulou, L., Chadjipapa, E.: <material> predicative adjectives in Greek NooJ module. In: Monti, J., Silberztein, M., Monteleone, M., Pia di Buono, M. (eds.) Formalising Natural Languages with NooJ 2014, pp. 49–54. Cambridge Scholars Publishing (2015)

8. Gavriilidou, Z., Papadopoulou, L.: Greek neoclassical compounds and their automatic treatment with NooJ. In: Gavriilidou, Z., Chadjipapa, E., Papadopoulou, L., Silberztein, M. (eds.) Proceedings of the NooJ 2010 International Conference and Workshop, pp. 73–83. Komotini (2011)

9. Gavriilidou, Z., Papadopoulou, L., Chadjipapa, E.: Numeral-noun and numeral-adjective construction in Greek. In: Silberztein, M., Donabédian, A., Khurshudian, V. (eds.) Formalising Natural Languages with NooJ, pp. 113–122. Cambridge Scholars Publishing (2013)

10. Gavriilidou, Z., Papadopoulou, L.: Derivation of multiply complex negative adjectives from verbal stems in Greek. In: Koeva, S., Mesfar, S., Silberztein, M. (eds.) Formalising Natural Languages with NooJ 2013: Selected papers from the NooJ 2013 International Conference, pp. 63–68. Cambridge Scholars Publishing (2014)

11. Gavriilidou, Z., Papadopoulou, E., Chadjipapa, E.: Processing Greek frozen expressions with NooJ. In: Vučković, K., Bekavac, B., Silberztein, M. (eds.) Automatic Processing of Various Levels of Linguistic Phenomena: Selected Papers from the NooJ 2011 International Conference (Dubrovnik), pp. 63–74. Cambridge Scholars Publishing (2012)

12. Papadopoulou, L.: Local grammars for pragmatemes in NooJ. In: Monti, J., Silberztein, M., Monteleone, M., Pia di Buono, M. (eds.) Formalising Natural Languages with NooJ 2014, pp. 122–128. Cambridge Scholars Publishing (2015)

13. Dictionary of Standard Modern Greek (1998). https://www.greek-language.gr/greekLang/modern_greek/tools/lexica/triantafyllides/index.html. Accessed Sept 2020

14. Κέντρο Ελληνικής Γλώσσας (n.d.). https://www.greek-language.gr/certification/dbs/teachers/index.html. Accessed May 2020

15. Council of Europe (2001). Common European Framework of Reference for Languages: Learning, Teaching, Assessment. https://rm.coe.int/1680459f97. Accessed May 2020

16. Mel'čuk, I.: Clichés, an understudied subclass of phrasemes. In: Buhofer, A. (ed.) Yearbook of Phraseology, pp. 55–86. De Gruyter, Berlin (2015)

The Lexical Complexity and Basic Vocabulary of the Italian Language

Annibale Elia, Alessandro Maisto, Lorenza Melillo[✉], and Serena Pelosi

University of Salerno, Fisciano, SA, Italy
{elia,amaisto,lmelillo,spelosi}@unisa.it

Abstract. The comprehensibility of a text depends mainly on two factors: the lexicon and the syntax. Thanks also to computational tools, we present here a research study that aims to assess the level of comprehensibility of the lexicon of the texts used for the linguistic education of primary school children. In the study presented in this paper, we formalized the New Basic Vocabulary (NVdB) [6] by including it within the Italian for NooJ [15]. An experiment was carried out on a collection of texts of approximately 312,000 tokens. It is composed of classic and contemporary narratives for children, aged between 8 and 10, attending the last three years of primary school. In our research we will present the preliminary results of the analysis, which will show the text classification according to their level of lexical complexity. This type of textual analysis finds several fields of application in language education studies.

Keywords: Lexicon complexity · Basic vocabulary · Vocabulary range

1 Introduction

In this study, we exploited the NooJ software in order to analyze unstructured texts from a lexical perspective. The paper will describe in detail the electronic dictionaries and local grammars that have been formalized in order to automatically deduce details about the comprehensibility of texts, starting with the vocabulary ranges of the words with which they are composed.

From a linguistic point of view, the evaluation of the comprehensibility of a text obviously needs to go through both lexical and syntactical analysis. Here, focusing on the lexical features of texts, we will present the preliminary results of an ongoing study, that we aim in the future to combine with syntactic investigation, as well.

We aim to automatically observe the level of knowledge of the language, intended as the number of words whose meaning is known and used, as a core parameter in the prediction of the comprehensibility of a text.

The experiment that has been carried out is related to a broader research framework concerning the understanding of narrative texts by children between 8 and 10 years of age.

In this respect, we refer to literature studies on the acquisition of lexicon, such as [9], among others, which claims that students' spontaneous lexicon acquisition cannot

B. Bekavac et al. (Eds.): NooJ 2020, CCIS 1389, pp. 14–23, 2021.
https://doi.org/10.1007/978-3-030-70629-6_2

be satisfactory for schools, since a large part of the basic vocabulary and the meanings of many frequent words remain unknown.

For all these reasons, it is essential, in the first years of primary school, to pay particular attention to the meanings of those terms that are new to children. In the process of lexicon acquisition, there are three main dimensions that must be taken into account: *scope*, which refers to the consistency of the lexical patrimony; *depth*, which is the knowledge connected with each word and, in the end, and *automaticity*, which concerns the inclusion of the word in the long-term memory [13].

De Mauro [5], who carried out the first lexicographic research on the identification of Italian lexical subsets based on usage frequency, developed a vocabulary of 7,500 words which are comprehensible to a large audience, even with low levels of education. The so-called NVdB (*Nuovo Vocabolario di Base*, New Basic Vocabulary) is divided into words from the basic vocabulary (FO: 2000), high-use vocabulary (AU: 3000), and high-availability vocabulary (AD: 2500). The NVdB marks each word with abbreviations of the different levels.

The relationship between the lexicon of a text and the words listed in the three classes of the NVdB can be used to assess the level of textual complexity in relation to the expected children's knowledge. For example, the high frequency in the examined text of words of the fundamental vocabulary can be considered a high index of comprehensibility, while the low frequency of the same typology of words should highlight a low index of comprehensibility.

The texts on which our hypothesis has been tested are *The Little Prince*, by of Antoine de Saint-Exupéry [8]; *Marcovaldo: The Seasons in the City*, by Italo Calvino [2]; and 5 scientific papers about Covid 19, written by various authors.

This paper will be structured as follows: Sect. 2 will deepen the description of the state of the arts; Sect. 3 will deepen the description of the lexical resource, and Sect. 4 will provide a conclusion and discuss future work.

2 The State of the Art

Tullio De Mauro's lexicographical work started in 1980 with the first publication of the Basic Vocabulary (VdB) of the Italian language.

Previous studies in this area, which are in many ways different from the VdB in terms of methodology, objectives, and number of entries, are Thompson (1927), who listed 500 words; Knease (1933), a selection of about 2,000 words from literary texts; Skinner (1935), a list of 3,000 words extracted from a textbook on Italian for foreigners; Russo (1947), a combined list of 3,137 words; Migliorini (1943), a list of 1,500 headwords selected on the basis of the linguist's intuition and not from a statistical analysis of the data.

Moreover, in the 1970s, Juilland and Traversa (1973) and Sciarone (1977) worked respectively on a frequency dictionary for the Italian language and on the fundamental vocabulary of the Italian language. The former work presented the 5,014 most frequent words that emerged from an analysis of 500,000 occurrences; the latter proposed a list of 2,500 words also obtained from the analysis of a corpus of 500,000 occurrences.

De Mauro, in the field of statistical linguistics, began to highlight the quantitative and numerical aspects of linguistic description. He created an epistemological break with the traditional approach to lexical study.

This study is rooted in French lexicographic studies, which already widely used statistical methods based on frequency in order to analyze and describe the *Francais Elementaire* (FF1) and to identify the highly available lexicon, that is, the lexicon highly available to speakers [10]. A *mot disponible* is defined as a word which, even though it is used and recurrent, is rarely found in spoken texts [11]: unlike having a statistically assignable probability of occurrence, it "comes to mind" easily when necessary. In fact, the term lexical availability refers to the property of a word of being more or less immediately recalled in mental associations.

The study of the available lexicon carried out by FF1 turns its attention to the mental dimension – towards the *esprit* – of the speakers. In fact, the investigation consists in the identification of a series of words referring to concrete objects that are most frequently associated by speakers with thematic areas close to the speaker himself or with centers of interest (*centers d'intérêts*). The sample on the basis of which the available French lexicon was investigated was composed of school students aged between nine and twelve, coming from four different geographical areas of the French territory.

In the case of the Basic Vocabulary of the Italian language, we can stress that it collects two categories of words: (1) the words of highest use in the texts of a language at a given moment, which can be extracted from the frequency dictionaries of the various languages, and (2) the words that, even if seldom used in the written and spoken language, are perceived as highly available even more than words of more frequent use.

The most commonly used words are derived from the statistical analysis of the texts, while the most available words can only be obtained from speech.

The first Basic Vocabulary of Italian, from now on VdB, was developed at the end of the 1970s and published as an appendix to Tullio De Mauro's *Guida all'uso delle parole*, n.3 of the "Basic Books," 1st edition, Rome: Editori Riuniti, 1980, pages 149–183 [5]. It was subsequently used in various lexicographic works such as GRADIT (Great Italian dictionary of the language of use, 2nd diction, 8 volumes, Utet, Turin 2007). (Great Italian dictionary of usage, directed by T. De Mauro, UTET, Turin 1999–2007) [12].

The list of words drawn up in 1980 was based on frequency data (the number of occurrences of a word in its conjugated and declined forms) and on data on the use of words taken from the LIF, the Lexicon of frequency of the contemporary Italian language, published by IBM in Pisa in 1970, elaborated by the team of Cnuce at Pisa (University Center for Electronic Computing) formed by Uberta Bortolini, Carlo Tagliavini, and Alberto Zampolli [1].

The LIF, consisting of 500,000 words of contemporary Italian in written use, led to the identification of 5,000 lemmas. The main feature of the LIF was that the texts which made up the corpus were characterized by synchronicity and currency. In fact, texts from the period between 1945 and 1968 were collected and organized into five groups: theater, novels, cinema, periodicals, and subsidiaries. Secondly, its definition highlighted the underlying problems of compiling frequency dictionaries. In addition to the LIF [1], the VdB benefited from a list of Italian spoken frequencies, LIP [7].

The fundamental vocabulary covers about 90% of the occurrences of words in both written and spoken texts, while the high-use vocabulary covers about 6% of the occurrences, even if their use is much higher than the 50,000 common words and the remaining lexicon.

The 3,000 words of high use in the LIF taken into consideration by the VdB were investigated through a comprehensibility test (edited by Massimo Vedovelli) [14]. Only those 2,750 included in the VdB have been accepted in the VdB included by at least half of students and eighth-grade students from various Italian regions. They alone constituted the high use vocabulary. Finally, the highly available vocabulary included approximately 2,300 words.

The VdB listed about 7,050 words in three main categories: fundamental, high use, high availability (in further text abbreviated as FO, AU, AD, respectively).

In the GRADIT, the above-mentioned categories, called usage marks, do not indicate the lemma, but each different meaning associated with the lemmas. FO, AU, and AD cover about 98% of the speeches. Other usage marks contained in the GRADIT are the following: Common (CO), technical-specialist (TS, followed by the knowledge domain of reference), literary use (LE), regional (RE), dialect (DI), exoticism (ES), infrequent use (BU), obsolete (OB).

The inclusion of the VdB in the GRADIT marks a lexicographic turning point in dictionary compiling. In fact, starting from the second half of the 1990s, the main Italian dictionaries used vocabulary ranges, although with different labels.

In any case, the use of the VdB was not limited to this: publishing houses like Giunti used it to direct the drafting of textbooks for primary school by improving their comprehensibility. Moreover, Editori Riuniti used it to ensure that authors used words from the basic vocabulary as much as possible. Also, foreign publishers, such as Langenscheidt, used the VdB for Bilingual dictionaries. Furthermore, the Department of the Sciences of Language of Sapienza University together with Emanuela Piemontese published an easy-to-read monthly, dueparole, which had the aim of supporting people with linguistic-cultural or intellectual difficulties by the systematic use of words from the basic vocabulary.

2.1 The New Basic Vocabulary of the Italian Language

In 2016, a renewed version of the VdB came out, the New Basic Vocabulary of the Italian language (NVdB) [4] with 7,500 words.

This need arises from the historical-linguistic evolution of the country. The processes of linguistic unification and homogenization increased over the years, and De Mauro himself underlined how the percentage values of the population that speaks exclusively Italian increased and above all the majority of the population speaks and writes Italian while at the same time speaking a dialect. In the evolution of Italian, characteristics that originally belonged only to speech were also consolidated in the written language. In the New Basic Vocabulary, several hundred words that are no longer used have been deleted and several hundred that were absent in the past have been inserted.

The NVdB is made up of about 2,000 entries of the Fundamental Lexicon (FO), 3000 entries of High Use (AU), and 2,500 entries of High Availability (AD). From the observation of the lemmas present in the NVdB, it can be seen that 73.3% of the old FO lexicon is present in this same category, and also 47% of the AU lexicon [14].

The acquisition of automatic analysis technologies and the use of computational linguistics applications made it possible to analyze and verify the lemmas on much larger corpora.

The NVdB is based on the analysis of a corpus specifically built for contemporary (written and spoken) Italian consisting of 18,000,000 words. The corpus has been organized into 6 sub-corpora of similar size: press (newspapers and periodicals), literature (novels, short stories, poems), non-fiction (textbooks, essays, encyclopedia), entertainment (theater, cinema, songs, and TV programs), computer-mediated communication (forums, newsgroups, blogs, chats, and social networks), and speech recordings. Its chronological interval of the texts goes from 2000 to 2012 [3]. One of the main innovations of the NVdB is the lemmatization of multiword expressions (idioms, fixed expressions).

The NVdB is divided between words of the fundamental vocabulary (FO: 2,000), high use vocabulary (AU: 3,000), and high availability vocabulary (AD: 2,500). Here each entry is marked with the abbreviations of different levels.

These three categories are not homogeneous, i.e. the fundamental and highly used vocabulary are based on lexical-statistical criteria, while the high availability is based on a sociolinguistic evaluation. In fact, the last one is composed by words with low frequency that native speakers feel to be very common in use. Examples are words like "slipper," "fork," and "pan," which are related to daily actions and are not actually pronounced or written often.

Over the years, the different editions of the *Guida all'uso delle parole* (Guide to the use of words) allowed the implementation of metalinguistic data.

In the 1983 edition, De Mauro inserted the grammatical categories (class, gender, number) that give help while distinguishing homographs (e.g. *ufficiale* s.m., *ufficiale* adj.; *deserto* s.m., *deserto* adj.) [5].

In 1989, meaning was added in quotation marks, and in 2003, it was inserted in order to disambiguate homographical terms (e.g. *riso* "food" s.m. *riso* "laugh" s.m.).

Despite this refinement, there are still cases of ambiguity, as far as the polysemy is directly proportional to the frequency of use of a lemma. This means that a great number of words have multiple meanings. It is clear that this strongly impacts on the performance of statistical analysis of the language.

3   Text Analysis and Vocabulary Ranges

In our experiment, we exploited NooJ functionalities in order to identify the vocabulary ranges from the NVdB in texts and in this way to deduce information about their comprehensibility.

The idea is to verify the presence of Fundamental Lexicon in texts usually intended for children. In order to test our hypothesis, we composed our Corpus selecting three different texts in Italian:

- The Little Prince, by Antoine de Saint-Exupéry;
- Marcovaldo, by Italo Calvino;
- 5 scientific papers about Covid 19, by various authors.

The corpus, codified in UTF-8 and divided into chapters, was analyzed in NooJ by applying the Italian Module [15] and by integrating it through two *ad hoc* resources:

a. Dictionary of Italian Simple Words tagged with De Mauro's NVdB marks, which include FO (*Fondamentale*, Fundamental), AU (*Alto Uso*, High Usage), and AD (*Alta Disponibilità*, High Availability) which represents the words that compose 98% of discourses, but also CO (*Comune*, Common), TS (*Tecnico-Specialistico*, Technical-Specialized), LE (*Letterario*, Literary), RE (*Regionale*, Regional), DI (*Dialettale*, Dialect), ES (*Esotismo*, Exoticism), BU (*Basso Uso*, Low Usage) and OB (*Obsoleto*, Obsolete). Figure 1 shows how the dictionary works when applied to a text. Here it can be observed that each word is tagged with multiple ranges, due to the strong presence of homographs in the Italian Dictionary;

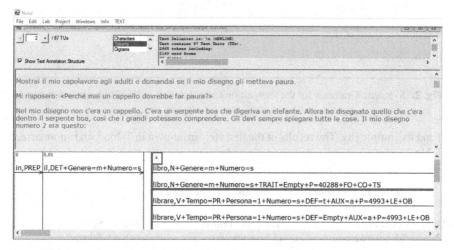

Fig. 1. Example of a portion of text analyzed with the NVdB ranges dictionary

b. Syntactic Transducer for the recognition and extraction of the tags associated with each mark. The grammar recognizes all the verbs, the nouns, the adjectives and the adverbs which are tagged with NVdB ranges in the dictionary. Then it extracts the vocabulary ranges and the Part-Of-Speech (POS) of the words, in order to produce, as exportable concordances, a list of all the vocabulary ranges related to the respective POS. Figure 2 shows the Syntactic Grammar.

We split the experiment into two steps: preliminarily, we extracted only the three basic vocabulary ranges, which represent 98% of the discourses. The primary goal of our work was to verify the existence of a correlation between the vocabulary used in a

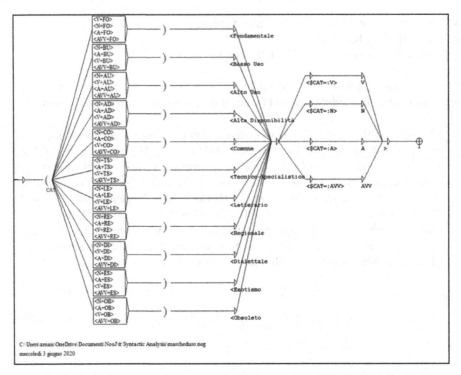

Fig. 2. Syntactic Grammar for the recognition and extraction of NVdB vocabulary ranges

text and its complexity. The results of the first step are shown in Table 1 and summarized in Table 2.

Table 1. Frequency of FO, AU, and AD vocabulary ranges in the corpus

Mark	Covid Papers (22020 tokens)		The Little Prince (17916 tokens)		Marcovaldo (41345 Tokens)	
	Frequency	%	Frequency	%	Frequency	%
FO	330	1.50	5300	29.58	10888	26.33
AU	216	0.98	1166	6.51	3533	8.55
AD	102	0.46	350	1.95	1609	3.89

The second step of our experiment concerned the extraction of NVdB Ranges together with the relative POS, in order to compare the three texts also by distribution of the Ranges over the grammatical category of the selected words. Table 3 and 4 show the results of the second step.

As we expected, the distribution of the frequency of the three vocabulary ranges considered in our analysis is coherent with the target of the three texts analyzed. *The*

Table 2. Diagram of FO, AU, and AD vocabulary range frequency for text

Table 3. Vocabulary ranges with POS distribution through texts

Mark	Covid Papers (22020 tokens)		The Little Prince (17916 tokens)		Marcovaldo (41345 Tokens)	
	Frequency	%	Frequency	%	Frequency	%
FO-V	101	0.46	2110	**11.78**	3806	**9.21**
FO-N	257	**1.17**	1214	6.78	3222	7.79
FO-A	186	0.84	851	4.75	1290	3.12
FO_AVV	28	0.13	587	3.28	1076	2.60
AU-V	72	0.33	348	1.94	893	2.16
AU-N	130	0.59	504	2.81	1591	3.85
AU-A	138	0.59	189	1.05	586	1.42
AU-AVV	0	0.00	32	0.18	75	0.18
AD-V	1	0.00	109	0.61	402	0.97
AD-N	83	0.38	135	0.75	831	2.01
AD-A	18	0.08	67	0.37	303	0.73
AD-AVV	3	0.01	39	0.22	73	0.18

Little Prince, whose target consists mainly in childere in early school years, contains, in percentage, the mayor number of words belonging to the FO mark. *Marcovaldo*, which actually targets teenagers and young adults, maintains a similar distribution of the vocabulary ranges. Contrariwise, Scientific papers about COVID, intended for domain specialists, contain only a small part of FO words.

Table 4. Diagram of vocabulary ranges with POS frequencies for text

4 Conclusion and Future Work

The results of our analysis confirm the hypothesis that a high frequency of words belonging to the FO vocabulary in a text can be considered a good indicator of high understandability. Our theory is supported by the data extracted, which demonstrate that texts intended for children or young adults, as *The Little Prince* and *Marcovaldo*, which must be more understandable, contain a great number of words from the FO vocabulary, while high specialized texts, rich of technical words, contain only a small part of this kind of words.

In future works we plan to develop specific tools for the recognition of textual categories based on the presence/absence of FO words. By enlarging our corpus with new texts and new analysis tools, we will delineate a more precise model of lexical understandability, which can include also a measure of the syntactic complexity of the text.

According to this model, it will be possible to design a tool able to perform the lexical screening of texts and capable of providing suggestions concerning the achievement of satisfactory levels of lexical comprehensibility, which must be related to readers grouped by age ranges. This model will be systematized in a set of indices that can give to the reader information about the readability of texts based on the reader's age.

A system based on this kind of indices could be very useful for editors, authors, or teachers regarding the production of new texts for a specific age or the adoption of a text for educational purposes.

References

1. Bortolini, U., Tagliavini, C., Zampolli, A.: Lessico di frequenza dell'italiano. Garzanti-IBM, Milano (1972)

2. Calvino, I.: Marcovaldo Edizioni Oscar Junior (1963)
3. Chiari, I., De Mauro, T.: The new basic vocabulary of Italian: problems and methods. Rivista di Statistica Applicata=Italian J. Appl. Stat. **22**(1) 21–35 (2012)
4. Chiari, I., De Mauro, T.: Nuovo vocabolario di base della lingua italiana. Casa Editrice Sapienza (2016)
5. De Mauro, T.: Il vocabolario di base della lingua italiana. In: Guida all'uso delle parole, pp. 146–172. Editori Riuniti, Roma (1980)
6. De Mauro, T., Chiari, I.: The New Basic Vocabulary of Italian as a linguistic resource. In: First Italian Conference on Computational Linguistics CLiC-it 2014 (2014)
7. De Mauro, T., Mancini, F., Vedovelli, M., Voghera, M.: A cura di. Lessico di frequenza dell'italiano parlato. Etaslibri, Milano (1993)
8. de Saint-Exupéry, A.: Il Piccolo Principe (Italiano) (1943) E. Trevi (a cura di) (2015)
9. Ferreri, S.: L'alfabetizzazione lessicale. Studi di linguistica educativa, Roma, Aracne, pp. 1–40 (2005)
10. Gougenheim, G.: Le Français Élémentaire the French Review, vol. 27, no. 3, pp. 217–220, 4 p. (1954)
11. Gougenheim, G., Michea, R., Rivenc, P., Et Sauvageot, A.: L'élaboration du français élémentaire. Etude sur l'établissement d'un vocabulaire et d'une grammaire de base, Didier, Paris (1956)
12. GRADIT (Grande dizionario italiano della lingua dell'uso, 2ª dizione, 8 volumi, Utet, Torino 2007). (Grande dizionario italiano dell'uso, diretto da T. De Mauro, UTET, Torino 1999–2007)
13. Sobrero, A.: L'incremento della competenza lessicale, con particolare riferimento ai linguaggi scientifici, Italiano LinguaDue, 1 (2009)
14. Vedovelli, M.: Confronti tra il LIP e le altre liste di frequenza dell''italiano. In: De Mauro, Mancini, Vedovelli e Voghera 1993, pp. 119–147 (1993)
15. Vietri, S.: The Italian Module for NooJ, pp. 389–393 (2014)

Formalizing Latin: An Example of Medieval Latin Wills

Linda Mijić[(⊠)] and Anita Bartulović

Department of Classical Philology, University of Zadar, Zadar, Croatia
{lmijic,abartulo}@unizd.hr

Abstract. Language modules for more than thirty languages have been created by NooJ, a linguistic development environment. So far, such projects have not included resources for the Latin language. This paper marks the beginning of creating a linguistic model for medieval Latin in the NooJ programme. Classical Latin continued to be used after the fall of the Western Roman Empire (476 AD), and it became a *lingua franca* of medieval Europe. Medieval Latin underwent spelling, morphological, syntactic, and semantic change, which was characteristic for all of Europe, but local variation also developed due to very specific historical and political frameworks and linguistic situations. For the purposes of this paper, we have processed a corpus consisting of 385 last wills and testaments, drawn up between 1209 and 1409 in the Zadar commune. Of these, 301 wills have already been published in hard copy and 84 are manuscripts kept in the State Archives in Zadar. We scanned and digitally processed all the printed wills in an OCR program, and we transcribed the unpublished handwritten wills. After we created a digitally readable text, we compiled a dictionary and processed nouns from that corpus. On the basis of this dictionary resource, we created a NooJ inflectional morphological grammar with 47 paradigms. Furthermore, we built a morphological grammar for the most frequent orthographical variants and a syntactic grammar, which solve the problem of damaged, i.e. reconstructed, texts.

Keywords: Medieval Latin Wills · Latin language · NooJ morphological grammars

1 Introduction

NooJ, a linguistic development environment, was released in 2002, and since then, language modules have been created for more than thirty languages [1]. These language modules refer mostly to modern languages, while some of them do refer to classical languages, but only in the processing of modern professional medical and botanical terms derived from Latin and/or Greek forms [2–4].

This paper is a preliminary work on creating lexical, morphological, and syntactic resources for the Latin NooJ module,[1] and it builds on our previous research of medieval

---

[1] We would like to express our gratitude to Kristina Kocijan and Max Silberztein, who helped us with their precious advice when we started grappling with the challenges of programming.

© Springer Nature Switzerland AG 2021
B. Bekavac et al. (Eds.): NooJ 2020, CCIS 1389, pp. 24–36, 2021.
https://doi.org/10.1007/978-3-030-70629-6_3

Latin used in the administration of the Zadar Commune in the thirteenth and fourteenth centuries [5–9].

Unlike other languages that have disappeared with their speakers, after the fall of the Western Roman Empire (476 AD), classical Latin continued to be used as a *lingua franca* of medieval Europe. It was used by the Church, in science, education, literature, administration, diplomacy, etc. In relation to classical Latin, medieval Latin underwent numerous orthographic, morphosyntactic, semantic, and lexical changes. Some of these changes were characteristic of all of Europe, but, because of the massive influence of different vernacular languages on medieval Latin, which no longer had native speakers, the language abounded with local specific features [10–13].

In this paper, we shall first describe the corpus and the preliminary work we conducted on it to obtain a computer-readable text. We shall then briefly outline the challenges we encountered in building dictionaries and grammars with regard to the external and internal characteristics of medieval notarial documents written in Latin. In the next section, we shall present the resources we have created in NooJ and how we overcame the most demanding problems by using morphological and syntactic grammar. Finally, we shall present the conclusion and perspectives of this work as a starting point for future projects.

2 The Corpus

In the Middle Ages, Latin was a prestigious language, and so in the period before the Renaissance, it was the language of the written word. Apart from texts of a higher stylistic level, Latin was used in the regulation of private and legal relations among members of different social strata of medieval communes. The Croatian State Archives in Zadar abounds in a variety of material from which scholars draw data for their research in the field of medieval studies. Wills, as a type of notarial legal document, provide an interesting insight into the various aspects of everyday life in the Middle Ages, such as urban, legal, economic, social, religious, and personal life [14–20].

A medieval will is a private legal document drawn up in a notary's office. It has a set diplomatic structure depending on whether it was written by a notary on behalf of the testator or subsequently written by a notary according to the oral testimony of four witnesses. Thus a written will consists of three parts:

(1) the introduction (*capitulum proemii/arenga*), which describes the circumstances and reasons for drawing up the will
(2) the part in which the testator determines the executors of the will (*capitulum providentiarum*); the legacies, i.e., specific things that the testator leaves to people (*capitulum legatorum*); the heirs (*capitulum institutionis heredis*); and the hereditary succession in the event of any heir's death (*capitulum substitutionis heredis*)
(3) the final part, which contains a clause citing the law that validates the will (*clausula codicillaris*) [21].

The last will expressed orally before witnesses has two parts:

(1) *expositio et petitio* – the part in which it is stated that the closest relative informed the rectors about the deceased's death and that the deceased could not draw up a will because there was no notary present, but that they announced their last will orally in front of four witnesses. This is followed by the relative's request that the rectors hear the witnesses and that the oral will be redacted according to statutory provisions.

(2) *citatio et testatio* – the rectors call witnesses and interrogate them under oath. The first witness gives a comprehensive statement, and the testimonies of the other witnesses are summarized in the sense that their statement confirms the testimony of the first witness.

Under medieval statutory law, the testator had the right to change part of his will during his lifetime, and such a document was called a *codicillum*, i.e., an addendum to the will. The structure of the codicil is very similar to a written will [7].

For the purpose of this paper, we processed a corpus consisting of 385 last wills and testaments (i.e., 378 "written" wills, 5 "oral" wills, and 2 codicils) drawn up between 1209 and 1409 AD in the Zadar commune. Of these, 301 wills have been published in hard copy in serial publications of historical sources over the past hundred years [22, 23], and 84 are manuscripts of ten Zadar notaries, whose notary records are kept in the State Archives in Zadar [24].

The wills were composed in Gothic script, the most widespread Latin script of the late Middle Ages, and the subtype is that of the Gothic cursive. This script is characterized by a large number of ligatures and abbreviations, which are a reflection of the notary's individuality, and they leave the impression of carelessness typical of quick writing. Therefore, transcribing individual words written in Gothic cursive is sometimes difficult [25–27].

In order to get a digitally readable text, we transcribed the unpublished handwritten wills, and we scanned and digitally processed all the printed wills in an OCR program. Our first problem with obtaining a readable text can be seen in Fig. 1. Many documents, especially those from earlier periods, are only partially legible because they have been very damaged, usually by moisture, so the gaps are marked in the transcription with dots.

The above-mentioned formulaic structure of the documents and their context helps transcribers in the reconstruction of most of the damaged places in the texts. When compiling his documents, a notary would use a set of legal formulae from the notarial handbook of the time, which he had learned during his studies, and each type of notarial document can be recognized by its characteristic formulae within its defined structure [21]. This often makes reconstruction of parts of words, whole words, or even whole sentences possible, and reconstructed parts are normally placed in brackets. We shall later illustrate in more detail the problem we encountered regarding brackets.

The corpus has almost 14,000 different tokens, but it should be pointed out that the number of tokens is actually smaller because, in the first phase of our work, NooJ counted each word broken off by brackets as two or more tokens. However, when we were creating the dictionary manually, we merged such words, and our dictionary of

Fig. 1. An example of a damaged text and its transcription (DAZD–HR–F31–BZ, PP b. IV, fasc. 16 (3), fol. 9r)

Latin nouns with all its variants consisted of 1,521 entries. Later, we shall present the methodology by which we reduced the number of entries of variants of individual words in the NooJ dictionary.

3   Creating the Dictionary

Our goal was to detect nouns and their variants in the text manually and to present a morphological grammar for inflectional paradigms. We associated each lemma with a designation of the word type (N), the gender (m I f I n), and the inflectional paradigm (FLX = paradigm). Latin nouns show number (singular and plural) and six cases (nominative, genitive, dative, accusative, vocative, and ablative), and according to their meaning, they are divided into common nouns and proper names.

For the purpose of this paper, common nouns were processed. This is an example of what a dictionary entry looks like:

```
comes,N+m+c+FLX=MILES
```

4   Grammars

In order to make dictionary entries recognizable in NooJ, we built three grammars. We shall describe each one below and point out the challenges we encountered in their application.

4.1   Inflectional Morphological Grammar

Based on the dictionary resource, we first created a NooJ inflectional morphological grammar (.nof files). Traditional Latin grammar distinguishes five declensions, but there are a number of exceptions to the basic rules. Due to different stems in oblique cases of regular nouns, especially in the third declension, as well as to peculiarities in declensions (such as *nomina indeclinabilia, nomina defectiva numero, nomina defectiva casibus*), we have had to compile 47 paradigms of noun declension. We wrote the description of paradigms according to the following model:

```
MILES = <E>/Nom+s + <E>/Voc+s + <B2>it(is/G+s + i/D+s +
em/Acc+s + e/Ab+s + es/Nom+p + um/G+p + ibus/D+p +
es/Acc+p + es/Voc+p + ibus/Ab+p);
```

4.2 Productive Morphological Grammar

As we mentioned in the introduction, medieval Latin is characterized on the one hand by a strong influence of spoken language of a certain geographical area and Christian Latinity, and on the other hand by the tendency towards grammatical correctness of classical Latinity. Such was also the historical linguistic situation in the medieval Zadar commune, a community in which many languages were in use, such as spoken Croatian, which became more and more dominant over time, and several spoken Romance dialects/idioms: Venetian as the language of the masters in the periods of Venetian domination over Dalmatian cities, spoken Jadertin (an autochthonous Romance idiom), which was gradually replaced by Venetian, and other Italian dialects spoken by newcomers from the Apennine Peninsula. Among the latter were most of the notaries providing their services in the Zadar commune, whose official language was Latin [28].

This illustrates the complexity of historical and political relations in different sociolinguistic contexts throughout medieval Europe, which inevitably led to the transformation of classical Latin. This can be seen in numerous changes at all linguistic levels, and even more so in their inconsistencies colored by regional peculiarities. Table 1 shows examples of the most common changes and inconsistencies from our corpus, such as the reduction of diphthongs, confusion in the writing of some letters, hypercorrection, etc.

Thus, various changes occurred in vocabulary; furthermore, some words change declensions. In our learning corpus, a large number of words had only one or two variants, but some of them had more than two. The majority of these words with more than two variants did not exist in classical Latin, but were borrowed either from vernacular languages, such as Italian and Croatian, or from Greek, which had a strong influence on the Christian vocabulary of the Bible, e.g.,

- domina, domna, dompna, dopna, dona, donna 'madam, missis'
- elemosina, elemosyna, elimosina, elymosina, helemosina, helymosina

  < gr. ™lehmosÚnh 'alms'

- gognaus, gognaius, gognayus, gonaius, gongnaius, gognalius

  < cro. Gonjaj 'unit of measure for area'

- guarnazia, guarnaça, varnacia, varnacio, varnaco, varnacon, guarnazonum

  < it. Guarnaca 'robe'

Table 1. The most common changes and inconsistencies in medieval Latin

Reduction	diphthong *ae > e*	*domine*
	diphthong *oe > e*	*pena*
Confusion	*i/e* and *u/o* etc.	*linteamen/lentiamen/lintiamen*
	double/single consonants	*apatrinus/**app**atrinus; villanus/vilanus*
	ti and *ci* before a vowel	*absolutio/absolucio; condicio/conditio*
	ch and *c*	*barca/barcha;* *monacha/monaca*
	ph and *f*	*orphana/orfana*
	th and *t*	*apothecarius/apotecarius*
	i and *y*	*cimator/cymator*
	c and *ct*	*dote/docte*
	s and *sc*	*consilium/conscilium*
	c, ç and *z*	*cancellarius/cançelarius/canzellarius*
	u and *v*	*servitrix/seruitrix*
	t and *d*	*calafatus/chalafadus*
	h	*hospicium/ospicium*
Epenthesis		*calumnia/calumpnia*
Hypercorrection		*etas/**h**etas* *platea/plat**h**ea* *protomagister/prot**h**omagister*

This last word, *guarnazia*, not only shows changes in letters, but also some of its variants change their declension class.

For most of the changes, it is difficult to find a pattern that would help NooJ to recognize different variants of the same word. In order to solve this problem, we intended to create a separate morphological grammar (.nom files) for each individual change, but, since several different changes can occur in the same word (such as *caligarius, calegarius, callegarius, chalegarius*), we created one morphological grammar (see Fig. 2) for the most frequent changes: confusion in writing double and single consonants, the syllables *ti* and *ci* before *a* vowel, *u* and *v*, *ch* and *c*, *ph* and *f*, *th* and *t*.

If we were to expand this grammar with other features of medieval Latin, even with the set limitations, it would significantly slow down the operation of the software. Therefore, we described word variants with other peculiarities in the dictionary using a superlemma, such as

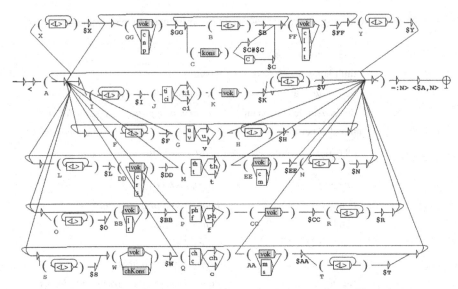

Fig. 2. Morphological grammar for the most common orthographic variants

```
cirugicus,N+m+c+FLX=LUPUS
cirogicus,cirugicus,N+m+c+FLX=LUPUS
cyrugicus,cirugicus,N+m+c+FLX=LUPUS
ciroycus,cirugicus,N+m+c+FLX=LUPUS
cyruychus,cirugicus,N+m+c+FLX=LUPUS
```

By applying this grammar to our corpus, we were able to remove a number of entries originally described from the NooJ dictionary by using a superlemma. Thus, the number of entries in the NooJ dictionary dropped from the initial 1,521 to 1,289.

While describing the dictionary, we came across another problem. In the text we found 70 words with different errors. We can distinguish between two types of errors:

(1) **misspellings** of nouns, i.e., wrong letters, substitutions, or dropped letters – e.g., *arepiseopum* instead of *archiepiscopum*, *mote* instead of *morte*
(2) errors in the **declension** of a noun which was already in our dictionary. For example, we found *aurifico* instead of *aurifice* for the word *aurifex* and *dota* instead of *dote* for the word *dos*, etc. One of the peculiarities of medieval Latin is the change in declension, but, since such examples are individual, we were more inclined to interpret them as errors than as peculiarities of the language, even though it was sometimes difficult to understand which case we were dealing with.

It sometimes remained unclear whether errors were made by the notary himself, a transcriber, or even an editor because they were not followed by an exclamation point, which is usually used to mark a word the notary misspelled. The problem is that NooJ cannot link them with the correct word. In dealing with this problem, we had two options:

(1) describing these words with a superlemma, as in the previous examples, in a special
     dictionary of misspelled words. However, mistakes were made only in some cases,
     e.g., the ablative singular *mote* from *mors, mortis*. Therefore, it would be mean-
     ingless to burden the NooJ with declensions of non-existent nouns, which would
     happen if we were to use this model: consangineus, TF + m + c + FLX = LUPUS
     + TB = consanguineus (where TB stands for 'what should be').
(2) updating the publishing policy: reviewing the whole text and correcting only those
     typing errors which were made by editors.

Describing these misspelled words with a superlemma would not be an adequate
solution because they do not exist in Latin dictionaries. Therefore, re-publishing the text
with a consistent methodology on how to treat the mistakes made by a notary is the only
acceptable solution.

In addition to these misspelled words, there are a number of unknown words which
are not recorded in medieval Latin dictionaries [29–31].

4.3 Syntactic Grammar

We now return to the issue of brackets that we mentioned in Sect. 2. Our challenge
was to eliminate brackets within reconstructed words, so that NooJ would be able to
recognize them as atomic linguistic units. The position, type, and number of brackets
in the word varies, as in the following examples: *(habita)trix, habi(tatrix, t(h)orum,
mi)s(sis), [in]dic[cione, habita-221trix*, etc. In the final example, we can see that a word
can also be broken up by the page number. We kept page numbers in the text where they
appeared in the printed editions so that the wills could be properly cited according to
the principles of historical scholarship.

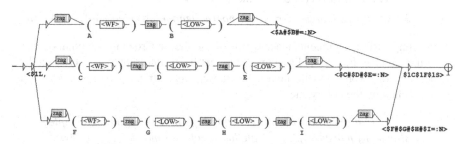

Fig. 3. Grammar used to delete brackets within words

We solved the problem of brackets and page numbers through the use of syntactic
grammar (.nog files). Each path of this grammar solves one of the problems regarding
brackets, in terms of their number, type, and position within a word (see Fig. 3).

Having applied this grammar to the text, we added annotations to the text, and NooJ
recognized words broken up by brackets as atomic linguistic units, in our case, as nouns.
Then it linked words and their flections, e.g.

```
tes)tamento/<testamentum,N+n+c+D+s+FLX=VERBUM>
mi)s(sis)/<missa,N+f+c+D+p+FLX=TERRA>
action[ibus]/<actio,N+f+c+D+p+FLX=RATIO>
```

We would now like to turn to another problem involving brackets. Namely, each diplomatic edition consists of a precise transliteration of a text with all its peculiarities, including all the errors made by the notary. For the purpose of clarity of archival sources, editors also intervene by resolving all abbreviations, correcting uppercase and lowercase letters, inserting punctuation, etc. Each country publishes historical sources according to its own tradition [32]. Moreover, publishing rules have changed over time. Our documents were published in several editions over a period of almost a hundred years (1905 to 2003). In these editions, publishing rules are inconsistent, so one type of brackets has different purposes or different types of brackets have the same purpose:

(3) Some old editions use round brackets for

    a. the reconstruction of the text

        Die duodecimo intrante (mensis)iunii. (1959)

(4) marking various interventions in the text by the notary, such as crossing out a part of the text, marking a part of the text written subsequently in the margins or between the lines of the text, or individual corrections. These individual interventions made by the notary were accompanied by the transcriber's comments in Croatian.

    *... in omnibus meis (paternis et maternis — **precrtano** [crossed out]).* (1959)

    *... et teneatur mihi facere tercium, septimum et tricessimum (primo anno — **između redova** [between the lines])* (1959)

    *... Presentibus... Iohanne Grec(o — **popravljeno u** [changed into])i...* (1969)

(5) inserting various comments made by the transcriber in Croatian, which may relate to the damage the text had sustained, the text being interrupted, empty space left between the words by the notary for subsequent entries, corrections of words misspelled by the notary, etc.

    *...... (**Na početku sasvim uništeno vlagom.**[The beginning completely destroyed by moisture]). .... Galellos, auunculos m(eos) ..... (1959)*

    *... in missis, helemosinis et aliis operibus (misericordie et pietatis) ..... (**dalje prekinuto** [the text ends here])* (1959)

    *Item (**u izvorniku ostalo prazno** [in the original this space is empty]) consangineus meus...* (1969)

    *... Qui nostrum superuixerit (**zapravo: superuierxit — znak kraćenja krivo stavljen** [actually: superuierxit the abbreviation mark is used incorrectly]).* (1969)

(6) Some old and some new editions use square brackets for the reconstruction of the text and round brackets for words crossed out in the original, but without any comments in Croatian, e.g.

> *... coram hiis vocatis et rogatis testibus, scilicet presbitero Stephano de Semao et Andree de [Co]topag[na]...* (1906)
>
> *[Testamentum Pribislavi condam Radosclavi de insula Bagni]* (2001)
>
> *Et si dicta Margarita eius vxor aut quecumque alia vxor sua in[posterum]...* (unpublished)
>
> *... per dictos suos comissarios (voluit)vnicumque...* (unpublished)

(7) In the latest edition, the crossed-out words have been relocated to footnotes, e.g.

> *Cum morte nil* <sit> cercius et [h]ora mortis ab omnibus ignoretur...*
> ***nil] add. Est M sed cancell. M2**

(8) Sometimes the editors did not even follow their own rules, which can be seen in the following example:

> *Item pro alijs [mille – **precrtano**](mi)ssis celebrandis pro anima mea relinquo (alios solidos XX grossorum – **precrtano**)libras XXIII paruorum...* (1969)

The only way to deal with typing errors, various kinds of brackets, and comments in Croatian in the middle of the Latin text is to reissue the texts as critical editions. Since then it would be a revised edition of the wills, the page numbers mentioned before would no longer be necessary.

5   Conclusion and Future Work

Our goal was to begin the work on creating NooJ resources for medieval Latin. The corpus consisting of 385 wills from thirteenth- and fourteenth-century Zadar proved to be quite fruitful for creating a dictionary and detecting problem points in the research of such texts, which have to do with the language itself, as well as with the publishing rules applied in the original editing of these texts.

Medieval Latin was not a standard language in the modern sense of the word because it was not standardized, and this is most apparent in the spelling. Its basic characteristic was the variation and inconsistency of forms in relation to classical Latin. Since it is sometimes difficult to find a pattern in these inconsistencies, the construction of dictionaries and grammars that would respect the peculiarities of medieval Latin was especially demanding. We were able to solve the most common changes in words by using morphological grammar. Since a single word can have several different orthographic and phonetic peculiarities and since this would slow down the software (e.g., the debugger offered 433 paths when analysing the word *apothecarius* and looking for the variants *appothecarius/appotheccarius/apotecarius*), we entered some word variants in the dictionary under a superlemma.

In conclusion, the application of the superlemma is not demanding for the NooJ programme, but it increases the preparatory work manifold in the sense that all possible variants have to be listed in the dictionary so that it could later be applied to other medieval Latin resources. Therefore, at later stages it might be better to process such examples with a superlemma as much as possible when processing other types of words in NooJ.

We overcame the problem of damaged (i.e., reconstructed) texts with syntactic grammar, which helped us eliminate different types of brackets within words. However, over the past century, publishing rules according to which the wills from our corpus were published in various editions of historical sources changed, so for future work it is crucial to arrive at a consolidated text by harmonizing these rules. For the time being, we have only made the most basic corrections in the text: (a) we have replaced the letter j with i, (b) we have relegated the words which the notary crossed out and which were printed in brackets in the printed editions with the comment "crossed out" and without the comment in unpublished ones to the footnotes in order to get as readable a text as possible.

Further work will need to find a solution for this or make a modification in the NooJ programme so that, after syntactic grammar has been applied to the annotated text in order to remove brackets, morphological grammar could be applied to find the peculiarities of medieval Latin, because NooJ first performs the morphological and then the syntactic analysis.

Apart from revising the text, the next phase in our work phase will include the development of inflectional morphological grammars to identify other types of inflectional words, including proper names. The resources created after this study is finished will be made available to the wider scientific community for further research, especially in the fields of medieval studies and digital humanities.

References

1. Silberztein, M.: Formalizing Natural Languages: The NooJ Approach. Wiley (2016)
2. di Buono, M.P., Maisto, A., Pelosi, S.: From linguistic resources to medical entity recognition: a supervised morphosyntactic approach. ALLDATA **82**, 81–85 (2015)
3. Seideh, M.A.F., Fehri, H., Haddar, K.: Recognition and extraction of latin names of plants for matching common plant named entities. In: Barone, L., Monteleone, M., Silberztein, M. (eds.) NooJ 2016. CCIS, vol. 667, pp. 132–144. Springer, Cham (2016). https://doi.org/10.1007/978-3-319-55002-2_12
4. Kocijan, K., di Buono, M.P., Mijić, L.: Detecting Latin-based medical terminology in croatian texts. In: Mauro Mirto, I., Monteleone, M., Silberztein, M. (eds.) NooJ 2018. CCIS, vol. 987, pp. 38–49. Springer, Cham (2019). https://doi.org/10.1007/978-3-030-10868-7_4
5. Mijić, L.: Latinitet inventara fonda Veličajne općine zadarske Državnog arhiva u Zadru (godine 1325–1385). Dissertation, Filozofski fakultet u Zagrebu (2014)
6. Mijić, L.: Internal structure and lexis of inventories in the fonds magnifica communitas iadre from the 14th century. SYSTASIS E-J. Assoc. Class. Philol. "Antika" **28**, 1–18 (2016)
7. Bartulović, A.: Paleografska, diplomatička i filološka analiza spisa zadarskoga notara Petra Perencana (1361–1392). Dissertation. Filozofski fakultet u Zagrebu (2014)
8. Bartulović, A.: O jezičnoj komunikaciji prema spisima zadarskoga notara Petra Perencana (1361–1392). Zbornik Odsjeka za povijesne znanosti Zavoda za povijesne i društvene znanosti Hrvatske akademije znanosti i umjetnosti, vol. 33, pp. 71–101 (2015)

9. Bartulović, A., Mijić, L.: Voda i s njome značenjski povezani leksemi u spisima srednjovjekovnoga zadarskog notara Petra Perencana. Folia onomastica Croatica **25**, 1–9 (2016). https://doi.org/10.21857/yrvgqtp179
10. Löfstedt, E.: Late Latin. H. Aschehoug & Co. W. Nygaard, Oslo (1959)
11. Norberg, D.: A Practical Handbook of Medieval Latin, trans. R.H. Johnson (1980). https://homepages.wmich.edu/~johnsorh/MedievalLatin/Norberg/index.html
12. Stotz, P.: Handbuch zur lateinischen Sprache des Mittelalters, 5 vols. Verlag C. H. Beck, Munich (1996–2004)
13. Dinkova-Bruun, G.: Medieval Latin. In: Clackson, J. (ed.) A Companion to the Latin Language, vol. 83, pp. 284–302. Wiley, Malden, MA–Oxford (2011)
14. Bennett, J.M., Whittick, C.: Philippa Russell and the Wills of London's late medieval singlewomen. Lond. J. **32**(3), 251–269 (2007). https://doi.org/10.1179/174963207X227569
15. Staples, K.K.: Identifying women proprietors in wills from fifteenth-century London. Early Mod. Women **3**, 239–243 (2008)
16. Cohn, S.: Renaissance attachment to things: material culture in last wills and testaments. Econ. Hist. Rev. **65**(3), 984–1004 (2012)
17. Mumby, J.: Property rights in Anglo-Saxon wills: a synoptic view. In: Nelson, J.L., Reynolds, S., Johns, S.M. (eds.) Gender and Historiography: Studies in the Earlier Middle Ages in Honour of Pauline Stafford, pp. 159–174. University of London Press, London (2012). https://doi.org/10.2307/j.ctv5139fw.18
18. Ladić, Z.: Last Will: Passport to Heaven. Urban Last Wills from Late Medieval Dalmatia with special attention to the Legacies pro Remedio Animae and ad Pias Causas. Zagreb, Tiskara Zelina (2012)
19. Bartulović, A.: Unusual details of everyday life from the notary registry of Petrus, called Perençanus, a notary from Zadar (1365–1392). Povijesni prilozi **56**, 201–228 (2019). https://doi.org/10.22586/pp.v56i1.8248
20. Bartulović, A.: Integracija došljaka s Apeninskog poluotoka u zadarskoj komuni (1365–1374). Radovi Zavoda za povijesne znanosti HAZU u Zadru, vol. 61, pp. 135–177 (2019). https://doi.org/10.21857/mwo1vczjry
21. Grbavac, B.: Notarijat na istočnojadranskoj obali od druge polovine 12. do kraja 14. stoljeća. Dissertation, Filozofski fakultet u Zagrebu (2010)
22. Codex diplomaticus Croatiae, Slavoniae et Dalmatiae, vol. 3–18, suppl. vols. 2. Zagreb (1905–2002)
23. Notarilia Jadertina, vols. 5. Državni arhiv u Zadru, Zadar (1959–2003)
24. Hrvatska–Državni arhiv u Zadru–fond 31–Zadarski bilježnici, Petrus Perençanus (1365–1392) / Vannes Bernardi de Firmo (1375–1404) / Petrus de Sarçana (1375–1416) / Iohannes de Casulis (1381–1417) / Articutius de Rivignano (1383–1416) / Raymundus de Modiis (1384–1389) / Vannes q. Dominici de Firmo (1389–1395) / Iordanus de Nosdrogna (1390–1400) / Theodorus de Prandino (1403–1441) / Iohannes de Trottis (1404–1407)
25. Cencetti, G.: Lineamenti di Storia della Scrittura Latina. Bologna, Casa editrice prof. Riccardo Patron (1956)
26. Stipišić, J.: Pomoćne povijesne znanosti u teoriji i praksi. Školska knjiga, Zagreb (1991)
27. Bischoff, B.: Paläographie des römischen Altertums und des Abendländischen Mittelalters. Berlin, Erich Schmidt Verlag (2009)
28. Vuletić, N.: Neka jezična pitanja autohtonoga zadarskog romanstva u 14. stoljeću. Rasprave Instituta za hrvatski jezik i jezikoslovlje, vol. 35, pp. 411–427 (2009)
29. Du Cange, C.D.F. et al.: Glossarium ad scriptores mediae et infimae latinitatis. Niort, L. Favre (1883–1887). https://ducange.enc.sorbonne.fr/. Accessed 18 July 2020
30. Niermeyer, J.F.: Mediae Latinitatis lexicon minus – Lexique Latin médiéval français/anglais. In: Leiden, E J.B. (ed.) A Medieval Latin-French/English Dictionary (1954–1976). https://linguaeterna.com/medlat/. Accessed 18 July 2020

31. Kostrenčić, M., Gortan, V., Herkov, Z.: Lexicon latinitatis medii aevi Iugoslaviae. Zagreb, JAZU (1969–1978)
32. Egdotika. Hrvatska enciklopedija, mrežno izdanje. Leksikografski zavod Miroslav Krleža (2020). https://www.enciklopedija.hr/Natuknica.aspx?ID=17136. Accessed 18 July 2020

The Morphological Annotation
of Reduplication-Circumfix Intersection
in Indonesian

Prihantoro[1,2(✉)] [ID]

[1] Lancaster University, Lancaster, UK
prihantoro2001@yahoo.com
[2] Universitas Diponegoro, Semarang, Indonesia

Abstract. In this paper, I report on the implementation of a morpheme-level annotation scheme for Indonesian [1], particularly the annotation of reduplications. Utilizing the NooJ program [2] and a set of novel linguistic resources, the majority of reduplications formed according to a number of distinct patterns were successfully annotated. However, one reduplication-circumfix intersection pattern could not be annotated. This is because the current NooJ morphological grammar is not designed to read the hyphen symbol, an orthographical cue that connects a root to its copy in Indonesian reduplication. Failure to read this symbol disconnects the opening and closing elements of the circumfix that surrounds its reduplication base. To overcome this problem, I introduced additional circumfix rules into the current morphological grammar without using any hyphen symbols in the rule definitions. The circumfix elements in the rules are linked as a single dependent unit using syntactic grammar whose rules NooJ allows to contain the hyphen symbol. However, this method promotes undesirable ambiguities. To overcome this side effect, I have modified the existing syntactic grammar to eliminate these ambiguities.

Keywords: NooJ · Annotation · Reduplication · Circumfix · Indonesian

1 Introduction

In this paper, I present some experimental results on the morphological annotation of Indonesian, focusing on the circumfix-reduplication interface. Indonesian is the official as well as the national language of the Republic of Indonesia, spoken by over 200 million people [3]. It is one of the standard varieties of Malay, found throughout Southeast Asia, and genetically affiliated to Austronesian languages [4].

In Indonesian, reduplication is one of the most productive word-formation operations. It is thus clearly important that reduplications should be accurately annotated. Other productive word-formation operations are affixation and compounding [4].

How are reduplications annotated by the currently available Natural Language Processing (NLP) tools built for Indonesian? Wicaksono and Purwarianti [5] constructed a POS tagger for Indonesian (IPOS). This NLP application invariably tokenizes both

© Springer Nature Switzerland AG 2021
B. Bekavac et al. (Eds.): NooJ 2020, CCIS 1389, pp. 37–48, 2021.
https://doi.org/10.1007/978-3-030-70629-6_4

monomorphemic and polymorphemic words as single-word tokens, as shown in Table 1. Input 1 is monomorphemic. Input 2 is polymorphemic, formed by fully reduplicating the root. Despite differing in shape, both are functionally tagged as NN (noun). The tool supplies no tags for categories of morphological form, such as whether a word is formed by reduplication or not. Therefore, for users who rely solely on this tool's output, it is impossible to run a query to find reduplications.

Table 1. IPOS tagger input and output samples

	Input	Word formation	Output
1	*buku* 'book'	Root word	buku/NN
2	*buku-buku* 'books'	Reduplication	buku-buku/NN

Let us now turn to MorphInd [6], an automatic morphological analyser for Indonesian. MorphInd supplies two types of tags: word tags and root tags. Larasati et al. [6] assert that MorphInd performs morphemic segmentation. However, we cannot observe this segmentation for reduplicated words in MorphInd's output, as shown in Table 2. The tokenization of the reduplication *buku-buku* 'books' is identical to the monomorphemic/non-reduplicated word *buku* 'book'. They are distinguished only by the word tag (NSD = singular noun versus NPD = plural noun).

Table 2. MorphInd input and output samples

	Input	Word formation	Output
1	*buku* 'book'	Root word	buku\<n\>_NSD
2	*buku-buku* 'books'	Reduplication	buku\<n\>_NPD

Only functional tags (like NSD and NPD) are present in MorphInd's tag inventory. The letter P (Plural) in the second position of the word tag can, in practice, be used to distinguish monomorphemic buku (NSD) and the corresponding reduplication buku-buku (NPD). In the MorphInd scheme, all reduplications are analysed as plurals. This analysis, however, can be inaccurate. Other than plurality, reduplication in Indonesian can mark a wide range of grammatical or semantic functions, including manner, distributive, and reciprocal. Thus, the singular versus plural analysis is not fully reliable and cannot fully compensate for the absence of formal morphological category tags. It is also apparent that certain reduplications that intersect with affixes are incorrectly analysed by MorphInd as two unrelated units.

In the example illustrated in Table 3, MorphInd incorrectly segments the input into two separate parts (the break being marked by the string DASH). The tag VSA (=

singular verb instead of VPA = plural verb) indicates, inaccurately, that each part is an independent word instead of a single morphological formation, i.e. a reduplication.

The above systems are widely used and are state-of-the-art systems (MorphInd for morphological analyser and IPOS tagger for POS tagger) for Indonesian, although others exist.

Table 3. Inaccurate analysis of reduplication-affix intersection from MorphInd

Input	Word formation	Output
pukul-memukul 'to hit one and each other'	Reduplication	pukul<v>_VSADASH ^meN+pukul<v>_VSA

2   Reduplication and Its Intersection with Affixes

The annotation in this experiment was implemented using NooJ v.5 [7] (June 2020 version). The morphological annotation scheme used in the experiment is that devised and presented in full detail in [1], henceforth abbreviated PM. To implement PM, I constructed NooJ dictionaries and grammars for Indonesian from scratch; to date, no Indonesian language resources are available for NooJ.

PM dictates that words must be tokenized into morphemes, and each morpheme must be associated with at least one morphological tag. The output format is <token, delimiter (comma), tag>. Thus, the annotation for the verbal root morpheme pukul, 'to hit', is as follows: <pukul, VER+ROOT>. The tag is a combination of analytic codes, demarcated by +.

PM follows the view of *morphological reduplication* proposed by Chaer [8]. Central to Chaer's concept of morphological reduplication is the distinction between a root and its copy. Thus, one of the fundamental principles of the annotation of reduplications in PM is that the annotation of a root and its copy must be clearly distinguished. In the implementation, the first segment of a full reduplication is considered to be the root, and the second its copy.

Each part must be encoded with a distinct analytic tag. The tag for the copy begins with the code RED (reduplication), while the tag for the original root starts with the root's POS tag (e.g., VER, ADJ, NOM for verbs, adjectives, and nouns, respectively) and is the same as the tag that that root would be assigned in a non-reduplicated context. The NooJ Task Annotation Structure (TAS) in Fig. 1 may serve to illustrate this.

The annotation of *tembak-menembak* in Fig. 1 is an example of a prefix-reduplication intersection, since the copy (but not the root) has the prefix *meN-*. This analysis was obtained in three steps. First, the NooJ dictionaries and morphological grammar were applied. The dictionaries supplied identical POS tags for the root tembak 'to shoot' and its copy as verbal roots. The morphological grammar supplied the tag for prefix *meN-*. This grammar can handle morphophonemic alternation for the allomorphs of *meN-* [9], of which *men-* (as in the above TAS) is one. Second, a syntactic grammar with an equality

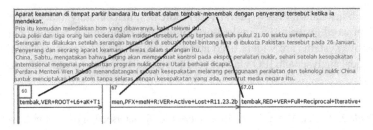

Fig. 1. NooJ TAS for a full reduplication: *tembak-menembak* 'to shoot one and each other'

constraint [2] was applied to introduce the annotation that indicates a copy (i.e. begins with <RED>) to the copy element. Third, a syntactic grammar with disambiguation rules was applied to the copy in order to remove all annotations except the annotation that begins with <RED>. In concert, these resources can annotate almost all patterns in which reduplications intersect with affixes. However, there was one pattern that these resources failed to annotate. Table 4 enumerates both the analysable and unanalysable patterns.

Table 4. An evaluation of Indonesian reduplication patterns tagged by NooJ

	Pattern	Correct tagging
1	<PFX> <ROOT> - <PFX> <RED>	Yes
2	<ROOT> - <PFX> <RED>	Yes
3	<ROOT> <SFX> - <RED> <SFX>	Yes
4	<ROOT> - <RED> <SFX>	Yes
5	<ROOT> - <IFX> <RED>	Yes
6	<PFX> <ROOT> - <RED> <SFX>	Yes
7	<CFX+A> <ROOT> <CFX+Z> - <CFX+A> <RED> <CFX+Z>	Yes
8	<CFX+A> <ROOT> - <RED> <CFX+Z>	No

The NooJ annotation in Fig. 2 exemplifies the eighth pattern. This is unsatisfactory because it analyses *beR-* and *-an* as two independent affixes (prefix + suffix) instead of as a single circumfix.[1] A circumfix is orthographically not distinct from a prefix and suffix combination, as a circumfix is composed of opening and closing elements. But although there are two elements, we must consider them as one set of affixes instead of as two independent affixes because the circumfix is functionally distinct.

---

[1] This is visible from the rule numbers. The rule numbers for *ber-* and *-an* in the TAS are different (R11.2.1 and R6.5, respectively). The numbers should be identical if the circumfix has been correctly analysed.

Fig. 2. TAS for the annotation of reduplication-circumfix intersection: *berpukul-pukulan*

Silberztein [2] shows how morphological grammar can be used to annotate reduplications in Quechua, in whose orthography the two elements of a reduplication are
agglutinated without any space or demarcating symbol. But the same approach is insuf-
ficient for the circumfix-reduplication example in Fig. 5. This is because the root and
copy in the pattern in question are separated by a hyphen, which is not recognized
by NooJ's morphological grammar parser. As a result, the two parts of the circumfix
cannot be linked (and therefore, incorrect results are produced). Any NooJ morphological grammar that targets the above pattern would thus necessarily fail to analyse the
interface.

3   Possible Solutions and the Current Experiment

3.1   Possible Solutions

I have identified several potential solutions (see Table 5), all of which maintain PM's
morpheme-level annotation. Option 1 is to build a kind of "unified grammar," which can
function as both a morphological and syntactic grammar.[2] This would be an elegant and
simple approach. Reduplications which are handled by using a series of rule applications
could instead be handled by just one simplified rule. While NooJ seems to be moving in
this direction, at present, the engine is not ready, and thus this solution is not presently
feasible (Silberztein, personal communication). Option 2, making the morphological
grammar read hyphens, would also require internal modification of the NooJ engine, but
might not be as time-consuming as option 1 to implement.

Option 3 is expected to compensate for the morphological grammar's restriction
on accepting a hyphen. However, in the current version of NooJ, encoding a hyphen
as a dictionary entry cannot override this restriction. This solution is thus not feasible.
Option 4, manually coding all full morphological analyses involved into the dictionary,
would work, but has the disadvantage of treating productive morphological operations
like non-productive morphological operations. This stands in contrast with the purpose
of automatic annotation, which is to minimize manual work.

In this paper, I explore option 5. Three major advantages of this approach are that (1)
it offers a greater degree of automation (no new dictionary entries need be introduced),
(2) it is feasible without modifying the current NooJ engine, and (3) the side-effects it

---

[2] In Nooj v.5, morphological and syntactic grammars are two separate types of grammar (.nom
and .nog, respectively).

Table 5. Possible solutions to annotate the reduplication-circumfix intersection.

	Option	Automaticity	Complexity	NooJ engine modification
1	Unify morphological and syntactic grammar	High	Low	Required
2	Allow morphological grammar to accept a hyphen	High	Low	Required
3	Encode hyphen as a dictionary entry	High	Low	Required
4	Manually list all full-form reduplications in the dictionary and manually incorporate the corresponding analyses	Low	Low	None
5	Incorporate additional rules that treat a circumfix like a prefix and suffix combination into the current morphological grammar	Low	High	None

causes can be predicted and anticipated. The introduction of rules that analyse a circumfix as a combination of a prefix and a suffix causes ambiguities to greatly increase as a side-effect. To eliminate this side-effect, the current disambiguation module is revised, as shown later in Sect. 3.2.

3.2 Current Experiment

In the experiment, all resources were simplified to target only the problematic sequence. The size of the text for this experiment is less than 50 words but contains samples relevant to the pattern in question; the reduced dictionary contains only those roots present in the experimental corpus (Fig. 3 and Table 6).

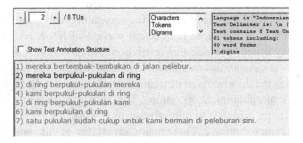

Fig. 3. Text for the experiment

The morphological grammar rules for this experiment were also adapted to contain only rules relevant to this experiment. In this grammar, the opening element <CFX+A>

Table 6. Sample root entry dictionary for the experiment

Entry
pukul, VER
pukul,
NOM
tembak,
VER
main, VER
cukup, ADJ

and closing element <CFX+Z> of the *ber–an* circumfix are introduced in conjunction with the prefix and suffix (on lines 3 and 5, respectively) (Table 7).

Table 7. Morphological grammar rules for the experiment

	Entry
1	Main = :ber | :an | :pe | :ber-an| :pe-an;
2	root = $(X <L>* $) (<E>/<$X=:ALU>) <E>/<$1L, $1C>;
3	ber = (ber/<ber, CFX+A> | ber/<ber, PFX>) :root;
4	...
5	an = :root (an/<an, CFX+Z>| an/<an, SFX>);
6	ber-an = ber/<ber, CFX+A> :root an/<an,CFX+Z>;
7	...

Let us target the most challenging sequence in this corpus, *berpukul-pukulan*, 'to hit each other repeatedly', whose root is *pukul*, 'hit'. This sequence is the most challenging for two reasons. First, the root is ambiguously analysed as both a verb (*pukul* 'hit') and a noun (*pukul* 'o'clock'), where the correct interpretation in this context is a verb. Therefore, the noun analytic code <NOM> has to be removed. Second, we need to remove the incorrect annotations (<PFX> and <SFX>) and replace them with correct analyses (<CFX+A> and <CFX+Z>). Overall, this experiment aims to convert the ambiguous annotations in Fig. 4 into the unambiguous annotations in Fig. 5.

The first step is to insert RED into the copy of the root using the syntactic grammar containing the rules shown in Table 8. At this point, there is no attempt at disambiguation: the analyses of both root and copy remain ambiguous, as shown in Fig. 6.

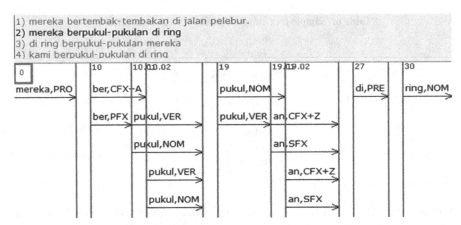

Fig. 4. Ambiguous annotations for *berpukul-pukulan* caused by the morphological grammar rules

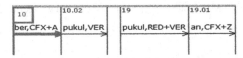

Fig. 5. Expected result for *berpukul-pukulan* after the application of syntactic grammar disambiguation rules

Table 8. The syntactic grammar rules to insert <RED> annotation

Rule
<CFX> $(A <NOM> $) - <E>/<$A_, **RED+NOM** $(B <VER> $) <E>/<$A_=$B_> <E>/> <CFX>;
<CFX> $(A <VER> $) - <E>/<$A_,**RED+VER** $(B <VER> $) <E>/<$A_=$B_> <E>/> <CFX>

The second step involves a syntactic grammar with the following tasks: (1) remove incorrect analyses of the root <NOM>, (2) remove the incorrect copy <RED+NOM>, (3) remove the incorrect analyses of the affixes (<PFX> and <SFX>). These three tasks are completed successfully via the rule shown in Table 9.

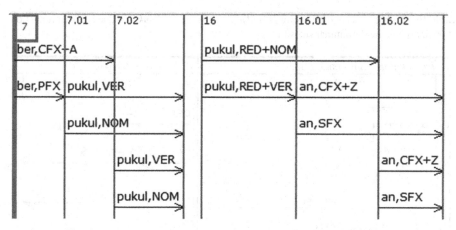

Fig. 6. The result of applying the syntactic grammar rules in Table 8.

Table 9. Syntactic grammar rules to remove ambiguities in circumfix annotations

Rule
Main = <CFX>/<CFX>
$(A <VER>/<VER> $) - $(B <RED+VER>/<RED+VER> $)
<E>/<$A_ =$B_>
<CFX>/<CFX> ;

Introducing new rules to target the problem has proven successful. The expected result in Fig. 5 was obtained. However, as mentioned previously in Sect. 3.1, this approach has a side-effect. Some morphemes that used to be unambiguously analysed have now become unexpectedly ambiguous. Table 10 shows examples of ambiguously annotated circumfix (reciprocal circumfix *ber–an* in *berpukulan*), prefix (intransitive verb marker *ber-* in *bermain*), and suffix (nominalizer suffix *-an* in *pukulan*), respectively. The roots in examples 1 and 3 are also ambiguous, adding yet more ambiguities to be resolved.

Table 10. Ambiguous annotations for *berpukulan, bermain,* and *pukulan* due to the introduction of the morphological grammar rules in

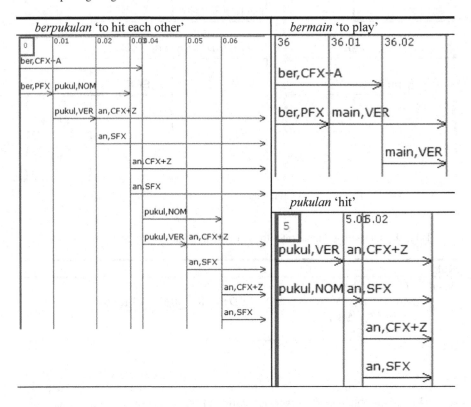

To disambiguate these annotations, the disambiguation rules in Table 11 must be applied in order. The rule in point 1 targets the annotations of the circumfix *ber–an*, while the rules in point 2 target the annotations of the prefix *ber-* and the suffix *-an*.

Table 11. Rules to disambiguate noisy annotations for *berpukulan, bermain* and *pukulan*

	Rules
1	Main = <CFX>/<CFX> <VER>/<VER> <CFX>/<CFX>;
2	Main = <PFX>/<PFX> <VER> <!-> | <!CFX+A> <VER>/<VER> <CFX+Z>/<SFX>;

The resulting disambiguated sequences are shown in Table 12.

Table 12. Unambiguous annotation of *berpukulan, bermain* and *pukulan*

Word	TAS

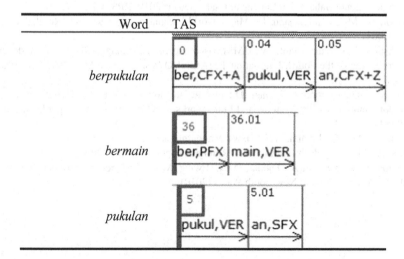

4 Conclusion

Despite the experimental nature of the work presented here, the application of the modified morphological analysis resources and disambiguation module has proven successful in overcoming the reduplication-circumfix intersection problem I observed in Sect. 2. The approach has also successfully eliminated the side-effect identified in Sect. 3.1. These results suggest that this is a promising approach worth extending to a full-scale trial.

Further research could explore the effectiveness of this approach when implemented to improve the resources presently used to perform morphological annotations on Indonesian texts. A precise measurement of the effectiveness of this approach would be obtained by evaluating the annotations of a full corpus to which the improved resources are applied.

Acknowledgments. This paper has been written during my PhD candidacy at Lancaster University, Lancaster, United Kingdom. I would like to extend my deepest gratitude to the Indonesia Endowment Fund for Education[3] (*Lembaga Pengelola Dana Pendidikan*, or LPDP) for its full sponsorship of my PhD study at Lancaster University. I am also highly indebted to Andrew Hardie, my PhD supervisor, for his useful feedback on this manuscript. All errors are mine.

References

1. Prihantoro: A new tagset for morphological analysis of Indonesian. In: International corpus linguistics conference, Cardiff (2019)
2. Silberztein, M.: Formalizing Natural Languages NooJ Approach. Wiley, London (2016)

---

[3] https://www.lpdp.kemenkeu.go.id/.

3. Badan Pusat Statistik, I.: Buku 7: Pedomen Kode Provinsi Kabupaten Kota Negara Suku Bangsa Kewarganegaraan Bahasa dan Lapangan Usaha Sensus 2010. BPS, Jakarta (2010)
4. Tadmor, U.: Malay-Indonesian. In: Major World Languages, pp. 791–818. Routledge, New York (2004)
5. Wicaksono, A.-F., Purwarianti, A.: HMM based part-of-speech tagger for Bahasa Indonesia. In: Proceeding of the Fourth International MALINDO Workshop (MALINDO2010), Jakarta (2010)
6. Larasati, S.-D., Kuboň, V., Zeman, D.: Indonesian morphology tool (MorphInd): towards an indonesian corpus. In: Systems and Frameworks for Computational Morphology, Zurich, Switzerland (2011)
7. Silberztein, M.: NooJ manual (2003). www.nooj4nlp.net
8. Chaer, A.: Morfologi Bahasa Indonesia. Rhinneka Cipta, Bandung (2008)
9. Sneddon, J.-N., Adelaar, A., Djenar, D.-N., Ewing, M.-C.: Indonesian Reference Grammar, 2nd edn. Allen & Unwin, New South Wales (2010)

Multiword Expressions in the Medical Domain: Who Carries the Domain-Specific Meaning

Kristina Kocijan[1]($\boxtimes$) (ID), Krešimir Šojat[2], and Silvia Kurolt[1]

[1] Department of Information and Communication Sciences, Faculty of Humanities and Social Sciences, University of Zagreb, Zagreb, Croatia
{krkocijan,skurolt}@ffzg.hr
[2] Department of Linguistics, Faculty of Humanities and Social Sciences, University of Zagreb, Zagreb, Croatia
ksojat@ffzg.hr

Abstract. This paper is a continuation of work in natural language processing in the medical domain for Croatian. After we have annotated single nouns from our corpus consisting of pharmaceutical instructions for medicaments, we are shifting the focus to multiword expressions (MWEs). The project still relies on the nouns from the previous step to detect MWEs where the noun is the main carrier of the medical meaning. However, in cases where the main noun is more general and not directly associated with the medical domain (e.g., *bubrežna* **funkcija** 'kidney **function**'), we use the power of NooJ morphology grammar to check if the preceding adjective root is associated with the noun found in the main dictionary and annotated as a medical domain noun. Thus, we are checking if the adjective (*endoskopski* 'endoscopic') has a corresponding noun (*endoskopija* 'endoscopy') that is already marked in the NooJ dictionary as a noun belonging to the medical domain. In such cases, we assume that the adjective belongs to the same domain as the noun and that the attribute for the medical domain can be inherited, not only for the adjective, but for the entire MWE as well.

The project hopes to help with the automatic extraction and annotation of single adjectives from the medical domain, but also to help identify medical MWEs. Additionally, we wanted to learn more about who carries the domain-specific meaning in Croatian MWEs.

Keywords: Medical domain corpus · Detecting MWE · Domain specific meaning · Morphology · Syntax · Croatian language · NooJ

1 Introduction

Some time ago, electronic health records were introduced to support decision making at a faster pace. This is facilitated by having records in digital format, which would allow for easier sharing of medical data and faster availability of data. Recently, we have started working on the medical domain for Croatian texts [6], hoping to provide the same possibilities and functionalities for Croatian medical workers. To get us started, we have prepared the 71,911,667-token corpus out of 6,500 Pharmaceutical instructions on

© Springer Nature Switzerland AG 2021
B. Bekavac et al. (Eds.): NooJ 2020, CCIS 1389, pp. 49–60, 2021.
https://doi.org/10.1007/978-3-030-70629-6_5

medicines, written for medical personnel. However, over 88,000 were words unknown to NooJ [10], which by that time had words belonging mainly to the general usage lexicon [12].

Due to the large number of unknowns, we chose the methodology *divide and conquer* and decided to first deal with the unknown nouns. Each noun was hand-tagged with the domain attribute MED, but also with one out of 12 sub-domain markers we have detected in the corpus. There were also a number of examples of a noun belonging to 2 different domains, in which case markers for both sub-domains were provided [7]. The same markers were also given to Latin nouns found in the corpus [6].

Still, we had to face other parts of speech that can be described as domain-specific, like verbs, adverbs, and adjectives, with nouns and adjectives being the more dominant ones. Since we wanted to address multiword expressions next, it was important that we first deal with adjectives, particularly because in some cases it is precisely the adjective that pushes the entire expression over to the side of the medical domain, e.g., *temperaturna lista* '**temperature** list'; *zdravstveni radnik* 'medical worker', *limfni sustav* '**lymphatic** system', or *bolesnički krevet* '**sick** bed'. The project will still rely on the nouns from the previous step to detect multiword expressions where the noun is the main carrier of the medical meaning (e.g. *akutna bol* 'acute **pain**') along with recognizing adjectives derived from such nouns.

This will bring us closer to detecting MWEs where the main noun is more general and not directly associated with the medical domain (e.g., *bubrežna funkcija* 'kidney function'; *farmaceutski podatci* 'pharmaceutical data'; *endoskopski nalazi* 'endoscopic results'; *gastrointestinalni sustav* 'gastrointestinal system'). To achieve this, we will use the power of the NooJ morphology grammar [10] to check if the adjective root is associated with the noun found in the main dictionary and annotated as a medical domain noun. In such instances, we will assume that the adjective belongs to the same domain and that the attribute for the medical domain can be inherited, not only for the adjective, but for the entire MWE as well.

The structure of this paper aims to give a brief theoretical overview of the derivational morphology for noun–adjective pairs in Croatian in general in Sect. 2, followed by a description of the main research settings for this project in Sect. 3, an overview of the analyzed data and the morphological grammar that was built upon the results of that data in Sect. 4, and a discussion of our results on the prepared corpus in Sect. 5. The paper concludes with an outline of future work.

2 Theoretical Overview and Related Work

As we began our research into multi-word lexical objects, we were met with the question of proper terminology usage in reference to such objects. Turning to other academic research done on the topic only raised more questions than it seemed to give answers, as there was a very clear terminological divide between two terms in particular and no apparent motivation or distinction in their usage. The two terms in question are *multi-word expressions*, or *MWEs*, and (the somewhat more dominant) *multi-word units*, or *MWUs*. So what exactly is happening here? Could these seemingly synonymous terms be taken at face value, or is there any semantic subtlety that should be taken into consideration before usage? To answer these questions, we yet again turned to research already done on the topic, but this time digging for definitions and characteristics associated with each term.

Regarding multi-word units or MWUs, the common consensus appears to be that "any sequence of words – semantically opaque or not – which is likely to be lexicalized" [4] can and should be considered a multi-word unit. Additionally, one of the most prominent defining traits of MWUs is that these units, despite being made up of more than just one word, carry a unitary meaning that is as strong as any single-word lexical unit [13].

Similarly, the agreed-upon definition for multi-word expressions or MWEs describes such linguistic objects as "lexical units larger than a word that can bear both idiomatic and compositional meanings" [9]. It should come as no surprise that the definitions for MWEs often rely on using the term *unit* to describe the nature of this linguistic object, as just by comparing the two definitions we can easily conclude that the two terms are essentially synonyms. This also explains the fact that the terms seem to be used interchangeably within the academic community.

Interestingly enough, the *multi-word unit / multi-word expression* dilemma appears to be but the tip of the iceberg in terms of the terminology of multi-word research. As Hüning and Schlücker [5] point out, abundant terminology is actually one of the biggest issues within multi-word object research. Aside from MWUs and MWEs, the field has a plethora of commonly used terms (which are either completely or partially synonymous), including the following: "collocation, extended lexical unit, fixed expression, formulaic sequence, idiom, idiomatic expression, lexical/lexicalized phrase, multi-word unit, phraseme, phraseologism, phraseological unit, phrasal lexical item, phrasal lexeme, prefabricated chunk, prefab" [5]. With such an extensive yet non-standardized terminology, any confusion over term usage is indeed understandable. As for the two terms we are concerned with, it does appear that multi-word expressions and multi-word units are synonymous and that the choice of one or the other seems to be more a matter of preference than definition. Silberztein [10] also argues that the definition of a multi-word unit shifts as the observing researcher does, causing it to vary between, e.g., a logician and a lexicographer, but goes further in providing three criteria that should help us differentiate between the two. However, considering our journey to better understand language use in the medical domain has only just begun, we opted for the term **multi-word expression** since we feel it gives us more room to explore all the possibilities available within NooJ.

That being said, we turn to the narrower topic of Croatian morphology. Croatian is a South Slavic language with very rich morphology, both in terms of inflection and word-formation. Inflection in Croatian is almost exclusively based on suffixation. Generally speaking, inflectional morphemes are bound morphemes expressing several grammatical categories; for example, gender, number, and case for nouns and adjectives; tense, person and number for verbs.

Numerous phonological changes take part at the boundaries of inflectional suffixes and the stems to which they are attached. The result of these processes is frequent allomorphy of forms. For example, in the MWE *srčani udar* 'heart attack', the adjective *srčani* is derived from the noun *srce* 'heart' by the addition of the suffix *–an(i)*, triggering phonological changes in the stem.

In MWEs like *histološke promjene* 'histological changes' containing adjectives of Latin or Greek origin, which are particularly common in the medical domain, Croatian reference books [1, 2, 11] stress that adjectives are derived from nouns (*histologija* 'histology') by adding the suffix *–ski*. At the same time, this suffix is a complex unit consisting of the derivational suffix *–sk–*, used for the derivation of adjectives, and the inflectional suffix *–i*. In this and similar examples, the suffix *–sk–* has undergone various phonological changes,[1] whereas the suffix *-e* expresses inflectional categories of gender (feminine), number (plural), and case (nominative). These and similar phenomena present a challenge in the creation of rules for the automatic recognition of particular morphemes and the precise definition of their status. Section 4 provides a detailed account of the morphological rules created to overcome such challenges.

In terms of grammatical gender, Croatian nouns can be masculine, feminine, or neuter. There are two numbers (singular and plural, in rare cases *singulare* or plurale tantum) and seven cases. Within noun phrases (NPs), consisting of nouns and adjectives or other determiners, there is always agreement in gender, number and case. The NP head (noun) determines the morphological form of adjectives and other preceding elements, such as pronouns.

In this article, we deal with the detection of NPs as candidates for terms within the medical domain. We primarily focus on NPs consisting of a noun and an adjective. The result of our preliminary analysis indicates that this is the most frequent term structure in our sample corpus. However, in numerous cases, nominal MWEs from the medical domain consist of various combinations of nouns with (potentially multiple) adjectives, adverbs, and other nouns, either in the same or a different case. We briefly tackle these MWEs in the Sect. 3.2.

At this time, we primarily deal with MWEs that consist of a noun and an adjective. In the majority of cases, it stands that adjectives co-occurring with nouns as their attributes in nominal MWEs modify their meaning. The meaning of nouns is more specified and narrower compared to cases without attributes – e.g., *atopijski, alergijski, kronični dermatitis* 'atopic, allergic, chronic dermatitis'. Thus, such MWEs are subtypes or hyponyms of a more general term (*dermatitis*).

Croatian morphology is also very rich in terms of word-formation processes. Whereas classes and paradigms of nouns, adjectives, and verbs are covered extensively by the Croatian NooJ inflectional dictionary and used for various NLP tasks as lemmatization, part of speech and morphosyntactic tagging etc., a derivational dictionary is still under construction. Due to the complexity and diversity of data, the development of word-formation resources is difficult and time-consuming work that requires much manual checking. Kyjánek [8] reports on derivational resources developed for various languages and points out that the number of such language resources is very small in comparison to the number of inflectional lexicons developed worldwide. Filko et al. [3] present the

---

[1] See Marković (morfofonologija) for more details.

development of the lexicon designed to mark derivational relations in Croatian. The authors of the present article plan to integrate these data into the Croatian NooJ module in the future.

As indicated, the analysis and annotation of word-formation processes is in many cases difficult due to their complexity and variety. In Croatian, two major word-formation processes are derivation and compounding. Derivation is predominately based on affixation; i.e. suffixation, prefixation, and simultaneous prefixation and suffixation. Among them, suffixation is the most frequently used derivational process in Croatian. The main difference between derivation and compounding is the number of involved stems: one stem is used in derivation, and two (or more) stems in compounding. Words are frequently formed via conversion, back-formation or various combinations of compounding and simultaneous affixation, as well.

Accommodating theoretical rules, in this stage of the project we aim to (1) automatically detect affixes (mainly suffixes) in the morphological structure of adjectives listed as candidates for the medical domain, (2) check whether there is a connection between these adjectives and nominal stems that are already tagged as MED in the Dictionary, and (3) use these data for the creation of broader morphological rules capable of dealing with larger corpora in the medical domain. Section 4 provides a detailed account of results and statistics for our endeavor.

When designing the rules, we took into consideration that the following processes take part in the word-formation of Croatian adjectives: suffixation, prefixation, simultaneous prefixation and suffixation, compounding, and combinations of compounding and affixation. The major process is suffixation. Babić [1] lists 160 suffixes used for this purpose. Croatian grammar and reference books [1, 2, 11] point out that adjectives are primarily derived from nouns. In a few cases, adjectives can be formed from adverbs, pronouns or other adjectives, as well. The most frequent prefix in the word-formation of Croatian adjectives is the prefix *ne-* (non-), denoting the opposition of meaning (e.g. *učinkovit–neučinkovit* 'efficient–inefficient'). Prefixes of mostly Latin origin (anti-, post-, contra- etc.) are partuculary common in the medical domain.

The morphological rules we designed for adjectival suffixes are based on a different direction. Basically, they take adjectives as a starting point and strip off derivational suffixes in order to establish derivational connections with corresponding nouns. The aim is to determine which adjectives can be assigned the MED tag due to derivational relations with already tagged nouns in the dictionary. The morphological rules we applied for prefixes aim to detect prefixes used in the medical domain. The number of these prefixes is limited and can be described in a more straightforward manner.

In the following sections, we describe the data used for this experiment and discuss the results we obtained. First, we give a brief overview of the preprocessing of data necessary for further steps.

3   Research Overview

3.1   Preparing the Data

The results presented in this paper were obtained from a test corpus – a smaller sub-corpus extracted from the large medical corpus as described in the Introduction. The prepared test corpus consists of 271,956 tokens.

The first phase of our project was to learn about the data (noun phrases) we had in the corpus. In order to accommodate this, a NooJ syntactic grammar was prepared to search for all the noun phrases that consisted of up to four adjectives[2] and a noun [A + N] taking into account that they match in number, gender, and case. In our test corpus, 16,930 examples[3] resulted from this grammar and were all annotated as <NP>.

However, we added additional information to each branch of the grammar since we wanted to learn if any of the nouns in an expression already had the domain-specific tag <N+MED>. In such cases, the recognized <NP> inherited the +MED tag, indicating that the entire phrase should belong to the same medical domain. On the other hand, if the noun in an expression was not tagged with the domain specific marker, the entire expression is only marked as an <NP>.

3.2   The Sandbox: Learning About the Data

The concordance was next moved to an area outside of NooJ where we could more easily manipulate the data and learn from it. Our preliminary results showed that 51.8% of noun phrases (8,769 NPs) already had a domain-specific marker, i.e., they carried the + MED tag.

(a.1.) *aktivno **krvarenje***
(a.2.) *akutna **toksičnost***
(a.3.) *alergijski **dermatitis***

Looking at the context of the detected noun phrases, we observed examples where the NP was followed by an additional noun in the genitive that was also from the medical domain, but these cases need additional care and will not be further discussed here. Such are the following examples:

(b.1.) *istodobnom primjenom **antacida***
(b.2.) *maloj grupi **bolesnika***
(b.3.) *medicinski karton **bolesnika***
(c.1.) *primarna **hiperhidroza aksile***
(c.2.) *pojačano **znojenje artralgija***
(c.3.) *simptomatsko **liječenje bolesnika***

---

[2] The analysis did not show matches for larger numbers of adjectives.

[3] This analysis was performed only via an algorithm that uses known adjectives. It is thus possible that a number of phrases were not recognized if any of the adjectives that form it are still unknown in NooJ.

The remaining 48.2% of noun phrases (8,160 NPs) that did not have any domain marker still needed to be reviewed since it was evident that a large number of them should carry the marker as well.

Among all the results, there were 2 with 4 preceding adjectives, 96 with 3 adjectives, 1,710 with 2 adjectives, and 15,122 with only one adjective as illustrated in the following examples (the number next to the adjective marker A, shows which adjective, if any, is from the medical domain, a lower number denoting an adjective closer to the noun):

- 4 preceding adjectives
  - *ostale manje česte zabilježene nuspojave* $<N_{MED}>$
- 3 preceding adjectives
  - *maksimalna preporučena dnevna doza,*
  - *otvorenom nekontroliranom kontinuiranom ispitivanju,*
  - *srednju korigiranu ukupnu koncentraciju* $<N_{MED}>,$
  - *teškom primarnom aksilarnom hiperhidozom* $<A1_{MED}+N_{MED}>,$
  - *različitih analgetskih djelatnih tvari* $<A2_{MED}>,$
  - *ozbiljnim kožnim infektivnim komplikacijama* $<A2_{MED}+A1_{MED}>,$
  - *specifična koštana alkalna fosfataza* $<A2_{MED}+A1_{MED}+N_{MED}>,$
  - *sterilnom normalnom fiziološkom otopinom* $<A3_{MED}+N_{MED}>,$
  - *terapeutskih mekih kontaktnih leća* $<A3_{MED}+N_{MED}>,$
- 2 preceding adjectives
  - *teške akutne reakcije,*
  - *pedijatrijski klinički podaci* $< A2_{MED}+A1_{MED}>$
  - *smanjenom bubrežnom funkcijom* $<A1_{MED}>$
  - *očni štetni događaji* $<A2_{MED}>$
  - *neliječena adrenokortikalna insuficijencija* $<A2_{MED}+ A1_{MED}+N_{MED}>$
  - *dječjom cerebralnom paralizom* $< A2_{MED}+ A1_{MED}+N_{MED}>$
  - *neobične abdominalne simptome* $< A1_{MED}+N_{MED}>$
- single adjective and a noun
  - *aseptičnim uvjetima* $<A1_{MED}>$
  - *cerebrovaskularnom bolešću* $<A1_{MED}+N_{MED}>$
  - *prolazna sljepoća* $<N_{MED}>$
  - *štitne žlijezde* $<N_{MED}>$

As these examples show, not only are nouns domain specific, but there are also adjectives that can carry this marker. Adjectives found co-occurring with nouns that were not from the medical domain were of special interest to us since we wanted to learn if the entire NP could inherit the domain from them. Such examples included the following expressions:

- **anatomska** *mjesta | područja | lokalizacije | strukture | promjene*
- **arterijska** *primjena | davanje | vod*
- **aseptička** *primjena | tehnika | postupci | uvjeti | miješanje*
- **bakterijska** *mutacija*
- **biološke** *aktivnost | učinci*
- **bolesnikova** *odgovornost*
- **bolno** *stanje |* **bolni** *impuls*

- **bolničko** *pakiranje*
- **bubrežna** *funkcija* | **bubrežni** *učinci*
- **dermatološki** *učinci*
- **dijagnostička** *primjena* | *potvrda* | *procedura* | *svrha* | *tehnika* | *cilj* | *podaci* | *postupak* | *rezultat* | *informacija.*

After manually checking our results, we detected the presence of 7,626 adjectives. Of those, only 2,346 were different word forms, or to be more precise, only 866 different adjectives, part of which should carry the domain marker. But our NooJ dictionary with 14,654 adjectives only has tags for the adjective type (i.e., whether the adjective is descriptive or possessive; whether it is definite or indefinite) as well as the paradigm name it uses to get all the inflective forms [12]. This is where we decided to use NooJ to augment the dictionary information with the domain markers for adjectives. In the next section we will explain the graph that helped us in that endeavor.

4   Building the Morphology Rules

During the analysis of our results, we noticed a number of NPs (2,686 of them) that were actually MWE from the medical domain but not due to the main noun. A closer look showed that in these cases it was the adjective that contributed to the medical marker. In order to try to (at least) semi-automatically annotate the existing adjectives,[4] we had to ask the following questions:

(1)   which adjectives can carry a medical domain marker?
(2)   is there a pattern for such adjectives?
(3)   can they be recognized from the medical nouns?
(4)   are there any special derivational prefixes used?
(5)   are there expressions in which non-medical adjectives and non-medical nouns form medical multiword expressions?

Answers to these questions helped us prepare a morphological grammar that would recognize such adjectives and automatically add + MED marker to our existing dictionary entries (Fig. 1). Thus, after detecting all the adjectives in our test corpus, we searched for the patterns. "Pattern" here refers to a string that is common to both N and A and another string that differs in morphologically connected words and exhibits some regular alternations (see Fig. 1, notation 1). For example: if an A ends in *-ivan* – the N will have the suffix *-cija* (e.g. *infektivan -> infekcija* 'infective -> infection'). These rules are mainly in line with the morphological rules for the suffixal and prefixal formation of adjectives. However, the way we embed these instructions in the algorithm differs from the rules described in reference books.

The search for patterns among these adjectives revealed that the majority of medical adjectival attributes can be recognized from nouns that have already been marked as medical nouns in our dictionary. Thus, we utilized NooJ to help us detect and mark

---

[4] It is important to notice here that, at this stage, we are only dealing with adjectives that are already known to NooJ – and not with new (i.e., to NooJ unknown) adjectives.

them. NooJ's morphology engine allowed us to design a grammar that recognizes if the root of an adjective can be associated with a MED noun in the main dictionary. If such a noun exists, the adjective inherits its domain marker. Let us see this using the example of *bakterijska mutacija* 'bacterial mutation':

- ***bakterijska*[Adj]** *mutacija* -> bakterij + {sk} + a
  IF *bakterija* EXISTS AS [N+MED] THEN MARK *bakterijska* AS [Adj+MED]
  The same is true for the following adjective–noun combinations:
- ***pedijatrijska*** [Adj] – pedijatrija [N]; ***arterijska*** [Adj] – arterija [N]
  Some morpheme variations may appear, as in *biološka aktivnost* 'biological activity':
- **biološka[Adj]** aktivnost -> biolo + {šk} + a
  IF *biologija* EXISTS AS [N+MED] THEN MARK *biološka* AS [Adj+MED]
  The same is true for the following adjective–noun combinations:
- ***epidemiološki*** [Adj] – epidemiologija[N]; ***dermatološki*** [Adj] – dermatologija [N]

Additional patterns were also detected, and using these patterns, we were able to connect other nouns to their corresponding adjectives. However, we wanted to make sure we were checking only against those nouns that already have a medical domain marker. Thus, an additional constraint node was added (see Fig. 1, notation 2).

In the following step, we detected prefixes that are characteristic for this domain and that occur in the corpus as well. These prefixes were provided as a list of possible patterns (see Fig. 1, notation 3). In some cases, a noun with a prefix also exists in the dictionary – in which case the grammar skips this list, but in the case where the noun exists without a prefix, it is detached from the main noun during the agreement check. Such examples include words like ***anti****diuretic* '**anti**diuretic', ***pred****operativan* '**pre**operational', ***post****operativan* '**post**operational', and ***netoksičan* '**non**toxic'.

[anti]	*diuretski/agregacijski;*
[pred \ post]	*menstruacijski/operativan/natalni/menopauzalni;*
[ne]	*rođenog/stabilne/steroidne/toksične;*
[van \ izvan]	*stanični/materini;*
[intra]	*uterine/venski/venozni...*

5 Results

The percentage of medical domain words at the beginning of this project stage for nouns was 25% out of all the nouns in the dictionary (27,813). For the adjectives (14,635) it was 0% since there were no adjectives with this marker when we started the project.

With our morphological grammar we were able to detect around 450 adjectives that complied with the rules given in the grammar. Out of those, 86% were correctly marked, and we semi-automatically added those annotations directly to the dictionary. This semantic layer now covers 5% of the adjectives in the dictionary (Fig. 2).

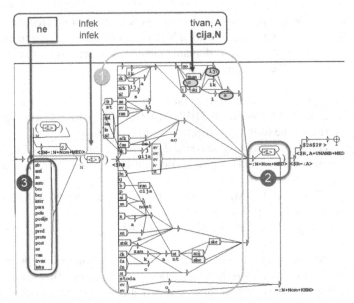

Fig. 1. Morphological grammar that recognizes and annotates medical domain adjectives from medical domain nouns

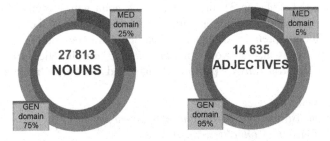

Fig. 2. Comparison of medical vs general domain nouns and adjectives in NooJ dictionary

After applying the medical domain attribute to the adjectives, its distribution in our test corpus (271,956 tokens) is 11.06% of all the adjectives. We get similar results on the larger corpus (19,059,018 tokens), where 10% of adjectives are domain specific.

Still, we have discovered three sets of exceptions to our rules. There are non-medical adjective and noun constructions that, when found together, give a MWE that is from the medical domain, as in the following examples:

- *žarišna točka* 'trigger point' (position on a muscle that hurts when you press it) or in a literal translation to English it would be 'hot spot' – where neither word is from the medical domain;
- *vodene kozice* 'chickenpox' or in literal translation 'little water goats' – again, neither word is from the medical domain.

After checking the results from our automatic morphological grammar – we found examples that seem like they are connected with a medical domain noun, but are actually not, for example:

- *prevratnički* – that the algorithm sees as a domain specific prefix (*pre*), noun (*vrat* – en. 'neck') and an adjectival suffix. However, this word has nothing to do with neck and its translation to English is 'revolutionary'.
- *prijeloman* – is recognized from a noun *prijelom* (en. 'fracture'), but it actually has to do with a turning point in time.

The special type of problem in this category are words that have multiple meanings as a noun, but those meanings do not cross over to the adjectives, as in the example below:

- *zatvorski* – referring to 'digestion problems', but also to "prison". However, the adjective *zatvorski*, refers only to the noun "prison".

Another similar example is the case of the noun *ciganin*, meaning 'Gypsy', but also a skin disease with the same name. However, the adjective '*ciganski*' only refers to the noun Gypsy.

The third challenge were adjectives that do not have a matching noun that we can use to recognize them, such as in the examples *kardiovaskularni, lumbalni, oralni, intestinalni,* or *renalni*. There is no noun like '*lumbal*' or '*renal*' in Croatian from which these adjectives can be recognized.

These three categories of exceptions should serve as a hint that, despite having a grammar that may recognize medical adjectives, the grammar alone is not enough to mark all the adjectives in our dictionary and some additional manual post-processing is required to fully annotate the list of adjectives.

6 Conclusion and Future Work

Since we were only dealing with the adjectives that exist in the NooJ dictionary, our next project will have to consider those adjectives that were left unknown so far. We will need to analyze them and again see how we can reuse existing resources to speed up the process of enlarging the NooJ dictionary of adjectives.

What type of expressions are more dominant in medical texts: ones where the noun carries the domain-specific meaning, or an adjective? Before we can give an answer to this question, we need to be able to recognize all the adjectives in our corpus. At that time we will be able to conclude what sets are more dominant in the corpus (ones with a noun or adjective from the medical domain) and who the true domain carrier is.

References

1. Babić, S.: Tvorba riječi u hrvatskome književnome jeziku. Hrvatska akademija znanosti i umjetnosti. Globus, Zagreb (2002)

2. Barić, E., et al.: Hrvatska gramatika. Školska knjiga, Zagreb (1995)
3. Filko, M., Šojat, K.; Štefanec, V.: Redesign of the Croatian derivational lexicon. In: Žabokrtský, Z.; Ševčíková, M..; Litta, E.; Passarotti, M. (eds.) Proceedings of the Second International Workshop on Resources and Tools for Derivational Morphology, pp. 71–80. Charles University, Faculty of Mathematics and Physics, Institute of Formal and Applied Linguistics, Prague (2019)
4. Grimm, R., Cassani, G., Gillis, S., Daelemans, W.: Facilitatory effects of multi-word units in lexical processing and word learning: a computational investigation. Front. Psychol. **8**, 555 (2017). https://doi.org/10.3389/fpsyg.2017.00555
5. Hüning, M., Schlücker, B.: Multi-word expressions. In: Müller, P.O., Ohnheiser, I., Olsen, S., Rainer, F. (eds.) Word-Formation. An International Handbook of the Languages of Europe, vol. 1, pp. 450–467. De Gruyter Mouton (2015). https://doi.org/10.1515/9783110246254-026
6. Kocijan, K., di Buono, M.P., Mijić, L.: Detecting Latin-based medical terminology in Croatian texts. In: Mauro Mirto, I., Monteleone, M., Silberztein, M. (eds.) NooJ 2018. CCIS, vol. 987, pp. 38–49. Springer, Cham (2019). https://doi.org/10.1007/978-3-030-10868-7_4
7. Kocijan, K., Kurolt, S., Mijić, L.: Building Croatian medical dictionary from medical corpus. Rasprave: Časopis Instituta za hrvatski jezik i jezikoslovlje **46**(2), 765–782 (2020)
8. Kyjánek, L: Morphological resources of derivational word-formation relations. Technical Report TR-2018–61. Institute of Formal and Applied Linguistics, Faculty of Mathematics and Physics, Charles University, Prague (2018)
9. Masini, F.: Multi-word expressions between syntax and the lexicon: the case of Italian verb-particle constructions. SKY J. Linguist. **18**, 145–173 (2005)
10. Silberztein, M.: Formalizing Natural Languages: The NooJ Approach. Cognitive Science Series, Wiley-ISTE, London (2016)
11. Silić, J., Pranjković, I.: Gramatika hrvatskoga jezika: Za gimnazije i visoka učilišta. Školska knjiga, Zagreb (2005)
12. Vučković, K., Tadić, M., Bekavac, B.: Croatian language resources for NooJ. CIT: J. Comput. Inf. Technol. **18**(2010), 295–301 (2010)
13. Zgusta, L.: Multiword lexical units. WORD **23**(1–3), 578–587 (1967). https://doi.org/10.1080/00437956.1967.11435507

Transformations and Paraphrases for Quechua Sentiment Predicates

Maximiliano Duran[1,2](✉) [iD]

[1] Université de Franche-Comté, Besançon, France
duran_maximiliano@yahoo.fr
[2] LIG, UGA, Grenoble, France

Abstract. In this paper, I present a study on the automatic generation of paraphrases of Quechua sentiment predicates. Using the transformational NooJ engine, I first build the rules corresponding to the elementary transformations for the Quechua language. I then describe in detail grammars performing pronominalization, reduction, and permutation of the arguments, passivation, and some others. Then, I show how they can combine with one another, respecting certain syntactic constraints, in order to obtain complex transformations. I present the electronic dictionary of Quechua sentiment verbs that I have built. Finally, I construct a particular subclass of transformations that will automatically generate paraphrases of a Quechua sentiment predicate.

Keywords: NooJ · Quechua · Syntactic analysis · Transformational analysis · Transformational grammar · Sentiment verbs · Sentiment predicates in quechua · Paraphrase · Machine translation

1 Introduction

Our goal is to construct a syntactic grammar that recognizes all the grammatically correct paraphrases of a Quechua sentiment sentence like {*Gervasio Romildata kuyan*/Gervasio loves Romilda}. As Languella [10], I adopt Harris's concept of paraphrase, which Harris [9] borrowed from the concept of morphism in mathematics. A morphism is a structure-preserving map from one mathematical set of objects to another. According to Harris, a sentence is a paraphrase of another one if a change occurs in the morphophonemic shape of the transformed sentence while preserving the original lexical morphemes and meaning. Paraphrasing has been used by many authors, such as Barreiro [1, 2], who used it to prepare texts for machine translation; Ben et al. [3], who used it for bilingual MT for Arabic-English translation of relative clauses; or Fehri et al. [8], who used it for Arabic–French translation of named entities.

Silberztein [11, 12] shows how, by combining a parser and a generator, and applying them to a syntactic grammar, one can build a system that takes one sentence as its input, and produces all the sentences that are morpho-syntactically or semantically related to the original sentence, or share the same lexical material with it. Figure 1 shows our NooJ grammar for the passive transformation:

© Springer Nature Switzerland AG 2021
B. Bekavac et al. (Eds.): NooJ 2020, CCIS 1389, pp. 61–73, 2021.
https://doi.org/10.1007/978-3-030-70629-6_6

- [Passive]{*Gervasio Romildata kuyan*/Gervasio loves Romilda} = {*Romildam Gervasiopa kuyasqan*/Romilda is loved by Gervasio}.

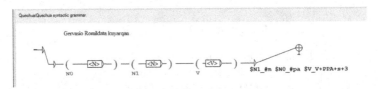

Fig. 1. [Passive]: {*Romildam Gervasiopa kuyasqan*/Romilda is loved by Gervasio}

The graph of Fig. 1 uses three variables, $N0 (the subject S), $N1 (the object O) and $V (the verb V). When parsing the sentence {*Gervasio Romildata kuyan* (N0 N1 V)/Gervasio loves Romilda}, the variable $N0 stores the word {Gervasio}, $N1 stores the word {Romilda} and $V stores the word {*kuyan*/loves}.

The grammar output "$N1_m $N0_#pa $V_V+PPA+s+3" produces the string {*Romildam Gervasiopa kuyasqan*/Romilda is loved by Gervasio}, where V+PPA+s+3 symbolizes the conjugated form past participle of the verb {*kuyay*/to love}, third person singular.

2 Syntactic PoS Transformations

2.1 Noun Transformations

In order to write a grammatical transformation of a sentence in Quechua, an agglutinative language, one needs to take into account the morpho-syntactic transformations of each PoS included in the sentence. This is because each PoS may be inflected or transformed by agglutination of one or more suffixes, acting as operators, coming from their corresponding class of suffixes.

For instance, *Calisto*, a proper name, may be inflected, as follows: {*Calistom*/it is Calisto} (*-m* is the suffix of assertion), {*Calistos*/people say that it is Calisto} (*-s* is the suffix of hearsay), {*Calistoqa*/It's Calisto} (*-qa* is the suffix of topic), {*Calistochá*/It is probably Calisto} (*-chá* is the suffix of uncertainty), etc.

All these inflected forms are obtained applying N-suff[1] operators using the NooJ grammar of Duran [7]. Many binary or ternary combinations of these suffixes may also generate grammatical transformations of (N). Figure 2 shows part of the grammar that generates the mono-suffix transformations of the proper name Calisto.

Let us consider the following direct sentence: {*Calisto wasinta llimpin*/Calisto paints his house}. Replacing the proper noun Calisto by some of its inflections, we obtain transformed sentences like:

---

[1] Suffixes for the inflection of proper nouns ending in a vowel: N-suff = {*-ch, chá, -cha, -chik, -chiki, -chu, -chu? -hina, -kuna, -lla, -má, -man, -manta, -m, -ntin, -niraq, niray, -ña, -p, -pa, -paq, -pas, -poss(7v), -puni, -qa, -rayku, -raq, -ri, -s, -ta, -taq, -wan, -ya!, -yá, -yupa*}.

- *{Calistos wasinta llimpin*/they say that Calisto paints his house}
- *{Calistoqa wasinta llimpin*/It's Calisto that paints his house}
- *{Calistochá wasinta llimpin*/it is probable that Calisto paints his house}

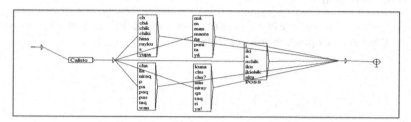

Fig. 2. Mono-suffix transformation of a subject

But this grammar may also generate some ungrammatical forms, such as *{*Calistop wasinta llimpin*/*Calisto's paints his house}, erroneous because *Calistop* is in the genitive case. That's why we need to add syntax constraints to this grammar in order to obtain more accurate outputs.

Furthermore, in Quechua, we may also get transformations by combining two or more N-suff suffixes. For instance, according to Duran [5 p. 73], using two agglutinated nominal suffixes, we obtain more than 320 grammatical transformations of a proper noun, like: {*Gervasio-cha-m llimpin*/little Gervasio does paint}; {*Gervasio-raq-mi llimpin*/Gervasio paints first}; {*Gervasio-lla-m llimpin*/only Gervasio paints}; etc.

For three agglutinated nominal suffixes, we obtain more than 720 grammatical transformations, such as {*Gervasio-cha-lla-m llimpin*/it's only little Gervasio who paints}; {*Gervasio-cha-lla-s llimpin*/they say that it's only little Gervasio who paints}; {*Gervasio-nchik-lla-s llimpin*/they say that it's only our little Gervasio who paints}; etc.

2.2 Pronoun Inflections

For a pronoun like {*pay (third person singular)*} we will have the following transformations:

- *{paymi*/it is him (assertion)}, *{paysi*/people say that it is him (hearsay)},
- *{payqa*/concerning him (topic)}, *{paychá*/It is probably him (uncertainty)}.

The class of pronominal suffixes contains 39 elements, which implies that we may obtain 39 mono-suffix inflections. However, only 28 of these suffixes generate transformed nouns that can be used as the subject of the transformed sentence.

If we take again the sentence: {*Calisto wasinta llimpi n*/Calisto paints his house} and replace the proper noun Calisto by some of these transformed pronouns, we obtain sentences like these:

- *{Paysi wasinta llimpin/*they say that he paints his house}
- *{Paychá wasinta llimpin/*it is probable that he paints his house}.

2.3 Verb Derivation

For any Quechua verb, we have two classes of suffixes which derivate verbs: interposition suffixes (IPS)[2] and postposition suffixes (PPS)[3].

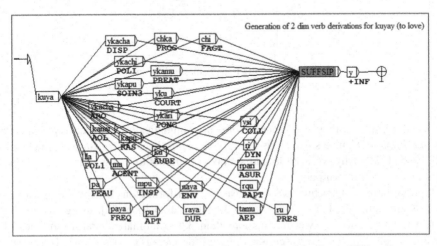

Fig. 3. *Kuyay* (to love) derived by two-dimensional combinations of IPS suffixes

Taking the sentiment verb {*kuyay/*to love}, and parsing it with the grammar of Fig. 3, we obtain 624 new derived verbs with {*kuya*} as the lemma and a combination of two SIP suffixes. They look like in the following sample:

```
# Dictionary generated automatically
kuyarichkay, V+FR="to start loving"+FLX=V_SIP_INF+DYN+CHKA
+INF;
kuyapayarquy,   V+FR="to   love   repeatedly   in   a   short
time"+FLX=V_SIP_INF+FREQ+RQU+INF;
kuyapayariy, V+FR="to love repeatedly in a delicate man-
ner"+FLX=V_SIP_INF+FREQ+RI+INF;
kuyaykachamuy,V+FR="to love in a dispersed manner"+FLX
=V_SIP_INF+ARO+MU +INF; …
```

---

[2] IPSsuff = {*chaku, chi, chka, ykacha, ykachi, ykamu, ykapu, ykari, yku, ysi, kacha, kamu, kapu, ku, lla, mpu, mu, naya, pa, paya, pu, ra, raya, ri, rpari, ru, tamu, rqa, rqu, spa, sqa, na, pti,stin, wa*}. Only the first 27 of them serve to derivate into a verb.

[3] PPSsuff = {*ch, chá, chik, chiki, chu(?), chu, chusina, má, man, m, mi, ña, pas, puni, qa, raq, s, si, taq, yá(!)*}. A total of 28 suffixes.

For three-layer combinations of IPS suffixes, we apply the algebraic grammar V_SIP_INF = :V_SIP1_INF|:V_SIP2_INF|:V_SIP3_INF; for details, see Duran [5], which generates 3,006 new derived verbs, in the infinitive form, ready to be derived or conjugated, as shown in the sample below:

```
kuyaparuchkay,V+EN="to   keep   loving   in   an   intensive
manner"+FLX=V_SIP_INF+PEAU+PRES+PROG+INF;
kuyaykachapayamuy,V+EN="to love repeatedly in a dispersed
manner"+FLX=V_SIP_INF+DISP+FREQ+ACENT+INF;
kuyapayaykarikuy,V+EN="to love mutually repeatedly and with
care"+FLX=V_SIP_INF+FREQ+PONC+AUBE+INF;
```

3   The Verbal PPS Transformations

For obtaining one layer of PPS inflections of a verb, we apply the grammar of Fig. 4.

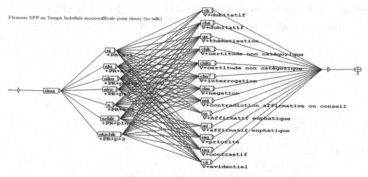

Fig. 4. *rimay* (to talk) inflected by one-layer postposition suffixation (PPS)

To generate all the binary PPS transformations of a verb, following the guidelines given in the work of Duran [5, pp. 255–257], I have constructed the NooJ grammar

- V_PPS2 = : PPS2 | :PPS2_F;

where **PPS2** contains 72 agglutinations for the present tense, such as the following: {*chusinam | manchá | manchik ... | punis | punitaq | ... raqchik | raqchu? | taqchu | taqmá | taqmi | taqsi | taqyá*}. **PPS2_F** corresponds to the future paradigms. This grammar produces 1,008 binary PPS transformations of the verb *kuyay*, such as those appearing in the following sample:

```
kuyankutaqchá, kuyanikuchusinam, kuyanikuraqchá, kuyanki
puni  chu, kuyankipunichu?, kuyankirajsi, kuyaniñachik,
kuyanipunimá, kuyairaqyá, kuyaikumanraq,...
```

One of the important properties of verb transformation in Quechua is that one can compose IPS and PPS transformations in order to obtain mixed transformations like this one:

- *{rima-**yku**-ni-raq-mi (rimaykuniraqmi/*First of all, I presented my greetings)}*

where we have one IPS (*-yku-*) between the lemma and the ending ***ni***, the first person singular and two PPS *(-raq, -mi)* after the ending.

The grammar of Fig. 5, constructed following Duran [5, pp. 257–258] and Duran [4], generates mixed transformations. In the example below, I apply a mixed-grammar composed of two-dimensional PPS and one-dimensional IPS transformations, to the verb {*rimay*/to talk}. We use the grammar V_MIX12, which generates all the transformations containing 1 IPS transformation and two PPS transformations. After parsing, we obtain 17,280 mixed transformed verbal forms like in the sample below:

- *rima***kamu**n**raqmi**,V+EN="*to talk*"+FLX=V_MIX12+AOL+s+3
- *rima***kacha**nkichik**manpas**,V+EN="*to talk* "+FLX=V_MIX12+ARO+p+2
- *rima***kacha**nkichik**paschá**,V+EN="*to talk* "+FLX=V_MIX12+ARO+p+2
- *rima***kacha**nkichik**paschik**,V+EN="*to talk* "+FLX=V_MIX12+ARO+p+2

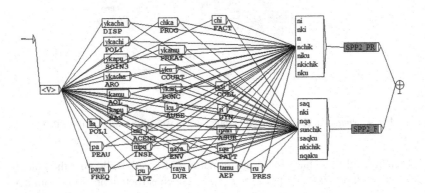

Generation of mixed transformations SIP1_SPP2 of a verb

Fig. 5. A mixed IPS-SPP transformation grammar for a direct transitive sentence

Let's consider some examples of transformations including these mixed inflections of the verb to talk {*Calisto mamanta riman*/Calisto talks to his mother}:

- *{Calistos mamanta rimaykunraq*/they say that, first of all Calisto talked to his mother}
- *{Calistoqa mamanta rimaykullanraq*/concerning Calisto, he first of all talked to his mother with much respect}
- *{Calisto mamanta rimariykunqaraq*/Calisto will talk whispering first to his mother}.

In Fig. 6, we show the syntactic grammar, which gathers these combined transformations. It is capable of recognizing more than one million transformed sentences of a direct transitive sentence such as {*Gervasio Romildata kuyan*/Gervasio loves Romilda}.

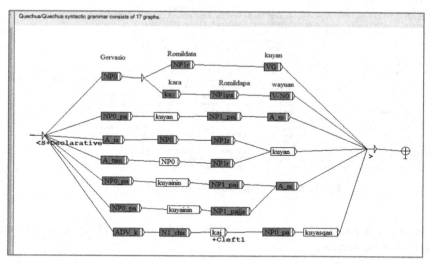

Fig. 6. A grammar which recognizes the transformations of "*Gervasio Romildata kuyan*"

3.1 The Class of Sentiment Verbs

Before introducing our study on paraphrases of sentiment predicates, we will present our dictionary of sentiment verbs. The multilingual electronic dictionary (QU-FR-QU) that we have been building during the last eight years has been enhanced with new linguistic information (namely, inflectional, derivational and morpho-syntactic properties) as well as with some semantic relations. This permits, among other linguistic phenomena, the generation of paraphrases. This dictionary includes the class of sentiment verbs, marked by "+sent". Figure 7 shows an excerpt of this class of verbs (QU-FR).

3.2 Elementary S-Transformation[4] of a Sentiment Sentence

Let us consider the declarative initial sentence of the type N0N1V:

$$\{Gervasio\ Romildata\ kuyan/\text{Gervasio loves Romilda}\} \tag{1}$$

which we want to paraphrase. We present some elementary transformations of a SOV sentence.

(1) The permutation N1_V: [PermN1_V]

---

[4] S-Transformation or Sentence-Transformation: "is an operator that links sentences that share common semantic material" – Harris [9].

```
# Language is: qu
# extract "+sent"
amirparisja-kay,V+Vq+itr+sent+DOM=PSY+FR="être dégouté"+FLX=V_ITR_CONJO
amisja-kay,V+sent+DOM=PSY+DOM=PSY+FR="en avoir marre"+FLX=V_ITR_CONJO
anayniy,V+Vq+tr+sent+FR="admirer"+SENS=encenser_ admirer+DOM=AAA+FLX=V_TR_CONJO
añayniy,V+Vq+tr+sent+FR="louer"+SENS=BBB+DOM=AAA+FLX=V_TR_CONJO
anchay-anchay_kay,V+Vq+itr+sent+DOM=PSY+FR="être arrogant"+FLX=V_ITR_CONJO
anchay-anchay_kay,V+Vq+itr+sent+DOM=PSY+FR="être hautain"+FLX=V_ITR_CONJO
anchayupay,V+Vq+tr+sent+sent+FR="apprécier"+SENS=BBB+DOM=AAA+FLX=V_TR_CONJO
asiriy,V+Vq+itr+sent+FR="rire doucement"+SENS=avoir expression gaie+DOM=SOM+FLX=V_TR_CONJO
atipasja-kay,V+Vq+itr+sent+DOM=PSY+FR="être abbatu"+FLX=V_ITR_CONJO
atipasja-kay,V+Vq+itr+sent+DOM=PSY+FR="être impuissant"+FLX=V_ITR_CONJO
atoj-kay,V+Vq+itr+sent+DOM=PSY+FR="être spiègle"+FLX=V_ITR_CONJO
auki_kay,V+Vq+itr+sent+DOM=PSY+mc+UNAMB+FR="être fougueux"+FLX=V_ITR_CONJO
aynikuy,V+Vq+tr+sent+DOM=PSY+DOM=PSY+FR="être solidaire"+FLX=V_ITR_CONJO
ayniy,V+sent+DOM=PSY+DOM=PSY+FR="coopérer"+FLX=V_ITR_CONJO
chikij-kay,V+Vq+itr+sent+DOM=PSY+FR="être envieux"+FLX=V_ITR_CONJO
chiqnichiy,V+Vq+tr+sent+DOM=PSY+FR="semer la zizanie"+SENS=semer la zizanie+DOM=AAA+FLX=V_TR_CONJO
chuya-kay,V+Vq+itr+sent+DOM=PSY+FR="être clair"+FLX=V_ITR_CONJO
ima-jukuj-kay,V+Vq+itr+sent+DOM=PSY+mc+UNAMB+FR="être indiférent"+FLX=V_ITR_CONJO
ima-jukuyakuy,V+Vq+itr+sent+DOM=PSY+mc+UNAMB+FR="devenir indiférent"+FLX=V_ITR_CONJO
quchukuy,V+sent+DOM=PSY+DOM=PSY+FR="devenir joyeux"+FLX=V_ITR_CONJO
jochukuy,V+Vq+itr+sent+DOM=PSY+FR="se rejouir"+FLX=V_ITR_CONJO
kaminakuy,V+Vq+tr+sent+FR="se insulter"+SENS=s'insulter réciproquement+DOM=AAA+FLX=V_TR_CONJO
kamiy,V+Vq+t+sentr+FR="gronder"+SENS=menacer+DOM=SOC+FLX=V_TR_CONJO
kusikuy,V+sent+DOM=PSY+DOM=PSY+FR="devenir heureux"+FLX=V_ITR_CONJO
kusinaj-kay,V+Vq+itr+sent+DOM=PSY+FR="être mécontent"+FLX=V_ITR_CONJO
kuyay,V+Vq+tr+sent+FR="aimer"+SENS=aimer_ chérir+DOM=PSY+FLX=V_TR_CONJO
llakikuy,V+Vq+itr+sent+FR="s'attrister"+SENS=se chagriner_ désoler+DOM=PSY+FLX=V_ITR_CONJO
```

Fig. 7. Excerpt of the class of QU sentiment verbs.

In QU it is possible to permute the verb and the object without modifying the semantics of the sentence:

- [PermN1_V] {*Gervasio Romildata kuyan/*Gervasio loves Romilda} = {*Gervasio kuyan Romildata/*Gervasio loves Romilda},
  which can be symbolized as: [PermN1_V] (N0N1V) = N0 V N1

(2) The permutation N0_V: [PermN0_V]

It is also possible to permute the verb and the subject without modifying the semantics of the sentence:

- [PermN0_V] {*Gervasio Romildata kuyan/*Gervasio loves Romilda} = {*Kuyan Gervasio Romildata/*Gervasio loves Romilda},
  which can be symbolized as: [PermN0_V](N0N1V) = V N0 N1

(3) Pronominalize the subject N0: [ProN0]. We will have:

  - [ProN0] {*Gervasio Romildata kuyan/*Gervasio loves Romilda} = {*pay Romildata kuyan/*He loves Romilda},
    which can be symbolized as: **[ProN0](N0NV) = pay N1 V**

(4) Pronominalize the object N1: [ProN1]. We will have:

  - [ProN1] {*Gervasio Romildata kuyan/*Gervasio loves Romilda} = {*Gervasio payta kuyan/*Gervasio loves her},
    which can be symbolized as: [ProN1](N0N1V) = N0 payta V

(5) Pronominalize both the subject and the object N0, N1: [ProN0N1]

We will have:

- [ProN0N1] {*Gervasio Romildata kuyan*/Gervasio loves Romilda} = {*Pay payta kuyan*/He loves her},
  which can be symbolized as: [ProN0N1](N0N1V) = pay payta V

(6) Nominalize the verb V: [Vnom_i]. We will have:

- [Vnom_i] {*Gervasio Romildata kuyan*/Gervasio loves Romilda} = {*Romildam Gervasiopa kuyainin*/Romilda is Gervasio's love},
  which can be symbolized as: [Vnom_i](N0N1V) = N1m payta V

(7) Nominalize the verb V: [Vnom_j]. We will have:

- [Vnom_j] {*Gervasio Romildata kuyan*/Gervasio loves Romilda} = {*Romildam Gervasiopa kuyaqnin*/Romilda is Gervasio's lover},
  which can be symbolized as: $[Vnom\_j](N0N1V) = N1m\ N0pa\ V+NV+POSC\_c+3+s$, where $NV+POSC\_c+3+s$ stands for: nominalized verb as agentive and possessive, in the third singular person.

(8) Passive of verb V: [Passive] or The Passive transformation. We will have:

- [Passive] {*Gervasio Romildata kuyan*/Gervasio loves Romilda} = {*Romildam Gervasiopa kuyasqan*/Romilda is loved by Gervasio,
  which can be symbolized as: $[Passive](N0N1V) = N1m\ \$N0pa\ \$V\_V+PPA+s+3$

(9) Cleft operator: [Cleft_0]

Here, a single message is divided into two classes. We will have:

- [Cleft_0] {*Gervasio Romildata kuyan*/Gervasio loves Romilda} = {*Gervasiom kachkan Romilda kuyaq*/It is Gervasio who loves Romilda},
  which can be symbolized as: $[Cleft\_0](N0N1V) = N0m\ kachkan\ N1\ V+NOM\_V+QS$

(10) Cleft: [Cleft_1].

- [Cleft_1] {*Gervasio Romildata kuyan*/Gervasio loves Romilda} = {*Romildatam Gervasioqa kuyan*/It is Romilda that Gervasio loves},
  which can be symbolized as: $[Cleft\_1](N0N1V) = N1tam\ N1qa\ V+PR+3+s$

(11)   Cleft: [Cleft_2]

- [Cleft_2] {*Gervasio Romildata kuyan/*Gervasio loves Romilda} = *{Gevasiom Romilda kuyaqqa/*Gervasio is the one who loves Romilda},
  which can be symbolized as: [Cleft_2] (N0N1V) = N0m N1 V+V+NOM_V+QS+THE

(12)   Adverb: [ADV_V]

We will have:

- [ADV_V] {*Gervasio Romildata kuyan/*Gervasio loves Romilda} = *{Gevasio Romildata achkallataña kuyan/*Gervasio loves Romilda really a lot},
  which can be symbolized as: [[ADV_V]] (N0N1V) = N0 N1ta achkata V+PR+3+s.

Table 1 shows a partial list of these transformations.

Table 1. Elementary transformations of {*Gervasio Romildata kuyan}*

[PermN1_V]	{*Gervasio Romildata kuyan}* = *{Gervasio kuyan Romildata/Gervasio loves Romilda}*
[PermN0_V]	{*Gervasio Romildata kuyan}* = *{Kuyan Gervasio Romildata/*Gervasio loves Romilda}
[Pron-O]	*{Gervasio Romildata kuyan}* = *{Pay Romildata kuyan/*He loves Romilda}
[Pron-1]	{*Gervasio Romildata kuyan}* = *{Gervasio payta kuyan/*Gervasio loves her}
[Pron-2]	{*Gervasio Romildata kuyan}* = *{Gervasio Romildata kuyaita qun/*Gervasio gives Romilda love}
[Cleft-0]	{*Gervasio Romildata kuyan}* = *{Gervasiom kachkan Romilda kuyaqnin/*It is Gervasio who loves Romilda}
[Cleft- 1]	{Gervasio *Romildata kuyan}* = *{Romildatam Gevasioqa kuyan/*It is Romilda that Gervasio loves}
[Nom-O]	{*Gervasio Romildata kuyan}* = {Gervasio Romildawan kuyanakun/Gervasio is in love with Romilda}
[Nom-V]	{*Gervasio Romildata kuyan}* = *{Gervasio kuyaita qatallin Romildapaq/*Gervasio feels love *f*or Romilda}
[Nom-1]	{*Gervasio Romildata kuyan}* = *{Romildam Gervasiopa kuyainin/*Romilda is Gervasio's love}
[Passive]	{*Gervasio Romildata kuyan/*Gervasio loves Romilda} = *{Romildam Gervasiopa kuyasqan/*Romilda is loved by Gervasio}

For many of these elementary transformations, it is possible to construct grammars that perform the reverse operation, as we can see in Fig. 8.

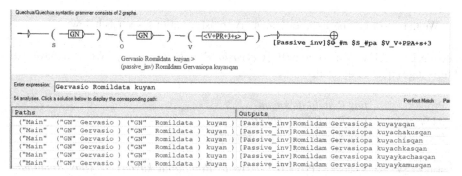

Fig. 8. Grammar for the passive-inv operation of {*Gervasio Romildata kuyan*} → *Romildam Gervasiopa kuyasqan*

4 Composition of Elementary Paraphrasers

In order to obtain composed paraphrasers C_PARPH, it is possible to construct a sequential composition of two or more elementary paraphrasers. They should, of course, respect certain syntactic constraints. Below are some examples.

(1) As said before, one or more of the PoS contained in each of these elementary transformations may be derived or inflected separately. For example, for (12) we may get {*Gevasio Romildata achkallataña kuyan*/Gervasio loves Romilda really a lot}, where the noun and the verb have been derived.

(2) The 12 operators presented earlier can be sequentially applied to a sentence, respecting the syntactic rules, in order to obtain composed paraphrasers, such as the following:

PermN1_V+ProN0
PermN1_V+ProN1
PermN1_V+ProN0N1
PermN1_V+ADV_achka
PermN0_V+PermN1_V
ProN0+PermN1_V
ProN1+PermN1_V
ProN0N1+PermN1_V...

To apply the first composed paraphraser of the list, [PermN1+ProN0], we apply first [ProN0]:

[ProN0] {*Gervasio Romildata kuyan*} = {*pay Romildata kuyan*}

Then we apply PermN1_V:

[PermN1_V] {*pay Romildata kuyan*} = {*pay kuyan Romildata*}

We may now compose three elementary transformations, such as below:

[PermN1_V+ADV_achka+ProN0] {*Gervasio Romildata kuyan}*. We will have the following sequence of results:

ProN0:   *pay Romildata kuyan*
ADV_achka: *pay Romildata achkata kuyan*
PermN1:   *pay Romildata kuyan achkata*

[PermN1_V+ADV_achka+ProN0] {*Gervasio Romildata kuyan*} = {*pay Romildata kuyan achkata*}.

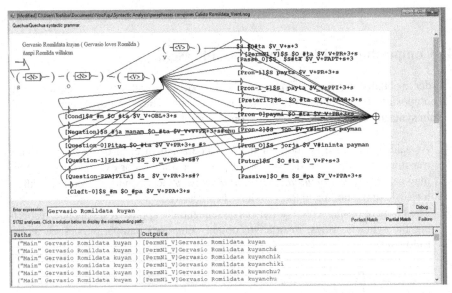

Fig. 9. Elementary paraphraser for an SOV sentence

The grammar of Fig. 9 concatenates these compositions. When applied, it generates 2,940 paraphrases like those appearing under the graph.

5 Conclusion

In this paper, I have shown several NooJ grammars capable of recognizing and producing a large number of sentences that are generated by transformations from an initial direct sentence. In particular, I presented grammars corresponding to elementary transformations of any direct sentiment predicate like {*Gervasio Romildata kuyan*/Gervasio loves Romilda}. By composing elementary paraphrasers, I have built a complex paraphraser which generates a large number of paraphrases.

I plan to construct a more comprehensive set of transformations and paraphrasing grammars, which I hope will help me in the implementation of the resources for our machine translation project for Quechua.

References

1. Barreiro, A.: ParaMT: a paraphraser for machine translation. In: Teixeira, A., de Lima, V.L.S., de Oliveira, L.C., Quaresma, P. (eds.) PROPOR 2008. LNCS (LNAI), vol. 5190, pp. 202–211. Springer, Heidelberg (2008). https://doi.org/10.1007/978-3-540-85980-2_21

2. Mota, C., Carvalho, P., Raposo, F., Barreiro, A.: Generating paraphrases of human intransitive adjective constructions with Port4NooJ. In: Okrut, T., Hetsevich, Y., Silberztein, M., Stanislavenka, H. (eds.) NooJ 2015. CCIS, vol. 607, pp. 107–122. Springer, Cham (2016). https://doi.org/10.1007/978-3-319-42471-2_10

3. Ben. A., Fehri, H. Ben, H.: Translating arabic relative clauses into english using the NooJ platform. In: Monti, J., Silberztein, M., Monteleone, M., di Buono, M.P. (eds.) Formalizing Natural Languages with NooJ 2014, pp. 166–174. Cambridge Scholars Publishing, Newcastle (2015)

4. Duran, M.: Morphology of MWU in Quechua. In: Proceedings of The 3rd Workshop on Multi-Word Units in Machine Translation and Translation Technology (MUMTTT 2017), pp. 32–42. Editions Tradulex, Geneva (2018)

5. Duran, M.: Dictionnaire électronique français-quechua des verbes pour le TAL. Thèse Doctorale. Université de Franche-Comté. Mars 2017 (2017)

6. Duran, M.: The annotation of compound suffixation structure of quechua verbs. In: Okrut, T., Hetsevich, Y., Silberztein, M., Stanislavenka, H. (eds.) NooJ 2015. CCIS, vol. 607, pp. 29–40. Springer, Cham (2016). https://doi.org/10.1007/978-3-319-42471-2_3

7. Duran, M., Morphological and syntactic grammars for recognition of verbal lemmas in Quechua. In: Proceedings of the 2014 NooJ International Conference and Workshop, Sassari (2014). Cambridge Scholars Publishing, Newcastle (2015)

8. Fehri, H., Haddar, K., Ben Hamadou, A.: Integration of a transliteration process into an automatic translation system for named entities from Arabic to French. In: Proceedings of the NooJ 2009 international Conference and Workshop, pp. 285–300. Centre de Publication Universitaire, Sfax (2010)

9. Harris, Z.: Mathematical Structures of Language. Interscience, New York (1968)

10. Langella, A.M.: Paraphrases for the Italian communication predicates. In: Barone, L., Monteleone, M., Silberztein, M. (eds.) NooJ 2016. CCIS, vol. 667, pp. 196–207. Springer, Cham (2016). https://doi.org/10.1007/978-3-319-55002-2_17

11. Silberztein, M.: Automatic transformational analysis and generation. In: Gavriilidou, Z., Chatzipapa, E., Papadopoulou, L., Silberztein, M. (eds.) Proceedings of the NooJ 2010 International Conference and Workshop, pp. 221–231. University of Thrace, Komotini (2011)

12. Silberztein, M.: Language Formalization: The NooJ Approach. Wiley, Hoboken (2016)

Arabic Psychological Verb Recognition Through NooJ Transformational Grammars

Asmaa Amzali[(⊠)], Mohammed Mourchid, Abdelaaziz Mouloudi, and Samir Mbarki

MISC Laboratory, Faculty of Science, Ibn Tofail University, Kénitra, Morocco
asmamzali@hotmail.fr, mourchidm@hotmail.com,
mouloudi_aziz@hotmail.com, mbarkisamir@hotmail.com

Abstract. This paper provides continuity with our previous work on the identification and classification of Arabic psychological verbs through lexicon-grammar tables. In this regard, we add transformational forms such as negation, passivization, and nominalization to enrich our lexicon grammar tables. However, these transformations link one sentence to another, keeping the same semantic material, such as أحبّ زيد ماري 'Zaid loved Marie' and its nominalized form أكنّ زيدٌ حبًّا لماري 'Zaid has love for Marie'. The two sentences share the same predicate (أحبّ 'to love') and the same arguments (زيد, ماري; 'Zaid, Marie'), even though their structure is different. We also extend our previous tool of recognizing Arabic psychological verbs in sentences that allowed us to detect those verbs in texts and corpora by transforming their lexicon-grammar tables into NooJ dictionaries and syntactic grammars. In this context, we create transformational grammars to make this tool more powerful by detecting the Arabic psychological verbs in texts in all their transformational forms.

Keywords: Arabic psychological verbs · Lexicon-grammar tables · Transformational grammars · Syntactic-semantic analysis · Dictionaries · NooJ

1 Introduction

Psychological verbs occupy an important part of the language vocabulary. They are extensively used in newspaper texts, novels, and social network messages (e.g., Facebook, Twitter, Messenger), etc. Therefore, the syntactic and semantic analysis of a text containing such verbs is very useful in NLP applications such as sentiment analysis or question-answering systems, etc.

Thus, the creation of an automatic tool allowing us to know people's concerns, feelings, tendencies, etc., is one of the most active research and development areas [1]. Such a tool would help those in charge to make their decisions.

Therefore, linguistic research had to be done on Arabic psychological verbs in order to extract all their properties that would be used in different steps of analysis. In our previous research [2], after the analysis of texts by our dictionaries and syntactic grammars, several psychological verbs were not recognized, since they appeared in some transformational forms such as passivization, negation, nominalization,

© Springer Nature Switzerland AG 2021
B. Bekavac et al. (Eds.): NooJ 2020, CCIS 1389, pp. 74–84, 2021.
https://doi.org/10.1007/978-3-030-70629-6_7

restructuring, etc. These transformations make the recognition of psychological verbs not so obvious.

In this regard, we need to add other linguistic resources, that is, transformational grammars, to make it possible to survey the opinions of Moroccan youth regarding their daily interests and concerns, which is our main objective.

Transformational grammars were introduced by Harris [11] to describe relations between sentences. His theory is that the syntax of the language is composed of basic sentences that receive a semantic interpretation. All the other sentences of the language are the product of transformation operations such as displacement, permutation, addition, elimination, etc. These operations are called transformational forms.

In this context, we will first list the transformations that can be applied to Arabic sentences containing psychological verbs. Then, we will implement a set of syntactic grammars modeling those transformations in the NooJ platform.

This paper is organized as follows: In the second section, we will present previous related research. In the third section, we will expose some transformations applied to sentences containing Arabic psychological verbs such as passivization, negation, and nominalization. Then, we will present an excerpt of our new lexicon-grammar table for Arabic psychological verbs enriched by transformational forms. In the fourth section, we will present the transformation grammars implemented in the NooJ platform. Finally, in the fifth section, we close our paper with a conclusion and some perspectives.

2   Related Work

In [2], we created a lexicon-grammar table of Arabic psychological verbs (see Fig. 1) with about 400 verb entries in three main classes: أفعال الشعور (Negative feeling verbs), أفعال الإحساس (Positive feeling verbs), and أفعال الرأي والتفكير (thought and opinion verbs).

Then we used NooJ to create an automatic tool by transforming the lexicon-grammar tables into NooJ dictionaries and syntactic grammars, allowing us to recognize those verbs in texts and corpora. But several psychological verbs are not recognized since they do not appear only in their basic forms, which makes their recognition not evident. Those verbs can appear in a transformed structure such as passivization, negation, nominalization, restructuring, etc.

Most of the existing research on transformational grammars has been done for the French language, unlike the Arabic language, which until now has suffered from a lack of research in this area.

In [3, 4], El Hannach proposed a syntactic analysis of Arabic qualitative verbs that have the structure 'VN0'anJl', and studied their transformational properties. He also presented several formal concepts to redefine the structure of the Arabic language, such as nominalization, adjectivization, and passivization. So he focused on "nominalization", which constitutes a basic fragment for the Arabic syntactic database.

In [5, 6], Max Silberztein created a large transformational grammar that can perform 91 transformations for French transitive sentences. In addition, he built a transformational grammar for the French language which allows the recognition of all the transformational forms of the French sentence "*Emma aime Gabriel*".

<OPT>explication	<OPT>example	VN0Prép1N1	VN0N1	VN0	Prép1=ل	Prép1=في	Prép1=ب	Prép1=على	Prép1=عن	Prép1=في	N1=Nnr	N1=Nhum	N1=Hum	N0=Nhum	N0=Hum	InTr	Tr	V	Category
عظمه و فرِحُ به و فخِرَ	بَجِحَ بالشيء	+	-	-	-	-	+	-	-	-	+	+	+	-	+	+	-	بَجِحَ	أفعال الإحساس
أفرح	بَجَحَهُ الخَبَر	-	+	-	-	-	-	-	-	-	+	+	+	-	+	-	+	بَجَحَ	
أفرح	أبْجَحَه الشيء	-	+	-	-	-	-	-	-	-	+	-	+	-	+	-	+	أبْجَحَ	
بَجِلَ:فرح	بَجِلَ أحمد بالخَبَر	+	-	+	-	-	-	-	-	-	+	-	+	-	+	+	-	بَجِلَ	
حَنَّ عليه:عَطَفَ	حنَّ اللَّؤُمُ على اللُّؤْم	+	-	-	-	-	+	-	-	-	+	+	+	+	+	+	-	حَنَّ	
أحَبَّ:وَدَّه و مال إليه.	أحَبَّ أحمد مريَم	-	+	-	-	-	-	-	-	-	+	+	+	-	+	-	+	أحَبَّ	
فرح به	أبْجَلَ الشيء	-	+	-	-	-	-	-	-	-	+	+	+	+	+	-	+	أبْجَلَ	
عَشِق:أحَبَّ	عَشِق لوك ماري	-	+	+	-	-	-	-	-	-	+	+	+	-	+	-	+	عَشِق	

Fig. 1. Excerpt of our Arabic psychological verb lexicon-grammar table created in [2]

3   Sentences Containing Arabic Psychological Verb Transformations

Transformations [7] describe the relations between the different structures of a sentence which can give a particular meaning, where those structures share the same lexical material. There are many transformational forms, including negation, nominalization, passivization, restructuring, adjectivization, etc.

In this paper, we were able to identify three transformational forms for Arabic psychological verbs: passivization, negation, and nominalization.

3.1   Negation (النفي)

This transformation is based on a logical operator of negation, such as: *laa* (لا 'no'), *lan* (لن 'not'), etc. A negative statement would have a true value that is opposite to the corresponding affirmative statement, e.g.,

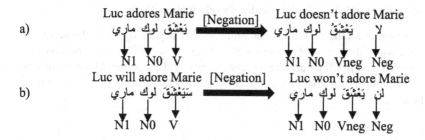

3.2 Passivization (المبنى للمجهول)

Arabic and French passivization syntax generally correspond to the same deep structure. The passive verb can be translated by a flexion form. The majority of psychological verbs have a passive form with the agent complement deleted [8], e.g.,

3.3 The Nominalization (Maçdarisation - تكوين جملة اسمية من جملة فعلية)

This property is considered as a transformational relation between sentences. It allows the transformation of a sentence with a verbal predicate into another sentence with a nominal predicate. It is based on support verbs [9], such as عبّر 'to express' or a support preposition like لدى 'have', e.g.,

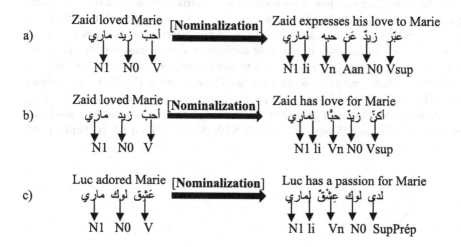

3.4   Lexicon-Grammar Tables of Arabic Psychological Verbs

In order to recognize all the sentences containing Arabic psychological verbs in text or corpora, even when they are not in their basic structure, we will enrich the lexicon-grammar table created in [2] by adding the transformational properties of the sentences (see Fig. 2). This operation makes our lexicon-grammar table more useful in various NLP applications.

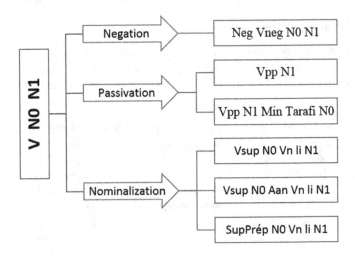

Fig. 2. Transformational forms of the basic structure "V N0 N1"

As illustrated in Fig. 3 below, based on our lexicon grammar tables realized in [2], we added the transformational forms of the sentences containing the Arabic psychological verbs, the support verb, the prepositions of negation, etc. All those properties must correspond with each entry in our table.

Our lexicon-grammar table is represented as a matrix in which the lines represent the lexical entries, the columns represent the lexical, syntactic, semantic, distributional, and transformational proprieties, and the cells contain either a lexical element, "+" or "−". In fact, each verbal entry of our table might have several transformational forms. As an example, the verb أَحَبَّ 'to love' is a transitive verb, or "Tr", that takes a human subject "N0 = Hum" and an object that accepts a human "N1 = Hum" or a non-human noun "N1 = Nhum"; in addition, it accepts two forms of negation (Neg V N0 N1, Neg V N0 Prép N1), two forms of passivization (Vpp N1, Vpp N1 min tarafi N0), and three forms of nominalization (Vsup N0 aan Vn li N1W, Vsup N0 Vn li N1 W, SupPrép N0 Vn li N1 W).

SupPrép N0 Vn Ii	Vsup N0 Vn Ii N1W	NégVN0Prép1N1	NégVN0N1	NégVN0	Vpp N1 min taraf N0	VppPrép1N1	Vpp N1	<OPT>explication	<OPT>example	VN0Prép1N1	VN0N1	VN0	SupPrép=	SupPrép=	Vsup=	Vsup=	Vsup=	Vsup=	Nég=	Nég=	Nég=V	Prép1=J	Prép1=	Prép1=	Prép1=	Prép1=	N1=Nnr	N1=Nhum	N0=Nhum	N0=Hum	InTr	Tr	V	Category
+	-	+	+	+	-	-	+	+	عظمه و فرح به و فخر	بهَج بالشيء	+	-	-	+	+	-	+	-	-	-	+	-	-	-	+	-	-	-	+	+	+	-	+	+	-	بهَج
-	-	-	-	+	-	+	-	+	أفرح	بهَجَهُ الخَبَر	-	+	-	-	+	+	+	-	-	-	+	+	-	-	-	-	-	-	+	+	+	-	+	-	+	بهَجَ
~	~	~	-	-	-	+	-	+	أفرح	أبْجَهَه الشيء	-	+	-	-	-	+	-	-	-	-	+	+	+	-	-	-	-	-	+	-	+	-	+	-	+	أبْجَعَ	أفعال الإحساس
~	~	~	-	-	+	+	+	+	بَجَلَ أَحْمَد بالخَيْر	بَجِلَ:فرِح	+	-	+	-	-	+	+	-	+	+	+	-	-	-	-	-	+	-	+	-	+	+	+	-	بَجِلَ
+	-	+	+	+	-	+	~	+	خَنَّ عليه:عَطف	حَنَّ الأُمُ على ابْنِها	+	-	-	+	+	-	+	-	-	-	+	+	-	-	-	+	-	-	+	+	+	+	+	+	-	حَنَّ
+	+	+	+	+	-	+	-	+	أَخَبَّ:وَلَدَه و مال إليه.	أَخَبَّ أَحْمَد مَرْيَم	-	+	-	-	+	+	-	+	-	-	+	+	-	-	-	-	-	+	+	+	+	-	+	-	+	أَخَبَّ
~	~	~	-	+	-	+	-	+	فرح به	أبْجَلَ الشيء	-	+	-	-	-	+	~	~	~	-	+	+	-	-	-	-	-	+	+	+	+	+	-	+	أبْجَلَ
+	+	+	-	+	+	-	-	+	عَشِقَ لوك ماري	عَشِق:أَحَبَّ	-	+	+	-	+	-	+	-	-	+	+	+	-	-	-	-	-	+	+	+	-	+	-	+	عَشِق

Fig. 3. Excerpt of the lexicon-grammar table of the class "أفعال الإحساس" (Positive feeling verbs)

4 Implementation

To integrate the lexicon-grammar tables in the NooJ platform [7], we first need to convert them into NooJ dictionaries, then build grammars that use the linguistic knowledge encoded in the lexicon-grammar tables, in order to identify the sentences in texts or corpora, or to generate the corresponding transformational forms from the basic structure.

4.1 From Lexicon-Grammar Tables to NooJ Dictionaries

In [2], we described the process of converting our lexicon-grammar tables of Arabic psychological verbs into a dictionary by a program that automatically generates NooJ dictionaries from lexicon-grammar tables, developed by Kourtin et al. [10].

As we mentioned in Subsect. 3.4, we enriched our previous lexicon-grammar table of the class "أفعال الإحساس", by adding the transformational properties (Fig. 3). In order to implement this table in NooJ platform, we generate its corresponding dictionary "PS_2.dic" (Fig. 4) by using the same tool used in [2]. This dictionary uses all the flexional and derivational grammars created in the file "qualitatif.nof" (Fig. 5).

Fig. 4. Excerpt of the new dictionary "PS_2.dic" of Arabic psychological verbs

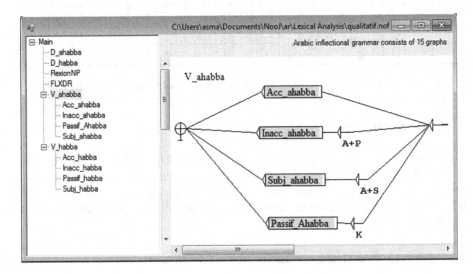

Fig. 5. Excerpt of flexional and derivational grammars

4.2 From Lexicon-Grammar Tables to NooJ Grammars

As indicated in [2], a lexicon-grammar table can be transformed automatically into NooJ dictionaries. However, the syntactic grammars that use the information presented in the lexicon-grammar tables must be created manually. For that, we have created syntactic grammars for three transformational forms – negation, passivization, and nominalization – of sentences containing Arabic psychological verbs.

As illustrated in Fig. 6, the syntactic grammar of negation that analyzes a basic sentence of psychological verbs and generates its negation depends on the tense of the verb. For example, when given the sentence سَيَعْشَق لُوك مَارِي 'Luc will adore Marie', which has the structure "V N0 N1", the grammar generated the negative sentence لن يَعْشَق لُوك مَارِي 'Luc won't adore Marie'.

The graph in Fig. 7, presents the grammar of reverse negation, which analyzes the transformed sentence and generates its basic form.

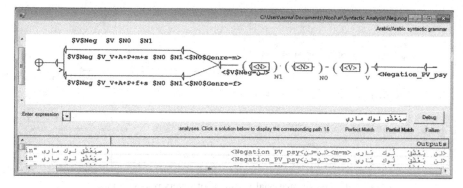

Fig. 6. Transformational grammar of negation.

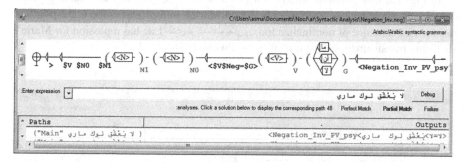

Fig. 7. Transformational grammar of reverse negation.

In Fig. 8, the grammar recognizes a given elementary sentence containing an Arabic psychological verb, عشق لوك ماري 'Luc adored Marie', then produces the corresponding transformed sentence of passivization, عُشِقَتْ ماري 'Marie is adored'. Also, in Fig. 9, the grammar is capable of parsing a passive form and then recon-structing its original active form.

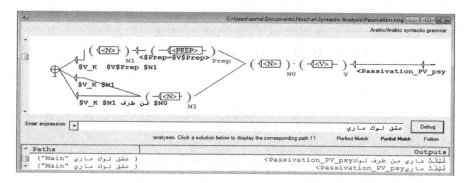

Fig. 8. Transformational grammar of passivization.

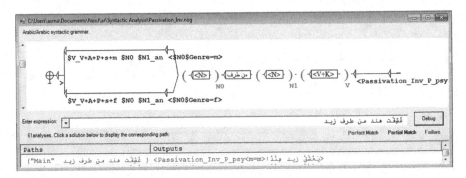

Fig. 9. Transformational grammar of revers passivization.

In Fig. 10, this grammar analyzes a given sentence containing an Arabic psychological verb such as أحبّ لوك ماري 'Luc loved Marie', and produces the corresponding transformed sentence of nominalization, لدى لوك حُبّ لماري 'Luc has a passion for Marie'. Also, this transformation is symmetric, as illustrated in Fig. 11.

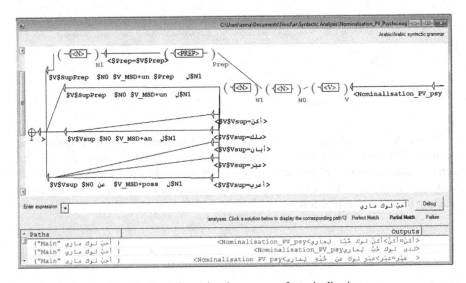

Fig. 10. Transformational grammar of nominalization.

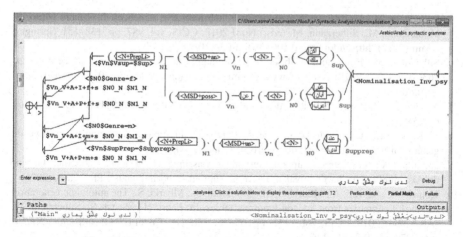

Fig. 11. Transformational grammar of reverse nominalization.

5   Conclusion and Future Work

In this paper, we studied the transformations that could be applied to sentences containing psychological verbs such as negation, passivization, and nominalization. Afterwards, we added these studied transformational properties to our previous lexicon-grammar table of the class "أفعال الإحساس" created in [2]. Furthermore, we integrated this table in the NooJ platform by generating its corresponding dictionary and implementing its transformational grammars.

This study enables the recognition of psychological verbs in their basic or transformational forms and will have a positive effect on the efficiency of textual and corpus analysis.

In the future, we will extend this linguistic study to cover all transformations in order to recognize all sentences containing psychological verbs in text and corpora, and to realize its application in surveying the opinions of Moroccan youth.

References

1. Yvette Yannick, M.: Interprétation par prédicats sémantiques de structures d'arguments. FEELING, une application aux verbes psychologiques. Thèse de Doctorat en Informatique fondamentale. Université Paris 7, France (1994)
2. Amzali, A., Kourtin, A., Mourchid, M., Mouloudi, A., Mbarki, S.: Lexicon-grammar tables development for Arabic psychological verbs. In: Fehri, H., Mesfar, S., Silberztein, M. (eds.) NooJ 2019. CCIS, vol. 1153, pp. 15–26. Springer, Cham (2020). https://doi.org/10.1007/978-3-030-38833-1_2
3. El Hannach, M.: Lexique-grammaire de l'Arabe: Classe des verbes qualitatifs (1989). https://books.google.co.ma/books?id=Nn7IjwEACAAJ
4. El Hannach, M.: Linguistics tools to develop an arabic syntax analyzer, innovations in information technology (IIT). In: 9th International Conference. IEEE (2013)

5. Silberztein, M.: Unary transformations for french transitive sentences. In: Mauro Mirto, I., Monteleone, M., Silberztein, M. (eds.) NooJ 2018. CCIS, vol. 987, pp. 138–151. Springer, Cham (2019). https://doi.org/10.1007/978-3-030-10868-7_13

6. Silberztein, M.: Emma aime Gabriel: une grammaire transformationnelle. Langue française **203**(3), 15–33 (2019). https://www.cairn.info/revue-langue-francaise-2019-3-page-15.htm. https://doi.org/10.3917/lf.203.0015

7. Silberztein, M.: La formalisation des langues: l'approche de NooJ. ISTE Editions, London (2015)

8. El Kassas, D.: Une étude contrastive de l'arabe et du français dans une perspective de génération multilingue. Ph.D. diss, Paris 7, France (2005)

9. Ahnaiba, A.: Les verbes supports en arabe classique et en arabe moderne: Le cas de'Akhadha/Ittakhadha l'équivalent du verbe support français prendre. Ph.D. diss (2006)

10. Kourtin, A., Amzali, A., Mourchid, M., Mouloudi, A., Mbarki, S.: The automatic generation of NooJ dictionaries from lexicon-grammar tables. In: Fehri, H., Mesfar, S., Silberztein, M. (eds.) NooJ 2019. CCIS, vol. 1153, pp. 65–76. Springer, Cham (2020). https://doi.org/10.1007/978-3-030-38833-1_6

11. Harris, Z.: Methods in Structural Linguistics. University of Chicago Press, Chicago (1951)

Grammatical Modeling of a Nominal Ellipsis Grammar for Spanish

Hazel Barahona[✉] and Walter Koza[✉]

Pontificia Universidad Católica de Valparaíso-Project FONDECyT, 1171033 Valparaíso, Chile
hazel.barahona.g@mail.pucv.cl, walter.koza@pucv.cl

Abstract. The objective of this work is to formalize nominal ellipsis in Spanish – a grammatical mechanism in which one element is silenced with its syntactic structure, under certain syntactic restrictions – through the creation of an algorithm that automatically recognizes and replaces elided elements in natural language texts. Based on the proposal by Saab [1, 2], this paper proposes a series of formalisms represented in NooJ [3, 4] to grammatically model this phenomenon. The methodology was tested on journalistic texts extracted from the Internet. The results obtained (100% precision; 82% coverage; 90.10% F-measure) show that the developed algorithm is useful for the recognition of ellipses.

Keywords: Nominal ellipsis · Generative grammar · Automatic identification · NooJ · Spanish Language

1 Introduction

This work describes a computational modeling of nominal ellipsis in Spanish. We begin with the theoretical assumptions of generative grammar following studies by Merchant [5]; Sag and Hankamer [6]; Culicover and Jackendoff [7]; and particularly, Saab [1, 2]. Specifically, the paper describes an algorithm developed for the automatic recognition of ellipses and the replacement of the elided element in natural language texts. Ellipsis consists of a grammatical mechanism avoidant of lexical redundancy [8], in which an element of the clause is not pronounced – i.e., it is elided – under certain syntactic restrictions. In this regard, Saab [1] and Merchant [9] point out that, in this phenomenon, the silenced element is recognized through a structural identity relationship with a preceding element that allows for the identification of said element and its position inside the clause.

This phenomenon has been addressed from different perspectives, including syntactic [5, 10–14] and semantic [6, 9] approaches, as well as within the frameworks of Head-Driven Phrase Structure Grammar [15] and Simpler Syntax [16]. Regarding research linked to computational linguistics, the works of Hardt [17]; Mitkov [18]; Nielsen [19]; Rello, Baeza-Yates, and Mitkov [20]; and McShane and Babkin [21] have undertaken analyses of ellipsis via corpus-labeling methodologies that identify and retrieve the elided element. However, those proposals tend not to include implicit syntactic mechanisms. To remedy this, this work seeks to formalize nominal ellipsis based on the processing

© Springer Nature Switzerland AG 2021
B. Bekavac et al. (Eds.): NooJ 2020, CCIS 1389, pp. 85–95, 2021.
https://doi.org/10.1007/978-3-030-70629-6_8

of morphosyntactic information. The contribution to the literature is double: on the one hand, we provide an efficient algorithm for applied computational linguistics tasks; and on the other, we develop a tool to evaluate the reach of theoretical generative studies as applied to nominal ellipsis.

For such purposes, we propose a formal description of ellipsis, modeled using an electronic dictionary under NooJ syntactic grammars, and tested on journalistic texts extracted from the Internet. The results obtained (100% precision; 82% coverage; 90.10% F-measure) show that the developed algorithm is useful for the recognition of ellipsis in natural language texts, while also showing that the generative theoretical proposals are adequate for the analysis of this phenomenon.

The article is organized as follows: first, we present the general context of ellipsis; second, we discuss the concepts relevant to the theory of Identity [1, 2], with special focus on aspects relevant to ellipsis; third, we describe the data processing tasks that we performed, considering the syntactic structure of determiner phrases (DP) in Spanish; and fourth, we present our results and conclusions.

2 Ellipsis: Definition and Types

Ellipsis is a syntactic mechanism through which, under certain structural particularities, an element is not pronounced (that is, it is elided) [1, 2, 5, 22]. In this regard, two types can be recognized: nominal ellipsis, in which a noun is elided (1a); and verbal ellipsis, in which a verb is elided (1b):

(1)   a. *El perro de mi madre y el ~~perro~~ del vecino mordieron al periodista*
       [my mother's dog and the neighbor's ~~dog~~ bit the journalist.]

   b. *Juan lee un libro y María ~~lee~~ una revista*
       [Juan is reading a book and María ~~is reading~~ a magazine.]

This mechanism acts at different syntactic levels. Thus, Spanish nominal ellipsis is a nuclear ellipsis of a DP; and, in Spanish verbal ellipsis, mechanisms of sentence ellipsis are involved. It is important to clarify that nominal ellipses do not only occur between coordinating DPs (2a), but also as part of a sentence ellipsis (2b-c). Here, the verbal assembling domains expand the locality between the preceding element (in bold) and its place in the phrase in which it is elided (strikethrough). In (3), the types of verbal ellipsis are shown. Since the objective of this work is not to address verbal ellipsis, only the verbal types that appear in the different studies are mentioned.

(2) a. *La guitarra acústica y la ~~guitarra~~ eléctrica*
[the acoustic guitar and the electric ~~guitar~~.]

b. *Los **niveles** de colesterol disminuyen y los ~~niveles~~ de azúcar aumentan*
[cholesterol **levels** decrease and sugar ~~levels~~ increase.]

c. *El **presidente** de Rusia homenajeó al ~~presidente~~ de China*
[Russia's **president** paid homage to China's ~~president~~.]

d. *Las **embarazadas** que asisten a terapia y las ~~embarazadas~~ que no asisten*
fueron internadas en el centro médico
[**pregnant women** who go to therapy and ~~pregnant women~~ who do not
were hospitalized in the medical center.]

(3) a. *Antonio **toca** el violín y Alex ~~toca~~ el chelo*
[Antonio **plays** the violin and Alex ~~plays~~ the cello.]

b. ***Antonio viajó** a Chile en enero y ~~Antonio viajó~~ a Brasil en agosto*
[**Antonio travelled** to Chile in January and ~~Antonio travelled~~ to Brasil in
August.]

c. *Antonio **gana mucho dinero** y María también ~~gana mucho dinero~~*
[Antonio **makes a lot of money** and Maria also ~~makes a lot of Money~~.]

d. *Antonio intentó entrar **al edificio**, pero no pudo ~~entrar al edificio~~*
[Antonio tried to enter **the building**, but he could not ~~enter the building~~.]

e. ***Antonio golpeó** a alguien, pero no sé a quién ~~golpeó Antonio~~*
[**Antonio punched** someone, but I do not know whom ~~Antonio punched~~.]

f. *– ¿Quién llamó?* [who called?]
–Antonio.

One of the theories that best explains nominal (2) and verbal (3) ellipses in Spanish is
that of Saab [1, 2], which is the basis for Distributed Morphology [DM, 23]. According
to this theory, ellipsis is defined as a non-insertion mechanism of lexical features in
which, during derivation, a particular feature, denominated as [I], blocks the insertion of
phonological features. The allocation of this feature [I] is the product of a transformational operation called *Identity*, whose result is the non-pronunciation – i.e., silencing
– of the elements that intervene in the syntactic operation. Saab [1] formally defines the
ellipsis domain as follows:

(4) a. An abstract morpheme α is identical to the abstract morpheme β if and only if α
and β match all their morphosyntactic and semantic features.
b. An A root is identical to a B root if and only if A and B share the same index.

This definition (4) establishes three contexts in which ellipsis intervenes: (i) cases of
partial identity with grammatical results; (ii) cases of partial identity with ungrammatical
results; and (iii) cases in which the identity is total, but the result is ungrammatical. This

work considered only the first two, which correspond to the features of number (5) and gender (6) in Spanish, respectively.

(5) a. Antonio quiere más a sus gatos que al gato de Pedro
     [Antonio loves his own cats more than Pedro's cat.]

     b. *Antonio quiere más a su gato que a los gatos de Pedro*
     [Antonio loves his own cat more than Pedro's cats.]

(6) a. *Antonio quiere más a su gato que a la gata de Pedro*
     [Antonio loves his own cat more than Pedro's [female] cat.]

     b. *Antonio quiere más a sus gatas que al gato de Pedro*
     [Antonio loves his [female] cats more than Pedro's cat.]

For Saab [1, 2], the ungrammaticalness of the examples in (6) is caused by the fact that, in Spanish, gender features are a property of the morphological root, in which the root is attached to the gender feature first, and then to the number feature. Therefore, for that author, number is a functional category that does not intervene in the domain of nominal ellipsis in Spanish, such as in (7).

(7)

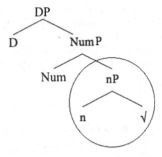

3   The Formalization of Syntactic Information

This work adopts Abney's [24] *DP hypothesis*, in which the determiner is a functional category that can take a noun phrase as a complement; namely, it is possible to represent a structure of constituents with a particular internal structure such as the one in (8).

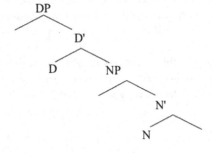

In Spanish, the determiner occupies the highest position, which allows the ellipsis of N in the lowest position. Furthermore, structurally speaking, the determiner is an important feature as the nucleus of the phrase, which is why it may not be an optional element (9a and 10b); and why it is also a mechanism for the recognition of the elided element, since it must agree with the elided N. In (10), the elided element is indicated with strikethrough text.

(8)   a. *guitarra roja
[red guitar]
b. La guitarra roja
[the red guitar]

(9)   a. La guitarra roja y la ~~guitarra~~ eléctrica
[the red guitar and the electric ~~guitar~~.]

Spanish data was analyzed under a constituent organization to outline the determiner phrase (8), resulting in three types of syntactic structures with nuclear ellipses (N). The first is that of *coordination between determiner phrases* (11a); the second, *coordination of clauses* (12a); and the third, *predicative argument* (13a). These three syntactic structures were formalized as shown respectively in pairs (11b), (12b), and (13c). The elided element is indicated with strikethrough text.

(10) a. El hijo de Juan y el ~~hijo~~ de Pedro
[Juan's son and Pedro's ~~son~~].

b. [[PRENOM]₁ N [POSTNOM]₁]**SDI Coord** [[PRENOM]₂ N [POSTNOM]₂]SDII

(11) a. El hijo de Juan fue al cine y el ~~hijo~~ de Pedro fue al teatro
[Juan's son went to the cinema and Pedro's ~~son~~ went to the theater.]

b. [[PRENOM]₁ N [POSTNOM]₁]SDI **[V + ARG (ADJ)]₁ Coord** [[PRENOM]₂ **N [POSTNOM]₂**]SDII [V + ARG (ADJ)]₂

(12) a. El presidente de Francia homenajeó al presidente de Perú
[the president of France paid homage to the president of Peru.]

b. [[[PRENOM]₁ N [POSTNOM]₁]SDI]_**arg0 PRED** [[[PRENOM]₁ N [POSTNOM]₁]SDI]_arg1

These structures explain the phenomenon of ellipsis as a mechanism presenting under two procedures: elision (in the case of production); and identification (in the case of comprehension).

3.1 Rules for Ellipsis: Elision and Identification

The process of *elision* defines the production of a nominal ellipsis, given its articulation of the syntactic and surface structures of Spanish (14).

(13) a. Given a coordination A^B, where A and B are DPs and B has a structure equal to A with a root object as an NP nucleus equal to that of A, elide the NP nucleus object of B.
b. Given a Predicate-Argument Structure (PAS) A, with arguments $\alpha, \beta, \gamma \ldots$, where α has a structure equal to that of the argument to its right and which has an NP whose root nucleus is equal to the NP in α, elide the nucleus of such NP.

On the other hand, *identification* describes the comprehension of the elliptical phenomenon, specifically, how the syntactic elements missing in the grammatical structure are computationally recognized (15).

(14) a. Given a coordination A^B, where B is a DP equal to A, and the NP nucleus is elided:

- Copy the nucleus root and the NP gender object of A
- Copy the Det number of B

b. Given a PAS A: P (α, β y γ), with an object to the right of α that represents the elision of its NP nucleus:

- Copy the root of the NP object of α
- Copy the determiner number of β or γ (according to the elided object)

This work computationally modeled (14) and (15). The creation of resources in NooJ is described below.

3.2 Computational Modeling in NooJ

The computational implementation used a general Spanish language dictionary [25] containing 72,593 entries. Lemmas corresponding to nouns, adjectives, and verbs were associated with inflected model grammars.

For the identification and replacement of the elided element in the nominal ellipsis, the following syntactic grammar was created.

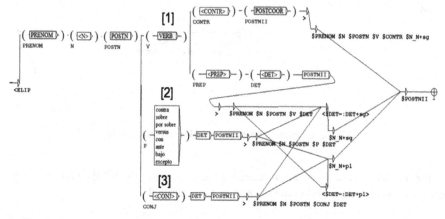

Fig. 1. Grammar for the identification and replacement of nominal ellipsis in Spanish.

The numbers in Fig. 1 indicate the types of ellipsis found in the corpus: with [1], cases of predication; with [2] and [3], coordination between determiner phrases.

The variables represented by parentheses embed grammars that contain syntactic restrictions; for example, the gender and number concordance typical of Spanish and which is preserved in nominal ellipsis [1]. Thus, the variable PRENOM (see Fig. 2) details the restrictions in the categories of the determiner and its concordance with the adjective.

PRENOM

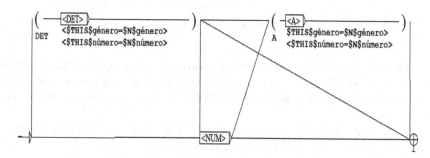

Fig. 2. Grammar embedded for determiner restrictions.

The POSTN variable indicates the restriction of the adjective with regards to its preceding N (see Fig. 3).

POSTN

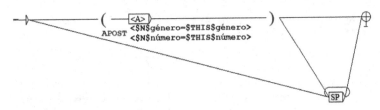

Fig. 3. Grammar embedded for adjective restrictions.

Finally, some grammars can be recursive (see Fig. 4). In the SP, the variation in the prepositional phrases found in the corpus can be described.

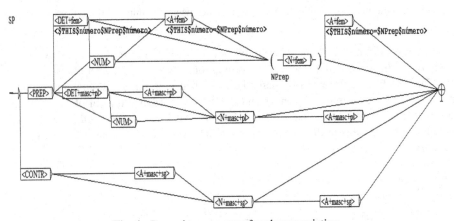

Fig. 4. Recursive grammars for phrase variation.

The indication of replacement implies a rewriting of the variables $PRENOM $NOM [1, 2, or 3] ($PREP) $DET; and later, of $NOM, although adjusted to the variables of number $DET. In cases in which a [1] $CONTR sequence appears, $NOM is replaced in the singular.

With the application of the grammar, it is possible to annotate (TAS) a grammatical sequence formally described with a corpus sequence (see Fig. 5).

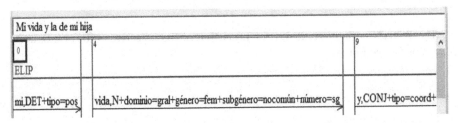

Fig. 5. Annotation of a grammatical sequence of the corpus

Furthermore, the implemented grammar recognizes, identifies, and replaces the elided element in the identified grammatical structure (see Fig. 6).

Mi vida y la de mi hija/<ELIP>Mi vida y la vida de mi hija

Tu salud y la de tu familia/<ELIP>Tu salud y la salud de tu familia

La lucha independentista y la de transformación/<ELIP>La lucha independentista y la lucha de transformación

los pañales desechables o los de tela/<ELIP>los pañales desechables o los pañales de tela

el número de aprobados supera al de suspensos/<ELIP>el número de aprobados supera al de número suspensos

Fig. 6. Results of the automatic recognition of nominal ellipses

4 Results

Table 1 summarizes the main results of the computational implementation based on the collected texts, a brief corpus of 5,000 words with 100 elided sentences.

Table 1. Results obtained

Unidentified sentences	9
Mistakes	0
Coverage	82%
Precision	100%
F-measure	90.10%

As can be observed, the algorithm did not result in any incorrect labeling. Moreover, while there were coverage problems caused by lexical units not listed in the electronic dictionary, the results obtained show that the syntactic restrictions under which the nominal ellipsis is structured are useful for automatic identification in natural language texts. We also note that, in addition to the applications for syntactic recognition to optimize results in computational linguistics [26], it is also a tool that, beyond numerical data, provides information on grammatical knowledge.

5 Closing Remarks

This paper presented a computational modeling of nominal ellipsis in Spanish, based on a proposal for generative grammar [2], using an electronic dictionary and morphological grammars. The resulting algorithm showed a high percentage of precision, coverage, and F-measure. This implies that the descriptions stemming from formal studies constitute an adequate basis for the elaboration of computational devices. Despite these initially promising results, the brevity of the corpus presents a limitation that merits further research.

Furthermore, in seeking to improve the ability of such models to resolve complex grammar when analyzing ellipses, future work will include comparative structures, such as (16), and those with preceding elements located in peripheral positions of the sentence, such as (17):

(15) *La gramática generativa es más compleja que la ~~gramática~~ de corte funcionalista*
[generative grammar is more complex than functionalist ~~grammar~~.]
(16) *Según los jugadores de Boca, los ~~jugadores~~ de River festejaron desmedidamente*
[according to Boca's players, River's ~~players~~ celebrated unreasonably.]

Lastly, we expect to include nouns in multi-word structures, as in (18).

(17) *La tasa de mortalidad de Chile es más alta que la ~~tasa de mortalidad~~ de Argentina*
[Chile's mortality rate is higher than Argentina's ~~mortality rate~~.]

For the latter, the complexity of the electronic dictionary will be increased with multi-word expressions that can also be linked to syntactic grammars.

Acknowledgments. This research was supported by a grant from the Proyecto Fondecyt Regular 1171033, from the Comisión Nacional de Investigación Científica y Tecnológica (Conicyt), Chile.

References

1. Saab, A.: Hacía una teoría de la identidad en la elipsis. Tesis de Doctorado. Universidad de Buenos Aires (2008)
2. Saab, A.: Nominal ellipsis. In: Craenenbroeck, J., Temmerman, T. (eds.) The Oxford Handbook of Ellipsis, pp. 526–561. Oxford University Press, Oxford (2019)
3. Silberztein, M.: Formalizing Natural Languages: The NooJ Approach. Wiley-Iste (2016)
4. Silberztein, M.: NooJ: a linguistic annotation system for corpus processing. Demo. In: Proceedings of the HLT/EMNLP2005 Conference, Vancouver (2005)
5. Merchant, J.: The syntax of silence: sluicing, Islands and identity in ellipsis. Tesis de Doctorado, Universidad de Santa Cruz (1999)
6. Sag, I.A., Hankamer, J.: Toward a theory of anaphoric processing. Linguist. Philos. 7(3), 325–345 (1984). https://doi.org/10.1007/BF00627709
7. Culicover, P., Jackendoff, R.: Ellipsis in simpler syntax. In: Craenenbroeck, J., Temmerman, T. (eds.) The Oxford Handbook of Ellipsis, pp. 172–187. Oxford University Press, Oxford (2019)
8. Brucart, J.: La elipsis. In: Bosque, I., Demonte, V. (eds.) Gramática Descriptiva de la lengua español, vol. 1, no. 43, pp. 2787-2863. Espasa-Calpe, Madrid (1999)
9. Merchant, J.: The Syntax of SILENCE: SLUICING, ISLANDS, and the Theory of Ellipsis. Oxford University Press, Oxford (2001)
10. Chomsky, N.: Syntactic Structure. Walter de Gruyter, Berlin (1957)

11. Chomsky, N.: Aspects of the Theory of Syntax. MIT Press, Cambridge (1965)
12. Chomsky, N.: Lectures on Government and Binding. Gruyter Mouton, Berlin (1981)
13. Chomsky, N.: The Minimalist Program. MIT Press, Cambridge (1995)
14. Lobeck, A.: Ellipsis: Functional Heads, Licensing and Identification. Oxford University Press, New York (1995)
15. Ginzburg, J., Miller, P.: Ellipsis in head-driven phrase structure grammar. In: Craenenbroeck, J., Temmerman, T. (eds.) The Oxford Handbook of Ellipsis, pp. 75–121. Oxford University Press, Oxford (2019)
16. Culicover, P., Jackendoff, R.: Simpler Syntax. Oxford University Press, Oxford (2005)
17. Hardt, D.: Verb phrase ellipsis: form, meaning, and processing. Tesis de Doctorado, Universidad de Pennsylvania (1993)
18. Mitkov, R.: The Oxford Handbook of Computational Linguistics. Oxford University Press, Oxford (2002)
19. Nielsen, L.: Verb phrase ellipsis detection using automatically parsed text. In: COLING 2004: Proceedings of the 20th International Conference on Computational Linguistics, Geneva, pp.1093–1099 (2004)
20. Rello, L., Baeza-Yates, R., Mitkov, R.: Elliphant: improved automatic detection of zero subjects and impersonal constructions in Spanish. In: Conference: Proceedings of the 13th Conference of the European Chapter of the Association for Computational Linguistics, pp. 706-715 (2012)
21. McShane, M., Babkin, P.: Detection and resolution of verb phrase ellipsis. LiLT 13(1), 1–34 (2016)
22. Merchant, J.: Ellipsis: a survey of analytical approaches. In: Craenenbroeck, J., Temmerman, T. (eds.) Handbook of Ellipsis. Oxford University Press, Oxford (2016)
23. Halle, M., Marantz, A.: Distributed morphology and pieces of inflection. In: Hale, K., Keyser, S. (eds.) The View from Building 20, pp. 111–176. MIT Press, Cambridge (1993)
24. Abney, S.: The English noun phrase in its sentential aspect. Tesis doctoral, MIT (1987)
25. Real Academia Española: Diccionario de la Real academia de la lengua Española. Espasa, Madrid (2014)
26. Hardt, D.: Ellipsis and computational linguistics. In: Craenenbroeck, J., Temmerman, T. (eds.) The Oxford Handbook of Ellipsis, pp. 342–356. Oxford University Press, Oxford (2019)

Digital Humanities and Teaching with NooJ

Where the Dickens Are Melville's Phrasal Verbs?

Peter A. Machonis(⌐)

Florida International University, Miami, USA
machonis@fiu.edu

Abstract. This study expands digital research in the humanities by using NooJ to examine Phrasal Verb (PV) usage in the complete works of the nineteenth-century British author Charles Dickens and his American counterpart Herman Melville. The goal is to ascertain if PVs are indeed a characteristic feature of early American English. To compare the PV usage of these two writers, we used a specially designed NooJ grammar, electronic dictionary, and a series of disambiguation grammars, adverbial and adjectival expression filters, and idiom dictionaries. Since usage could be attributed to subject matter, we analyzed usage per 1,000 words of text in the complete works of both Melville (1.3 million words) and Dickens (4 million words), obtained from Project Gutenberg. To avoid excessive noise, the NooJ PV dictionary was limited to 1,148 expressions using the particles *out*, *up*, *down*, *away*, *back*, and *off*. The NooJ platform successfully identified PVs with a precision of 98.8% for the novels of Dickens and an overall accuracy of 98.3% for the works of Melville. After eliminating this residual noise, we conclude that Dickens uses more PVs than Melville: 3.32 PVs per 1,000 words of text as compared to 2.49 PVs per 1,000 words of text.

Keywords: NooJ in the humanities · Dickens · Melville · Multiword expressions · Phrasal verbs · English verb-particle combinations

1 Introduction

English phrasal verbs (PVs) or verb-particle combinations, such as *ask in*, *get up*, *push away*, *roll down*, and *take out*, are considered a distinctive trait of the Germanic languages and a major difficulty for non-native learners of English. Although particles existed as early as Old English and were first described by eighteenth-century grammarians, PVs began attracting the attention of linguists in the early twentieth century with Kennedy's [1] classic study. Since Kennedy's seminal monograph, however, PVs have often been classified as pleonastic or colloquial variants of simple verbs (*count out*, *count up* vs. *count*; *burn out* vs. *exhaust*). Many linguists have reiterated his historical analysis, such as Konishi [2], who also finds a steady growth of these combinations after Old English, a slight drop during the Age of Reason – with authors such as Dryden and Johnson who avoided such "grammatical irregularities" – followed by a new expansion in the nineteenth century. Today though, grammarians often attribute PVs to an American

© Springer Nature Switzerland AG 2021
B. Bekavac et al. (Eds.): NooJ 2020, CCIS 1389, pp. 99–110, 2021.
https://doi.org/10.1007/978-3-030-70629-6_9

influence. For example, *The New Fowler's Modern English Usage* [3] states, "Frequent in American English, it is clear that the use of phrasal verbs began to increase in a noticeable manner in America from the early nineteenth century onward. From there, many have made their way to Britain during the twentieth century, to widespread expressions of regret and alarm".

It appears that many English grammars continue to promote the myth that PVs are colloquial and typical of American English, in spite of the work of Bolinger [4], who associates these structures with a "creativeness that surpasses anything else in our language", and Fraser [5], who first portrayed the complex transformations these verbs can undergo. Furthermore, Hampe [6], in her corpus-based study of semantic redundancy in English, suggests that compositional phrasal verbs (e.g., *drink up the milk, lock up the car*), where the overall meaning of the expression can be derived from that of the regular verb, can function as an "index of emotional involvement of the speaker". That is, the use of the particle can at times play a pragmatic role, adding a subjective element of meaning – an indirect way of communicating the speaker's attitude or emotion.

More recently, Stephan Thim [7] claims "little evidence for the universal assumption that phrasal verbs are more typical of American English". In fact, he highlights "the little attention Late Modern English – in particular the nineteenth century – has received". As Brinton [8] concludes: Thim "undercuts much received notion on the phrasal verb" and should very well serve as a "springboard" for more detailed analyses. This study thus proposes to expand digital research in the humanities by using the NooJ platform, along with a specially designed PV grammar, electronic dictionary, and a series of disambiguation grammars, adverbial and adjectival expression filters, and idiom dictionaries to parse the complete works of two prominent nineteenth-century authors – the English writer Charles Dickens and his American counterpart Herman Melville – and compare their actual PV usage. Although digital humanities date back to the first concordances, this project is unique in that it involves identifying a precise type of verb which can appear in both continuous (e.g., ***roll down*** *all the windows*) and discontinuous (e.g., ***roll*** *all the windows **down***) format.

2   Previous Research

Previous research [9–12] showed how NooJ could successfully annotate English PVs in large corpora, including discontinuous PVs involving insertions of one to four word forms. In particular, [9, 10] introduced the NooJ PV grammar and dictionary constructed from Lexicon-Grammars, while [11] illustrated how to reduce noise by incorporating additional dictionaries and disambiguation grammars, modifying them with unique NooJ functionalities such as $+EXCLUDE$ and $+UNAMB$. Most importantly, the PV grammar, as displayed in Fig. 1, uses the NooJ functionality $THIS = V\$Part$, which assures that a particular particle must be associated with a specific verb in the PV dictionary in order for it to be recognized as a PV in NooJ's Text Annotation Structure (TAS). While this may limit the overall coverage, or recall, of every PV in any corpus, since the NooJ PV dictionary does not contain every PV of the English language, it does assure better precision than programs that use taggers, which necessarily produce a certain percentage of tagging mistakes. With further refinements to the NP node of the NooJ

PV grammar (see Fig. 2 and Fig. 3), [12] demonstrated that it was possible to accurately identify PVs in NooJ's sample corpus (the 1881 H James novel *The Portrait of a Lady* containing 233,102 word forms) with a 90% precision rate, with precision defined as: True Positives/(True Positives + False Positives).

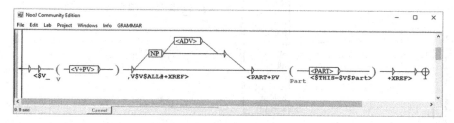

Fig. 1. The NooJ PV grammar [11]

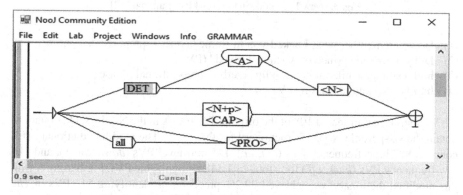

Fig. 2. Revised NP node in the NooJ PV grammar [12]

3 Limiting the Particle Search for Better Precision

Although this PV Grammar is fairly accurate, for this study we wanted to have a higher precision rate, which was achieved by limiting our PV dictionary to the six particles *out, up, down, away, back, off*. While this may not accomplish the ultimate NLP goal of annotating every PV in a large corpus, it does provide a valuable base for examining the evolution of PV usage throughout the history of the English language. In fact, the linguist Hiltunen [13] examined English texts limiting searches to seven typical particles representing three levels of PV frequency: high (*out, up*), mid (*down, away*), and low (*back, off, forth*). By doing the same, except for the particle *forth*, we can create a fairly accurate snapshot of PV usage in numerous nineteenth-century novels with improved precision. Specifically, we wanted to avoid the excessive noise from the particles *in* and *on*, which are frequently used as prepositions in similar syntactic constructions, as the following sentences illustrate:

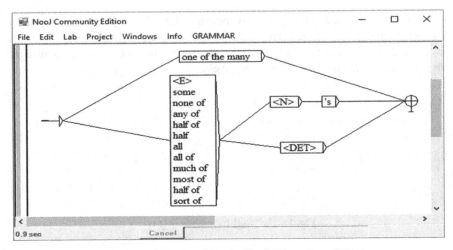

Fig. 3. New DET node in the NooJ PV grammar [12]

(1) Do you remember what I **asked** you **in** Rome? (verb + prepositional phrase)
(2) Did you **ask** the prince **in** when he arrived? (PV)
(3) **had** a strange smile **on** her thin lips (verb + prepositional phrase)
(4) **had** her hat and jacket **on** (PV)

We therefore eliminated 108 of the original 1,256 PVs in the NooJ PV Dictionary to obtain the six-particle NooJ PV dictionary for this study. The modified dictionary still contains 887 high-frequency PVs (*out, up*), 145 mid-level PVs (*down, away*), and 116 low-frequency PVs (*back, off*) for a total of 1,148 recognizable PVs. Furthermore, with this modified dictionary, we achieved 99.2% precision in identifying 517 PVs in *The Portrait of a Lady*. In fact, the following examples were the only noise produced:

(5) I should spend the **evening out** I sent him a
(6) of the relation was to **make** her reach **out** a hand
(7) for the present try to **make** her take **up** the cudgels
(8) proposed that they should **take** a run **down** to Spain

4   PV Usage in the Complete Works of Dickens and Melville

With this increased precision, we next applied a NooJ Linguistic Analysis to 16 novels by the British writer Charles Dickens (4 million words) and 12 novels by the American author of the same time period Herman Melville (1.3 million words), which were obtained from Project Gutenberg. Using NooJ's PV grammar and dictionary, along with its disambiguation grammars and other resources, we created concordances of all the expressions that contained a PV notation in their TAS. We next identified and eliminated by hand any PVs that were incorrect. This involved verifying 13,299 likely PVs in Dickens and removing 158 false positives, and examining 3,342 potential PVs in Melville and eliminating 56 incorrectly annotated as PV. We also included nominalizations of PVs, as well as gerundive forms in our tabulations:

(9) a very neat **turn out**
(10) in the **handing down** of a capacious baking dish

4.1   Accuracy of Discontinuous PVs in NooJ

What is unique about NooJ, though, is its capability of correctly identifying discontinuous multiword expressions in large corpora. In our data, we noticed many discontinuous PVs, varying from one to six word forms (WFs) inserted between the verb and the particle. Although one-word discontinuous PVs are the most common, two or more WFs between the verb and the particle are also frequent in the novels examined. For example, in Dickens's *David Copperfield* (363,485 words), out of the 1,243 correct PVs, 245 (20%) involved one WF between the verb and the particle, 61 (5%) contained two WFs, 9 (1%) contained 3 WFs between, with one case of a discontinuous PV with 4 WFs between. Likewise, in Melville's *Moby Dick* (218,390 words), out of the 571 accurate PVs identified, 72 (13%) involved one WF between the verb and the particle, 23 (4%) had 2 WFs, 9 (2%) involved 3 WFs, with one instance of a discontinuous PV with 4 WFs between.

The following are some of the more interesting cases involving more than one WF from the novels examined:

(11) I still **held** her forcibly **down**; (*Great Expectations*) [2 WFs]
(12) She **pushed** the candle impatiently **away**; (*Oliver Twist*) [3 WFs]
(13) The sea had jeeringly **kept** his finite body **up**, *(Moby Dick)* [3 WFs]
(14) and **wear** his daily life **out** grain by grain (*The Mystery of Edwin Drood*) [3 WFs]
(15) and **laid** her weary head **down**, weeping (*Dombey and Son*) [3 WFs]
(16) **throwing** his long arms straight **out** before him, *(Moby Dick)* [4 WFs]
(17) He never **took** two articles of clothing **out** together, (*Nicholas Nickleby*) [4 WFs]
(18) she **drove** her wheeled chair rapidly **back** (*Little Dorrit*) [4 WFs]
(19) Shall I **put** any of those little things **up** with mine? (*The Pickwick Papers*) [5 WFs]
(20) **felt** his empty sleeve all the way **up**, from the cuff, (*Great Expectations*) [6 WFs]

Using NooJ's *Statistical Analyses > Frequency* feature, we could see in our concordances that *take* is the most commonly used verb in PV formations, which furthermore appears very often discontinuously with any of our six particles, as the following examples from *David Copperfield* illustrate:

(21) **Take** me **away**.
(22) **Take** him **back** unconditionally,
(23) **take** me **up** directly
(24) **Take** the top one **off**,
(25) who had **taken** Agnes **down**
(26) She had **taken** them **out** now,

However, there are cases of *take* followed by prepositions from the same novel, which brings us to one of the major difficulties in correctly identifying PVs:

(27)   and **take** a stroll **down** one of those wire-arched walks
(28)   he **took** his crooked thumb **off** the spot where he had planted it,

4.2   Difficulty Distinguishing Between Preposition and Particle

As in previous studies, much of the noise came from the overlapping of particles and prepositions, since NooJ keeps all possible analyses in its TAS. Here are some examples of noise (verb + preposition) that contrast with true PVs among our data, showing that the fuller context is needed to decide if the PV TAS is accurate or not:

(29)   the tears **rolled down** the poor child's face (verb + prepositional phrase)
(30)   **rolling back** the table-cloth (PV)
(31)   She **took** her feet **off** the fender, pushed back her chair (verb + prepositional phrase)
(32)   He **took off** the cocked hat again (PV)
(33)   able to **get up** the narrow stairs without Bob (verb + prepositional phrase)
(34)   was somewhat noisily **getting** his steam **up** for departure (PV)
(35)   **lighted** the traveller **up** a steep and narrow staircase; (verb + prepositional phrase)
(36)   had **lighted up** two candles in the hall (PV)
(37)   Nevertheless, as they **wound down** the rugged way (verb + prepositional phrase)
(38)   she had entered it, and **wound** their way **down** among the (PV)

Whereas the preceding cases are fairly clear, we did have to choose between borderline cases in deciding if a potential PV should be considered acceptable or classified as noise. When in doubt, we used movement as a test for PV acceptability. For example in 29 above, you cannot say the tears *rolled the poor child's face down*. Consider the following possible PVs identified by NooJ from *Little Dorrit*:

(39)   Arthur **pulled off** his hat to him
(40)   **pushed** his hat **up**
(41)   Mr Flintwinch, [...] **looked up** his hat, and lighted Mr Blandois across the hall

Only sentences 39 and 40 are considered true PVs. In those two cases, you can move the particle and restate: *pulled his hat off* and *pushed up his hat*, but if you were to paraphrase example 41 as *looked his hat up*, it would be ungrammatical and was thus considered noise. Similarly, this is an acceptable PV:

(42)   in backing against a pump, that he **shook** his hat **off** (*Martin Chuzzlewit*)

Consider, however, these borderline cases from *Martin Chuzzlewit*:

(43)   I come to him after I've **taken** the edge **off** my own hunger, you know
(44)   and presently came stamping and **shaking** the wet **off** his hat and coat,

Since you can say *taken the edge off of my own hunger*, or simply *taken the edge off*, example 43 is considered satisfactory. Although example 44 is more dubious, we did accept it, since you can say: **shaking off** *the wet from his hat and coat*, or even **shaking** *the wet* **off**, without any further modification.

Likewise, the following example from *Piazza Tales* was determined to be adequate, since both **wipe** *this ugly stuff* **off**, as well as **wipe** *the razor* **off**, are acceptable:

(45)   while I **wipe** this ugly stuff **off** the razor

The fuller context, however, is needed to verify the acceptance of some sentences, such as this one from *Israel Potter*:

(46)   and thinking to myself what leaky fire-buckets they would be to **pass up** a ladder

Although you can say **pass** *leaky fire-buckets* **up**, you cannot say **pass** *a ladder* **up** in this particular context, and thus this case was considered noise. As Talmy [14], who refers to English particles as "satellites" states, "a problem arises for English which, perhaps alone among Indo-European languages, has come to regularly position satellite and preposition next to each other in a sentence". In fact, a broader context is sometimes needed that no NLP platform can provide to clearly distinguish preposition from particle.

5   Noise Removal: A Continual Process

As we examined the concordances for possible noise, we continually refined many of NooJ's dictionaries, disambiguating grammars, filters, and other linguistics resources. For example, when we encountered variations of the many expressions that already existed in the nouns and frozen expression dictionary, *nouns and frozex.dic*, we continued to add these to remove further noise. In *Bleak House*, for example, we encountered the noun *lattice-work*, which we accordingly designated as *N+Conc+s+UNAMB* to avoid being misidentified with the PV to **work up**:

(47)   deal of attention, the lattice-**work up** her back having widened

Likewise, the expression *close up to* was designated *PREP + UNAMB* and thus not to be confused with the PV to *close something up*:

(48)   over more carefully; then went **close up** to him, and took
(49)   the walls, forced Gabriel Varden **close up** to the door.

Finally, the many expressions involving variations on *up and down the stairs* had to be listed in this dictionary as *ADV + UNAMB*. This included *up the stairs, up the staircase, up stairs, up-stairs, up or down stairs, down the stairs, down stairs, down-stairs*, and *down the staircase*. This assures that NooJ does not give the PV TAS to the following:

(50)   uttered but one word, and **called** that **up** the stairs
(51)   He **followed** the child **up** stairs.

(52) was **passing up** the staircase,
(53) **took** her classical features **down**-stairs
(54) to have an intention of **hurling** them **down** stairs on speculation

In the future, we may have to create a grammar that recognizes all of the *stair/staircase* expressions, since the following are still incorrectly identified as PVs:

(55) **made** his way **up** the little staircase
(56) They **followed** the girl **up** some steep corner-stairs
(57) and **followed** her **up** a dark bare staircase
(58) **lighted** the traveller **up** a steep and narrow staircase;

In fact, there are already two dictionaries that work in tandem with grammars that target more complex idiomatic expressions to which we added more expressions: *take one's eyes off*, *keep one's eyes off*, *turn one's back on*, *turn one's back against*, *turn one's back as*, and *turn one's back* followed by punctuation <P>. These expressions were thus given the Idiom TAS by NooJ, which automatically eliminated the following previously incorrectly annotated PVs:

(59) wholly consisted in her never **taking** her eyes **off** his face
(60) I couldn't **keep** my eyes **off** him.
(61) and he **turned** his **back**.
(62) an instant blinding me, and **turned** his powerful **back** as he

In addition to specifying new locatives in the dictionary, such as *lane* and *road*, we also modified the Locative Disambiguation Grammar's NP node to take into account preceding adjectives, as well:

(63) **turned down** a dirty lane, where
(64) as they **turned down** a narrow road, (*Hard Times*)

We still kept the NooJ feature +*EXCLUDE* for the particle *up* in the Locative Disambiguation Grammar, so as not to create silence such as:

(65) calm again, numbers of people **choked up** every avenue of access

In fact, care must be taken not to put too many locatives in this dictionary. For example, including *road* enabled us to automatically remove noise from *Hard Times* (example 64), yet at the same time created one case of silence in another Dickens novel:

(66) **pointing out** the road that I was taking (*Our Mutual Friend*)

5.1 Unresolved Noise

Among the PV noise that has not been automatically removed by NooJ's grammars and filters, the most common involves prepositions being incorrectly identified as particles.

The second most common type of noise still not resolved entails cases where the potential PV is really a noun or even an adverb, such as the following:

(67) wearing a very large sword, and **boots up** to his hips,
(68) as she blew a little **dust off** the pickled pork
(69) Fog everywhere. **Fog up** the river, where it
(70) the bright **gas** springs **up** in the streets
(71) to pass one **hand down** one side, and confuses
(72) and he'd shave her **head off**.
(73) little steamboat got her **steam up** in London
(74) Jo looks about him and **even** glances **up** some ten feet
(75) Lane on both sides, and **even out** in Holborn,

Finally, there are a few cases in which PVs overlap in the TAS, such as:

(76) not a little indignant to **hear** a young urchin roaring **out** some jolly song

While example 76 is noise, the following is correctly identified by NooJ:

(77) **roaring out** some jolly song

Other miscellaneous noise is created when the past particle *fallen*, which is also categorized as a plural noun (e.g., *the fallen*), is identified as a noun in the TAS:

(78) It might **have** fallen **out** so,
(79) one of us have been so happy if it **had** fallen **out**

The PV *to **have** something **out*** is fairly productive, however, and should not be removed, as the following correctly identified PVs show:

(80) Of course if you are sure that you **have** no personal security **out**,
(81) and **had** a tooth **out**
(82) **have** it **out** with Mr. Peggotty.

6   Results and Future Research

6.1   Results

In spite of residual noise in our concordances, we achieved an overall precision of 98.8% in Dickens and 98.3% in Melville, as can be seen in Fig. 4 and Fig. 5. Each novel is listed with the number of words per novel, along with the number of genuine PVs (i.e., noise deleted), followed by the number of words per 1,000 words of text. In the last three columns, we show the number of PVs that NooJ detected in its TAS, the noise we removed manually, and the PV identification precision for each novel. At the bottom of each figure, we calculate the actual PV usage per 1,000 words of text in each author's complete works, along with NooJ's precision in accurately identifying PVs. Our final results show that the British author, Dickens, uses more PVs than his American counterpart, Melville: 3.32 PVs per 1,000 words of text as compared to 2.49 PVs per 1,000 words of text. Although this entailed only two authors from the same time frame, it clearly demonstrates that PV usage cannot be considered to be a uniquely American influence.

DATE	TEXT	WORD FORMS	Phrasal Verbs (noise deleted)	Phrasal Verbs per 1,000 words of text	Phrasal Verbs identified by NooJ (incl. noise)	NOISE	PRECISION
	CHARLES DICKENS						
1836	The Pickwick Papers	308,843	1051	3.40	1068	17	98.4%
1837	Oliver Twist	161,518	636	3.94	648	12	98.1%
1838	Nicholas Nickleby	330,990	952	2.88	960	8	99.2%
1840	The Old Curiosity Shop	221,855	672	3.03	679	7	99.0%
1841	Barnaby Rudge	259,931	893	3.44	899	6	99.3%
1843	A Christmas Carol	29,185	113	3.87	115	2	98.3%
1843	Martin Chuzzlewit	345,529	1036	3.00	1052	16	98.5%
1846	Dombey and Son	363,526	1148	3.16	1170	22	98.1%
1849	David Copperfield	363,485	1243	3.42	1257	14	98.9%
1852	Bleak House	361,983	1200	3.32	1209	9	99.3%
1854	Hard Times	105,682	304	2.88	307	3	99.0%
1855	Little Dorrit	344,932	1116	3.24	1132	16	98.6%
1859	A Tale of Two Cities	138,157	427	3.09	433	6	98.6%
1860	Great Expectations	188,948	795	4.21	798	3	99.6%
1864	Our Mutual Friend	333,783	1254	3.76	1270	16	98.7%
1870	The Mystery of Edwin Drood	97,844	301	3.08	302	1	99.7%
	TOTALS and PVs per 1,000 WF	3,956,191	13141	3.32			
	OVERALL PRECISION				13299	158	98.8%

Fig. 4. Actual PV usage and NooJ precision for works of Dickens

6.2 Future Research

To avoid an author bias, future research will examine more American and British authors to see to what extent an American influence, if any, was involved in the expansion of PV usage. In addition, future plans involve expanding the PV dictionary with the particles

DATE	TEXT	WORD FORMS	Phrasal Verbs (noise deleted)	Phrasal Verbs per 1,000 words of text	Phrasal Verbs identified by NooJ (incl. noise)	NOISE	PRECISION
	HERMAN MELVILLE						
1846	Typee: Romance of the South Sea	114,984	238	2.07	246	8	96.7%
1847	Omoo: Adventures in South Seas	103,665	336	3.24	339	3	99.1%
1849	Mardi: And a Voyage Thither (v.1)	98,388	218	2.22	221	3	98.6%
1849	Mardi: And a Voyage Thither (v.2)	103,691	235	2.27	239	4	98.3%
1849	Redburn. His First Voyage	120,504	390	3.24	396	6	98.5%
1850	White Jacket	145,547	401	2.76	410	9	97.8%
1851	Moby Dick	218,390	571	2.61	575	4	99.3%
1852	Pierre; or The Ambiguities	156,630	280	1.79	285	5	98.2%
1853	Bartleby, The Scrivener	14,650	34	2.32	38	4	89.5%
1855	Israel Potter	67,047	188	2.80	191	3	98.4%
1856	The Piazza Tales	80,998	163	2.01	169	6	96.4%
1857	The Confidence-Man	95,602	232	2.43	233	1	99.6%
	TOTALS and PVs per 1,000 WF	1,320,096	3286	2.49			
	OVERALL PRECISION				3342	56	98.3%

Fig. 5. Actual PV usage and NooJ precision for works of Melville

out, up, down, away, back, and *off*. Sydney La Valley [15] has recently created a Lexicon-Grammar of PVs using the particle *away* (e.g., *frighten away, wear away*), which is currently underrepresented as a mid-level frequency particle in our NooJ PV dictionary. Likewise, more tables will be created to enhance the representation of the two low-level frequency particles *back* and *off* (e.g., *roll back, take back, knock off, pull off*).

Once the NooJ PV dictionary is further enhanced, we will then expand the data to include authors from the early, mid, and end of the nineteenth and beginning of the twentieth century, both American (James Fenimore Cooper, Washington Irving, Nathaniel Hawthorne, Harriet Beecher Stowe, Mark Twain, Edith Wharton) and British (Jane Austen, Walter Scott, the Bronte sisters, George Eliot, Thomas Hardy, Oscar Wilde), as well as Henry James, who was born in the USA but acquired British citizenship.

Since our program would be able to recognize PVs in large corpora with improved accuracy, it could become the best instrument to measure actual PV usage in different genres – novels, plays, nonfiction, technical material, daily life texts (e.g., news articles, blogs), etc. – and at different periods in the history of the English language. Furthermore, all NooJ programs are open-source, so that our PV program would be available to other researchers around the globe. It would play a central role in using digitalized resources in the humanities – connecting the past to the present and future of research.

References

1. Kennedy, A.G.: The Modern English Verb-Adverb Combination. Stanford University Press, Stanford (1920)
2. Konishi, T.: The growth of the verb-adverb combination in English: a brief sketch. In: Araki, K., Egawa, T., Oyama, T., Yasui, M. (eds.) Studies in English grammar and linguistics: A miscellany in honour of Takanobu Otsuka, pp. 117–128. Kenkyusha, Tokyo (1958)
3. Burchfield, R.W.: The New Fowler's Modern English Usage. Rev. 3rd ed. Oxford University Press, Oxford, New York (2000)
4. Bolinger, D.: The Phrasal Verb in English. Harvard University Press, Cambridge (1971)
5. Fraser, B.: The Verb-Particle Combination in English. Academic Press, New York (1976)
6. Hampe, B.: Superlative Verbs: A Corpus-Based Study of Semantic Redundancy in English Verb-Particle Constructions. Gunter Narr Verlag, Tübingen (2002)
7. Thim, S.: The English Verb-Particle Construction and its History. De Gruyter Mouton, Berlin, New York (2012)
8. Brinton, L.J.: Review of phrasal verbs: the english verb-particle construction and its history. By Stephan Thim. Lang. **89**(3), 664–667 (2013)
9. Machonis, P.A.: English phrasal verbs: from lexicon-grammar to natural language processing. Southern J. Linguist. **34**(1), 21–48 (2010)
10. Machonis, P.A.: *Sorting* NooJ *out* to *take* multiword expressions *into account*. In: Vučković, K., Bekavac, B., Silberztein, M. (eds.) Automatic Processing of Various Levels of Linguistic Phenomena: Selected Papers from the NooJ 2011 International Conference, pp. 152–165. Cambridge Scholars Publishing, Newcastle upon Tyne (2012)
11. Machonis, P.A.: Phrasal verb disambiguation grammars: cutting out noise automatically. In: Barone, L., Monteleone, M., Silberztein, M. (eds.) NooJ 2016. CCIS, vol. 667, pp. 169–181. Springer, Cham (2016). https://doi.org/10.1007/978-3-319-55002-2_15
12. Machonis, P.A.: Linguistic resources for phrasal verb identification. In Barreiro, A., Kocijan, K., Machonis, P., Silberztein, M. (eds.) COLING 2018 Proceedings of the First Workshop on Linguistic Resources for Natural Language Processing, pp. 18–27. Association for Computational Linguistics, Stroudsburg (2018)
13. Hiltunen, R.: On phrasal verbs in early modern english: notes on lexis and style. In: Kastovsky, D. (ed.) Studies in Early Modern English, pp. 129–140. Mouton de Gruyter, Berlin (1994)
14. Talmy, L.: Lexicalization patterns: semantic structure. In: Shopen, T. (ed.) Lexical Forms in Language Typology and Syntactic Description, pp. 57–149. Cambridge University Press, New York (1985)
15. La Valley, S.G.: A lexicon-grammar analysis of "away" expressions. MA in Linguistics Final Projects. 10. Florida International University, Miami, FL (2020). https://digitalcommons.fiu.edu/linguistics_ma/10

Depictions of Women in "Duga" and "Tena": A Computational Analysis

Lorena Kasunić and Gordana Kiseljak[✉]

Faculty of Humanities and Social Sciences Zagreb, University of Zagreb, Zagreb, Croatia
lorena.kasunic@gmail.com, gkiselja@ffzg.hr

Abstract. By combining two contrasting fields, the humanities and digital technologies, a new discipline was born – that of digital humanities. After a long period of constantly using a single approach in literary science – interpretation – in recent years, a new approach has been introduced in this field of science – an empirical type of research, that of computational analysis. Not many efforts have been made in Croatia to implement or even introduce computational analysis as a possible approach in literary studies. This paper analyzes the depiction of women in two particular short stories: "Tena" by Josip Kozarac and "Duga" by Dinko Šimunović. These texts are considered appropriate and representative because their main characters are women whose portrayals are given in great detail. That is the reason why analyzing such texts can be fruitful for deriving data for the construction of the general model. Both texts are written in Croatian, which points to one of the main purposes and intentions of this paper – the use of canonical literary texts from Croatian literature to build a model for the quantitative analysis of female characters and hopefully apply it to other texts in the future. The methods which are used in this paper are computational analysis (a quantitative approach) and interpretation (a traditional, qualitative approach) of quantitative results based on literary science. This paper represents a pilot study of sorts, in which the authors will use the NooJ environment to take the initial steps toward building the aforementioned model.

Keywords: Computational analysis · Depictions of women · Digital humanities · Croatian language · NooJ

1 Introduction

Studying and analyzing literary texts is the domain of the study of literature, which uses interpretation as its main method. Through the long and rich history of interpretation of literary texts, literary scholars developed a variety of literary schools, directions and interdisciplinary approaches. Some of them focus more on the text itself (e.g., Russian formalism); others are more interested in the cultural, historical, or political background and context (e.g., cultural studies). Although these approaches differ in the initial point of view on the literary text, they all use interpretation as an approved method of analysis. They also fall under the rubric of qualitative approaches.

© Springer Nature Switzerland AG 2021
B. Bekavac et al. (Eds.): NooJ 2020, CCIS 1389, pp. 111–122, 2021.
https://doi.org/10.1007/978-3-030-70629-6_10

On the other hand, the comparatively newer method of computational analysis is a quantitative approach. The question that arises is whether computational analysis can find its place among these qualitative approaches. Can it become a new individual approach (such as structuralism, new criticism, etc.) or will it be an additional method that will be helpful for literary critics to widen their analyses? What can computational analysis give to literary scholars? Firstly, it enables distant reading, which enables scholars to analyze a much larger amount of text at the same time. For example, a person can create a corpus of one hundred realist novels without having to closely read each of them. In this way, the quality and importance of some previously neglected texts (ones that do not form the literary canon) can be discovered. Secondly, statistical data can cast new light on a certain question that a literary scholar might wish to find answers for. In this study of female depictions, for example, statistical data can show which are the most frequent adjectives, nouns, or verbs that occur next to a certain female character. These empirical data can perhaps make the interpretation of literature more objectively grounded, meaning that interpretation can sometimes be biased and prejudiced based on ideological, political, national or other aspects which are often intertwined in a literary text. Furthermore – building on the first statement about the ability of reading large amounts of text in a short time period – computationally analyzing a corpus of a certain author can be a great way to detect the specific literary style of a writer. There is also a possibility of attributing authorship by looking at the grammatical, syntactical, and stylistic features of an anonymous text and comparing it with the corpus of a potential author.

2   Related Work

2.1   Literary Background

Looking at the history of Croatian literature, Božidar Petrač [7] observed that female characters were in it from the beginning. Different literary periods had different under-standings and representations of women. Although Croatian literature is rich in female characters, Petrač [7] claims that these characters have not been analyzed enough. Just as other forms of interpretation often rely on the literary canon, this also applies to character analysis – literary scholars reach for novels, poems, short stories, and plays that have already been analyzed in detail. Most of these analyses have unfortunately neglected to focus on female characters; therefore, Petrač [7] claims that the richness of female characters in Croatian literature has not yet been explored to its full potential.

In the following section, a sort of a typology of female characters will be presented, based on Petrač's article "The Figure of the Woman in Croatian Literature" (Cro. "Figura žene u hrvatskoj književnosti"). The first type is *the woman as a mother*. During the Middle Ages, Croatian writers mostly wrote poems. The main motif and object was one particular woman – The Virgin Mary. Accordingly, Marian poetry was developed and started to prevail. Women were presented as mothers, moral pillars, and keepers of life [7]. With the arrival of the Petrarchian influence and the Renaissance, a new type of woman appeared – *the ideal woman*. Poets described women as perfect creatures – both in the physical and the spiritual sense. They were fair ladies who were now also keepers, but keepers of the lover's heart [7]. Petrač calls this type of character the *angel-woman*, alluding to her innocence, purity, and piety. At the same time, poets, especially epic poets, developed the *heroic woman*. She is a strong and exemplary figure who sacrifices for the common good, for her nation, for her faith [7]. Croatian Baroque literature differentiates between three types of female protagonists – *the fair lady, the fallen woman,* and *the penitent woman* [7]. The first type is similar to the ideal woman of the Renaissance, while the other two types are often intertwined. First, the female protagonist is in the stage of impurity; then, she experiences a religious conversion and turns into the penitent woman. Her sins are oftentimes connected with carnal pleasures. The penitent woman is an example and a warning for all sinners – that is, baroque readers. She shows how anybody can be forgiven if they repent [7]. Finally, the nineteenth century provides more developed female characters. Authors begin to create psychologically complex and individuated protagonists, and these characters are often female. In Realism, the *femme fatal* appears, a destructive, diabolic, and dangerous figure. In this regard, Croatian authors of the period were under great influence from the European masters – Flaubert, Balzac, Zola, Ibsen, etc. [7].

At the end of his article, Petrač wonders whether the modern age brings with it a new type of female character. He concludes that the modern novel cannot shape a particular type of a character because it forgoes the female psychology and creates men and women who are "abstractions, void, abyss, and despair" [7].

2.2 Computational Research

The field of digital humanities – and computational analysis as a part of it – is still not really present in the work of Croatian literary scholars. At present, no research deals with anything similar to the topic of this study. For this reason, this section will look into some interesting studies and approaches from the English-speaking scientific community.

Massey et al. [6] made a study that is the starting point for building automatic methods for the prediction of relations between characters in a literary text. They had four fields of interest: "... we collect judgments as to the **coarse-grained category** (professional, social, familial), **fine-grained category** (friend, lover, parent, rival, employer), and **affinity** (positive, negative, neutral) that describes their primary relationship in a text. We do not assume that this relationship is static; we also collect judgments as to whether it **changes** at any point in the course of the text" [6:1, emphasis in the original]. They used 109 literary texts from different time periods for the collection of annotations (that is, summaries of those texts available on SparkNotes). Annotators used them to judge the relationship between two characters. The authors provided a questionnaire divided on four parts: Affinity (how the characters are related – Social, Professional, Familial), Kind (a more detailed assessment of the relationship – e.g., friend, husband), Change (to detect how the relationship changes), and Detail (if some additional information should be included) [6].

Arhur M. Jacobs [4] presented two computational studies about sentiment analysis for words and fiction characters. What is of special interest in the context of researching character depiction is the part of Jacobs's paper which talks about personality profiles of characters in stories, novels, plays, etc. These personality profiles were implemented for characters in the *Harry Potter* books. Estimation of an emotional profile was done combining the name of the character and the emotion word specific for this fictional character [4].

Another study dealing with characters is shown in [5]. Their main focus was relation extraction. The method had four steps: utterance attribution, vocative detection, relation extraction, and relation propagation. The authors think family relations are a stable phenomenon which can therefore be automatically extracted. Furthermore, family relations and their extraction "can assist literary analysis by providing basic facts for further reasoning on the story" [5].

The studies presented above mostly focus on relations between characters or their emotional profile and are not trying to make a complete review of the character, with all their aspects. However, it is interesting to see different approaches and methods for character analysis, as it is useful for contextualizing the research of this paper in this field.

3   The Dataset

The research about the depiction of female characters was conducted on the literary texts, "Tena" and "Duga." Both are short stories, one written by Dinko Šimunović ("Duga") and the other by Josip Kozarac ("Tena"). The stories were originally written in Croatian and were analyzed in that language. To put the texts into a literary context, it should be noted that "Duga" belongs to the literary period of Modernism. It has 8,850 tokens and 32,098 annotations in NooJ. "Tena" belongs to the literary period of Realism. It is almost twice as long as "Duga," which has 17,929 tokens and 67,384 annotations in NooJ. Table 1 shows the data for both literary texts.

Table 1. Basic information about the analyzed texts

	"Duga"	"Tena"
Author	Dinko Šimunović	Josip Kozarac
Year	1907	1894
Literary period	Modernism	Realism
Literary genre	Short story	Short story
No. of tokens	8,850	17,929
No. of annotations	32,098	67,384

"Duga" tells the story of a little girl named Srna, who has different hopes and desires from the other girls in her village. A big part of the text talks about another girl called Sava and her tragic fate. That is why Srna and Sava are considered the main characters of the story. "Tena" is a coming-of-age story about a young country girl in Slavonia, an eastern region of Croatia. The main motif of the story is a marriage that causes disruptions between all of the characters.

These literary texts were chosen for this study because they have quite strong female protagonists who are highly present in the texts. The main focus of the authors is the detailed and complex representation of female characters. Although the stories are not from the same literary period, both of them create well-rounded characters and present female characters in a non-stereotypical way. That is the reason why analyzing such texts is helpful in building a more general model. In addition, there are many minor female characters, which increases the occurrence of expressions we can categorize as ones depicting femininity.

4 Grammar Models

Both short stories were downloaded from the *eLektire* website in.pdf format. The first step was to manually annotate expressions that were considered important for the depiction of female characters. In addition, all the female names that a NooJ grammar needed to recognize were collected. Subsequently, a NooJ dictionary of female personal names and other names that refer to female characters (examples will be shown in the Results section) was built. This dictionary was added to the resources for lexical analysis for Croatian that already exist in NooJ [10].

The next step was building a syntactic grammar in NooJ [8]. The grammar was split in two major parts: the *She* and the *Fem* part. The layout of this initial grammar structure is shown in Fig. 1. The *She* part was used to detect expressions that have the female personal pronoun in its center. The *Fem* part was used to locate phrases that have personal names of female characters or other names that refer to them. Although there were expressions which contained both a female personal pronoun and, for example, a personal name of a female character, the expression's grammatical construction was described either in the *She* part or in the *Fem* part, depending on the simplicity and clarity of the path.

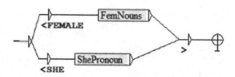

Fig. 1. The separated *She* and *Fem* subgraphs

The expression "path" is used to denote a special syntactic structure of a certain expression. The goal was to make a specific path for each expression, which was manually annotated. Two major nodes were created – one for objects and the other for verbs, or rather, predicates. Because of this, two grammars were made (one for each text) in order to capture these specific expressions. Figure 2 shows the grammar for the text "Duga," *She* part. As can be seen, the female personal pronoun is the central part of speech around which different paths were built. In some examples, verb forms came before the pronoun, and in others, they came after the pronoun. All these cases had to be accounted for.

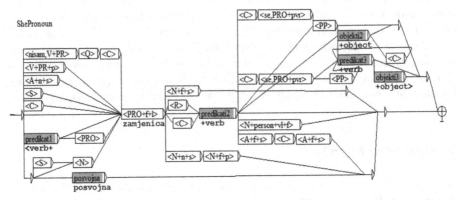

Fig. 2. An example of the grammar structure for "Duga" (*She* part)

The subgraphs for objects and predicates are the central syntactic elements surrounding the main female noun or pronoun (female personal names, female personal pronoun, specific namings of female characters). The *Fem* part of the grammar consists of another subgraph called *zena* (En. 'woman') denoting expressions containing pronouns and adjectives that describe the main female noun. Its complexity is shown in Fig. 3. This subgraph also has a graph called *zenska imena* ('female names'), where female personal names are listed. The *She* part is constructed in a similar way. Only, instead of the above-mentioned subgraphs, there is one special subgraph called *posvojna* (denoting the possessive female pronoun). It has a slightly simpler structure than the subgraph *zena*, as can be noticed when comparing Fig. 3 and Fig. 4. The expressions were built around the personal female pronoun. The grammar models for "Duga" and "Tena" differ slightly in their structure (due to the difference in the specific expressions) but are based on the same principles.

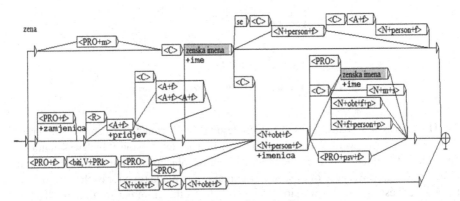

Fig. 3. Subgraph *zena* from the *Fem* part

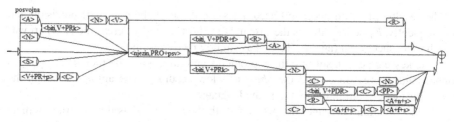

Fig. 4. Subgraph *posvojna* from the *She* part

5 Results

After the creation of separate grammars, the first step towards analyzing was calculating
the truthfulness and accuracy of the grammar models, i.e., the execution of empirical
appraisal. Synthetic one-dimensional indicators – precision, recall and F_1-score – are
typically used for estimating the conduct of natural language processing (NLP) or information retrieval (IR) systems [3]. "[R]ecall is a measure of effectiveness in retrieving (or
selecting) performance and can be viewed as a measure of effectiveness in including relevant items in the retrieved set" and "precision is the number of retrieved relevant items
as a proportion of the number of retrieved items … a measure of purity in retrieval performance, a measure of effectiveness in excluding nonrelevant items from the retrieved
set" [1]. Lastly, F_1-score or F-measure "represents the harmonic mean of precision and
recall" [9]. Table 2 shows the results of the aforementioned three measures; each of the
them was calculated for the individual *She* and *Fem* parts of both short stories.

Table 2. The accuracy of grammar models

	"Duga"		"Tena"	
	She	*Fem*	*She*	*Fem*
Precision	0.5	0.883	**0.639**	**0.939**
Recall	**0.864**	0.883	0.704	**0.956**
F_1-score	0.633	0.883	**0.696**	**0.948**

The main purpose of the results in Table 2 is the detection of flaws in constructed
grammar models, i.e., to conclude what was more correctly annotated. Moreover, it was
done so as to uncover the reason why a certain text is more correctly annotated than
another. The analysis was executed on two separate levels: the individual (between a
personal female pronoun and nouns indicating female characters of the same novel) and
the collective (between the stories "Duga" and "Tena").

The results indicated that the grammar model for "Tena" was more successful than
the one for "Duga," particularly the *Fem* part. The results were surprising because of
the assumption that the larger the text (corpus), the more problems with designing the
grammar model there would be (contributing to a possible lower accuracy rate). However, that was not the case – "Duga" was far more difficult to annotate, as is evident

in the results. Most unsuccessful accuracies are those of the *She* part: precision and consequently, F_1-score – that is the case in both short stories, whereas the *Fem* part was much more successful (again, "Tena" has slightly better results).

The key element in solving these problems and improving the models is trying to understand the reason behind the *She* part's low accuracy. The answer is not in the grammar models, but in the text, i.e., the language.

In the Croatian language, the problem with the pronouns[1] is that a certain female pronoun exists in various gender[2] forms; some pronouns can even indicate another part of speech. The singular form (in the nominative case) of the female personal pronoun (*ona*[3]) is the same as the plural form (in the nominative case) of the neuter personal pronoun. Furthermore, the genitive form of the female personal pronoun has two versions, one of which (*je*[4]) can be used as a verb. The same applies to one of the accusative forms of the personal female pronoun, which has three versions (one is also *je*). Similarly, the dative form of the female personal pronoun has two versions, and one is the word *joj*[5], which can be used as an exclamation word.

Word ambiguity is also common among Croatian nouns but is much more easily solved than that concerning pronouns. These are just some of the instances in which detailed knowledge of the language plays a crucial rule in understanding language traps. For improving further analysis, two possible literary techniques were introduced: *She/Fem* ratio and graphs with female name occurrences.

Figure 5 presents the graphs containing the ratios of two focus categories: female personal pronouns and nouns indicating female characters (first names, roles, family positions, etc.). "Duga" has more *Fem* (144; 79%) phrases than *She* (38; 21%) phrases – close to four times more *Fem* than *She* phrases.

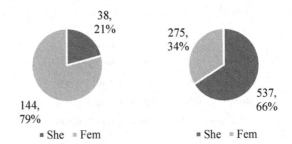

Fig. 5. "Duga" (left) and "Tena" (right) – *She/Fem* ratios

One possible reason behind the pronoun shortage is the introduction of numerous supporting characters who played a significant role in the structure of the story, necessitating the explicit use of main characters' first names or regularly emphasising their

---

[1] In the Croatian language there are eight types of pronouns, which vary depending on the declension (seven grammatical cases) and conjugation.

[2] The Croatian language has three genders: feminine, masculine, and neuter.

[3] En. 'she'.

[4] As a pronoun, it means 'she'; as a verb, it can also mean '*to be*'.

[5] As a pronoun, it indicates the word *she*; as an exclamation word it means 'oops', 'oh', or 'ouch'.

positions (as mothers, daughters, girls, grandmothers, women, ladies, widows etc.). In "Tena", the case was the complete opposite, as there were far more *She* (537; 66%) phrases than *Fem* (275; 34%) phrases – a ratio of almost double. This might indicate that some characters are considerately more developed or talked about than others.

One of the possible areas for utilizing these numbers and graphs is predicting authorship attribution. That is, based on preferences of the usage of *Fem* or *She* expressions, we could conclude who is the author of some anonymous text, or verify the author of some newly found text.

Lastly, Fig. 6 and Fig. 7 show graphs with the numbers of occurrences of the female characters' explicit names. These techniques, used in the final stage of the analysis, represent the most concrete usage of the numbers extracted from the NooJ results. As in the previous cases, the results (the number of names) are separated based on the short story they belong to. The focus was solely on trying to detect the potential meaning of the results from a particular short story.

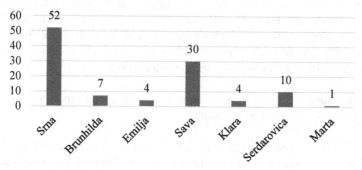

Fig. 6. "Duga" – number of name occurrences

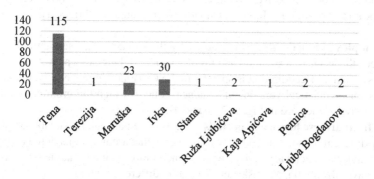

Fig. 7. "Tena" – number of the name occurrences

The most interesting findings were centered around three female characters, one from "Tena" – Tena herself, and two from "Duga" – Srna and Emilija. As expected, Tena and Srna, as the protagonists, were the names that occurred most frequently in each text. Alongside these names, each one of them has a full name which also occurred in the text, but considerably less frequently. Tena's full name is Terezija and it occurred only once. Srna's full name Brunhilda also occurred less than her nickname – seven times. Preferences between the usage of the full name or the nickname can open up possible further research questions about our protagonists and their surroundings. The third name, Emilija, refers to Srna's mother, who also appears in the text as Serdarovica, which is derived from her surname after marrying Srna's father, Janko Serdar. Her position in the text was determined by her being a married woman.

6 Conclusion

This study was an attempt at merging two contrasting fields (the humanities and digital technologies) into a singular inquiry. This was executed with a new, experimental type of literary analysis – the usage of a linguistic program for analyzing the depictions of the female characters in two specific short stories ("Duga" and "Tena"). The primary goal was to accomplish a general model for female characters, with the mission that this model be meaningful and respectfully present all female characters in a three-dimensional manner – as Forster [2] would describe them in his book *Aspects of the Novel*, round characters as opposed to flat ones. After the results and the analysis follows an overall examination of the entire research process. There were a few obstacles in the procedure of building the grammar models using the Croatian language:

- **ambiguity** is one of the main reasons for making separate grammars for the two short stories; as in the following two examples:
  - *Sava*: in "Duga" it refers to the name of a female character, but in "Tena" there is no character with that name; it only indicates the name of a river in Slavonia (a region in eastern Croatia);
  - *Srna*: also the name of a female character in "Duga"; while this word does not appear (as a name) in "Tena", it can also refer to an animal (a dear);

- the **complex syntactic structure** caused by the syntactic and semantic differences between the usage of a standard and literary variety of language; as well as the significant syntactical freedom that is specific to the Croatian language (e.g., the manifold of possible syntactical versions of sentences, due to which the grammar models are as extensive as they are in Fig. 1, 2, 3, and 4);
- **texts from diverse historical periods** – the use of a particular a vocabulary which is vastly different than that used today (e.g., words that are now considered archaic; the use of dialects which vary across regions; uncommon character names such as Duga, Srna, Sava, Brunhilda, Maruška, etc.), slightly different syntax;
- **unsolved problems** – the repetition of annotations for the same word (the final results were less than it showed in an initial concordance); the necessity of developing a proper methodology for combining the humanities and the empirical disciplines; the imperfections of the tools used; the overall novelty of the approach; etc. The end goal is to resolve as many possible issues and make a more compact and efficient grammar model for future work.

After listing all the possible dilemmas which were encountered while building the grammar models, it is worth reflecting on the corpora used for this project. What was the purpose of analyzing such a modest corpus? The ideal end goal would be a universal grammar model which could accommodate for a considerable quantity of corpora. The analysis of grammar models made specifically for a particular text is only a first step, but it can give us valuable insight for further research.

"Tena" and "Duga" are short stories, so they belong to the genre of prose. Prose as a literary genre has a lot of benefits for computational analysis, as opposed to drama or poetry. Computational analysis cannot handle ambiguity, irony, sarcasm, or any kind of figure of speech. Poetry, especially modern and postmodern poetry, usually uses abstract and irregular language forms and structure. The literary period of the extracted books is also a significant factor, because texts from Romanticism and Realism onwards generally share a language variety that is similar to the contemporary one (in the case of the Croatian language). Therefore, one version of the grammar model should be sufficient for works of prose belonging to the aforementioned periods.

In the Croatian academic sphere, the combination of empirical analysis and the humanities is newly emerging. However, it is evident that all the work and progress made in the field of digital humanities is not as present in the study of literature as it is in information sciences and linguistics (even though the name of discipline – digital humanities – alludes to an interdisciplinary relationship between the humanities and information and/or computer science). The traditional (qualitative) approach is strongly present within literary departments at most faculties in Croatia, as well as at foreign universities. The reason behind this are centuries of established and cherished tradition. Advancements in the expansion of methodology used in literary science are hard-won, because common practice almost always equals the right praxis. The development of the most efficient methodology which can benefit both disciplines (literary science and information sciences) needs to be the primary concern so that they can complement each other, without the violation of either's integrity and importance.

Nowadays, the digitalization of books is a common practice, which easily provides materials for computational (or similar) analysis. The only question which remains is that of accessible and usable tools. Most of the people working in the humanities are not experienced enough in programming languages like C, C++, or Python to write their own programs for analysis. This is why it is necessary to provide a designated program with instructions, such as the NooJ program, which was used in this study. With the implementation of these ideas, the integration of computational methods in literary science – in the form of an easily available literary method – can hopefully be achieved.

References

1. Buckland, M., Gey, F.: The relationship between recall and precision. J. Am. Soc. Inf. Sci. **45**(1), 12–19 (1994)
2. Forster, E.M.: Aspects of the Novel, 1st edn. Penguin Books, London (1988)

3. Goutte, C., Gaussier, E.: A probabilistic interpretation of precision, recall and F-score, with implication for evaluation. In: Losada, D.E., Fernández-Luna, J.M. (eds.) ECIR 2005. LNCS, vol. 3408, pp. 345–359. Springer, Heidelberg (2005). https://doi.org/10.1007/978-3-540-31865-1_25
4. Jacobs, A.M.: Sentiment analysis for words and fiction characters from the perspective of computational (neuro-)poetics. Front. Robot. AI **6**, 53 (2019)
5. Makazhanov, A., Barbosa, D., Kondrak, G.: Extracting family relationship networks from novels (2014)
6. Massey, P., Xia, P., Bamman, D., Smith, N.A.: Annotating character relationships in literary texts (2015)
7. Petrač, B.: Lik žene u hrvatskoj književnosti. Bogoslovska smotra **60**(3–4), 348–354 (1990)
8. Silberztein, M.: Formalizing Natural Languages: The NooJ Approach. Cognitive Science Series, Wiley-ISTE, London (2016)
9. Tharwat, A.: Classification assessment methods. New England J. Entrep. **ahead-of-print**(ahead-of-print) (2020)
10. Vučković, K., Tadić, M., Bekavac, B.: Croatian language resources for NooJ. CIT J. Comput. Inf. Technol. **18**, 295–301 (2010)

The Use of Figurative Language in an Italian Dream Description Corpus
Exploiting NooJ for Stylometric Purposes

Raffaele Manna[✉], Antonio Pascucci, Maria Pia di Buono, and Johanna Monti

UniOR NLP Research Group, "L' Orientale" University of Naples, Naples, Italy
{rmanna,apascucci,mpdibuono,jmonti}@unior.it

Abstract. Computational Stylometry develops techniques that allow scholars to find out information about authors of texts by means of an automatic stylistic analysis. Indeed, each author's style is unique, and no two authors are characterized by the same set of stylistic features. Several scholars focus on the analysis of different stylistic features and specific linguistic phenomena. The complex semantic aspects of figurative language remain one of the less investigated stylistic features, due to the lack of precise mapping between linguistic realizations and the concepts underlying the figurative language. Metaphors, similes, metonymies, and figurative language as a whole play an important role in how we mold our day-to-day reality, and they are represented through specific linguistic phenomena suitable to expressing specific conceptualization. Several linguistic devices and markers may highlight the presence of metaphorical expressions and other figures of speech. In this paper, we present research that exploits NooJ software and its linguistic resources to identify metaphors, oxymorons, and similes using a corpus of Italian dream descriptions, built by collecting dream descriptions from several blog users. Our goals, using NooJ's features, are to build a domain dictionary able to represent lexical and semantic characteristics of metaphorical expressions, and to build model grammars able to recognize, extract, and tag these metaphors and figures of speech on the basis of different linguistic devices.

Keywords: Figurative language processing · Computational stylometry · Stylistics

1 Introduction

Human language shapes our experience. It makes our thoughts, our opinions, and our way of feeling experienceable with words towards the human community in which we live [20]. Recently, our community has expanded to a virtual one allowing us to spread and share experiences to a larger community around the world. With social media and personal blogs, the technological support has changed, but not the desire to confess and tell our deepest thoughts, our fantasies, our dreams [25].

The dream can be understood in different ways, bearer of different semantic characteristics and different referents. We can think, for example, about dreams as hope that some event will happen or as the production of images and consequent events during

B. Bekavac et al. (Eds.): NooJ 2020, CCIS 1389, pp. 123–133, 2021.
https://doi.org/10.1007/978-3-030-70629-6_11

the phase of night rest. Specifically, in these nocturnal neural activities [29] and narrative productions (dreams), human beings try to find meaning, an indication of their
daytime actions, or in some cases, simply a narrative exercise in describing the events
that occurred once they returned to an awakened state [13, 37].

In this contribution, dream texts are intended as a private narrative production showing the creativity of human language. In dreams, the dreamer narrates his experience
and inner world through a personal style, often resorting to a set of stylistic features
and rhetorical devices to communicate a given narrative segment [16]. Indeed, dreams
are recognized as having their own narrative structure and organization different from
other textual productions [16]. In particular, in this paper, we describe a first attempt at
formalizing the linguistic realizations of three types of figurative language, exploiting
the functionalities of the NooJ language environment. In addition, we investigate the
possibility of using stylometric features to recognize some realizations of rhetorical figures. With the aim of identifying linguistic realizations and tagging examples of simile,
oxymoron, and simple metaphor in a corpus of Italian dream texts, we add some semantic features to the basic Italian NooJ dictionary by projecting information from external
lexical resources.

This paper is organized as follows: in Sect. 2, we list the related work. In Sect. 3, we
present the NooJ approach, first describing the corpus used for the experiments, and then
the construction of the NooJ domain dictionary by projecting semantic properties from
external lexical resources. In Sect. 4, we present the modeling of NooJ grammars for
simile, oxymoron, and simple metaphor, and we discuss some critical points regarding
the NooJ grammars used. Finally, in Sect. 5, we draw our conclusions and discuss future
research.

2   Related Work

In this section, we focus on related work about corpora, linguistic resources, and content
analysis concerning descriptions of dreams. In addition, we list some studies investigat-
ing the link between the activity of narrating and writing dreams and the production of
figurative language.

One of the earliest studies on the content of dreams was carried out by Hall and Van
de Castle [14], proposing a classification based on empirical categories. The scholars
categorize the events in dreams according to frames associated with the roles involved
in the category. As an example of empirical categories, the most common are "friends,"
"aggressive interactions," "physical activities," "misfortunes," and "successes." Among
these categories, for example, aggressive interactions are categorized in terms of an
aggressor and a victim.

On the basis of the empirical categories used by Hall and Van de Castle [7], Domhoff
and Schneider [8] develop a novel corpus of dreams. Domhoff and Schneider describe
their search engine, their large archive of dream descriptions, and their website containing
more than 17,000 dream reports. Furthermore, in a subsequent article [9], the same
authors underline the similarity of patterns and properties in the social networks between
the characters involved in users' awake life and nocturnal activity; they also analyze the
contents of dreams, finding a persistence and consistency of these contents over the long
term for each user.

Based on the studies reported above, the content of dreams can be considered as a narration of events that happened to the user during the day or during a more-or-less long period of time. In [16], the research question shifts to how distinguishable dream descriptions are from other personal narrative productions. The researchers use several natural language processing techniques to reveal the textual and stylistic characteristics associated with dream texts. The results show how dreams have "uncertain" characteristics, that is, by the use of linguistic markers of "uncertainty" (as opposed to time indications and conversational expressions) and by the preponderance of scene descriptions.

To get closer to the topic presented in this paper, we mention a study [3] that investigates and analyzes the relationships between Conceptual Metaphor Theory (CMT) [20] and the activity of dreaming. Furthermore, through the case of the analysis of dreams produced by study subjects, the researchers are able to underline the connection between metaphors as a verbal tool to consolidate emotional, affective, and cognitive contents, on one hand, and identity and mental contents, on the other hand.

3 The NooJ Approach

NooJ software[1] offers tools for the development, management, and analysis of linguistic resources and corpora to a large community of linguistics, corpus linguistics, and computational linguistics scholars [32]. Through the use, refinement, and enrichment of NooJ dictionaries, scholars are able to address different research hypotheses by adapting and adding lexical-semantic information to the entries of their dictionaries in the different languages supported by the NooJ community [30, 36]. Furthermore, NooJ supports the development of syntactic grammars [31], which enable the use of lexical information resources and dictionaries to generate and recognize linguistic realization patterns in a corpus of texts.

Since our aim is to identify and tag the linguistic realizations of some types of figurative language in the corpus presented below, we use both the NooJ dictionary for Italian and the editor for syntactic grammars by building three of them for our purposes. Therefore, in this section, we present our approach to addressing the problem of identifying the uses of figurative language with the aid, in part, of stylometry.[2] First, we describe the corpus used to conduct the linguistic analyses and some statistics about its composition. Then, we describe the refinement of the Italian NooJ dictionary [35] by the integration of unknown words detected in our corpus. After that, we list the annotation steps performed to tailor the Italian NooJ dictionary with semantic information related to the abstractness and concreteness of words [24] and, further, with information regarding sentiment polarity. To perform and incorporate this type of semantic information into the NooJ dictionary, we use two external linguistic resources developed in other experimental contexts. Finally, we describe in detail the syntactic grammars constructed to identify and tag the linguistic realizations of the three types of rhetorical figures: simple metaphor, simile, and oxymoron.

---

[1] https://www.nooj-association.org/index.html.

[2] Computational Stylometry is the statistical analysis of writing style, and it is used to identify or profile the author of a text.

3.1 The Italian Dream Report Corpus

In order to build our corpus, we downloaded dream descriptions from an Italian blog[3] of a community of dreamers. Specifically, the blog consists of a collection of lucid dreams[4] [2], which dreamers recall using specific techniques [19].

The corpus is balanced both in terms of genre and in terms of the number of texts per author. In fact, the corpus contains dreams from a total of forty-eight authors, divided into twenty-four male authors and twenty-four female authors. Furthermore, during the development of the corpus, we decided to observe a limit of fifteen dream texts for each user in order to include the greatest number of authors, given the quantitative variation of dream narrative production among the authors of the blog.

As a pre-processing step, the dream texts were reduced to lowercase; then, URLs and any HTML tags were removed from the texts. Since they are web texts and subject to typing errors, to include every word available from the texts, a check on word forms was carried out, and in some cases, spelling correction was performed.

To describe the amount of linguistic data available in the corpus, we calculated the total number of tokens, the number of word types, the type/token ratio (TTR), and the average number of tokens for each text dream. We present these statistics in Table 1.

Table 1. Statistics of the Italian dream report corpus.

Number of tokens	*138,302*
Number of Word Types	*23,412*
TTR	*16.9%*
Token Average	14.37 tokens/sentence

3.2 Dream Domain Dictionary

One of the main resources in NooJ for inferring lexical-semantic information is the lexical database, better known as the NooJ dictionary. The NooJ language development environment, through the resources published on the corresponding page of the official website,[5] already comes with a collection of linguistic resources and dictionaries compiled by the international research community.

In this section, we describe the steps we took to enrich the Italian NooJ dictionary with semantic information extracted from two different lexical resources developed in other experimental projects[6] and generated automatically by aligning different resources.[7]

---

[3] https://www.sognilucidi.it/forum/.

[4] *Lucid Dream* is a situation in which dreamers are aware that they are dreaming.

[5] https://www.nooj-association.org/resources.html.

[6] https://megahr.ffzg.unizg.hr/.

[7] https://github.com/clarinsi/megahr-crossling.

We started by using the NooJ dictionary provided in the Italian language module [35]. Then, we identified the lemma entries of the Italian NooJ dictionary corresponding to the words contained in the Italian dream report corpus. In this way, we identified 11,865 words in the Italian NooJ dictionary, which represent the basis for the development of our domain dictionary. Indeed, most of the words refer to nouns, adjectives, and verbs. So, after performing these steps and having identified the words in our corpus, we started enriching the entries of the Italian NooJ dictionary with new types of semantic information regarding Concreteness/Abstractness and Sentiment Polarity information.

Beginning with the addition of semantic information regarding the Concrete/Abstract aspect of words, and acquainted with studies in distributional semantics on these same aspects [11], we used a resource built in an experimental context covering 77 languages. In [22], two models were trained to predict and transfer concreteness and imageability ratings of words via supervised learning, using word embeddings as explanatory variables. From [22], we extracted the generated resource for the Italian language, in which the ratings of concreteness and imageability have been transferred via cross-lingual word embeddings. Then, we integrated this resource into the Italian NooJ dictionary through two steps: first, the words in the domain dictionary were matched with the lemmatized words in the resource in [22]; then, the system-predicted scores (from 1 to 5, with 1 standing for abstract, 5 for concrete) for each word were converted to labels readable by the NooJ dictionary compiler. As an example, we present a word with the scores of the external resource used and the corresponding integrated entry in the NooJ dictionary:

$$macchina \ 4.234466611789336 \tag{1}$$

$$macchina, N + FLX = N41 \tag{2}$$

In the example (1), the word *macchina* 'machine' has a score of 4.23, so it is annotated as a concrete word on the 1–5 scale. Consequently, the corresponding entry in the NooJ dictionary has +**Conc** as a semantic tag indicating the concrete property of the word, after the indication of the Italian inflection class. In cases when a word is determined to be abstract, the semantic tag +**Abst** is added to its NooJ dictionary entry. Intuitively, we consider words with scores higher than 3 as concrete words, while for abstract words the score should be lower than 3.

As a second step, we added sentiment polarity information to each matched entry of the NooJ dictionary using a sentiment lexicon for the Italian language called Sentix.[8] This lexicon is the result of the alignment of other lexical resources: WordNet, MultiWordNet, BabelNet, and SentiWordNet. Each entry of Sentix consists of the Italian lemma, the part of speech corresponding to the lemma, the WordNet synset ID, the score from SentiWordNet, a sentiment polarity score ranging from −1 to 1, and an intensity score ranging from 0 to 1. Among the scores listed, we chose to use the indication about the sentiment polarity for each word. Therefore, we proceeded by matching the lexical entries of Sentix with the lemmas in our NooJ dictionary, adding to each matched entry the sentiment polarity scores already converted into the corresponding labels: +**Pos**, +**Neu**, and +**Neg**. The +**Pos** label is attributed to positive polarity lemmas having a score

---

[8] https://valeriobasile.github.io/twita/sentix.html.

of 1.0, and the +**Neg** label is selected for those with negative polarity (-1.0), while for neutral words (0.0) we use +**Neu**.

4 Modelling Grammars with NooJ

After having enriched the NooJ dictionary with the lexicon-semantic information regarding Concrete/Abstract and sentiment polarity information, we designed three different NooJ grammars, as discussed in the next corresponding sections, to identify three types of basic linguistic structures associated with the realization of similes (Sect. 4.1), oxymorons (Sect. 4.2) and simple metaphors [5] (Sect. 4.3) in the Italian language. Our aim is to investigate the production of these three types of figurative language, introduced and signaled by specific stylometric clues and by certain linguistic markers [12, 15] that can help the processing by machines. In the context of our research, we have of course exploited NooJ grammars to recognize and isolate some linguistic realizations associated with the phenomena taken into consideration in a corpus of dream texts on the basis of stylometric features and linguistic markers. For the purposes of this paper, we manually inspected the corpus to identify the linguistic phenomena considered in order to verify if, once applied, the developed grammars would correctly identify and tag them. Our corpus contains 47 examples of simile introduced by come, (see Sect. 4.1), 126 examples of simple metaphor (see Sect. 4.3), and 30 examples of oxymorons (see Sect. 4.2).

4.1 The Simile Grammar

On the conceptual nature of similitude and its relationship with metaphor, its history in rhetorical theory and the conceptual relations that simile poses between two concepts has been widely discussed in relatively recent fields of research, such as cognitive neuroscience, philosophy, philosophy of the mind, linguistics, and philology [1, 17, 21, 26]. In this paper, by *similitude,* we mean a logical operation or function in which certain properties of a given word are highlighted and related through rhetorical artifice and linguistic markers resulting in a very clear linguistic realization [23]. We are aware that the simile can have several linguistic markers that signal the linguistic realization [34]. For example, in English, we have *like* and *as* as linguistic markers of simile, as in the following examples:

$$\text{Sparkle } \underline{\text{like}} \text{ diamonds - } \textit{Brillante } \underline{\textit{come}} \textit{ un diamante} \tag{3}$$

$$\text{Busy } \underline{\text{as}} \text{ a bee - } \textit{Indaffarato } \underline{\textit{come}} \textit{ un'ape} \tag{4}$$

For the linguistic realization of the simile in Italian, we consider the preposition *come* as a style clue to introduce and point out the two concepts and properties related by the logical function of the simile.,

In Fig. 1, we show the structure of the NooJ grammar regarding simile in Italian. The grammar uses the conjunction *come* as a pivot, which relates some selected grammatical categories. In fact, we select the type of linguistic category (nouns, verbs and adjectives)

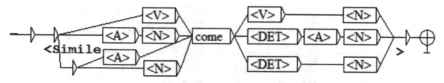

Fig. 1. The syntactic grammar of the simile in Italian. As the image shows, in the grammar we included the linguistic categories useful for the construction of the figure by hinging on the most common linguistic marker, in Italian, for the formation of the simile.

to which a given word could belong in the linguistic realization, not including additional semantic information contained in the NooJ dictionary. Constructing and designing the linguistic structure and realization of the simile, we rely on the stylometric clue coming from the main linguistic marker *come*.

In particular, three are the most productive paths followed by our grammar: P1. **Adjective** come **DETerminer + Noun**; P2. **Adjective + Noun** come **DETerminer + Noun,** and P3. **Noun** come **DETerminer + Noun**.

$$\textit{Leggero come una foglia} \quad \text{'Light as a leaf'} \tag{5}$$

$$\textit{Sua vita come un rene} \quad \text{'His life like a kidney'} \tag{6}$$

$$\textit{Neonato come una gomma da masticare} \quad \text{'Newborn as a chewing gum'} \tag{7}$$

As a result, these three paths are able to automatically identify all 47 examples of similes in our corpus.

4.2 The Oxymoron Grammar

In terms of semantic relations, an oxymoron can be defined as the juxtaposition of two mutually contrasting meanings [10]. Since the oxymoron combines contrasting meanings to make the semantics of the linguistic unit univocal [27], replacing the proposition with a combined linguistic expression, the NooJ grammar concerning the oxymoron is composed of couples of words in which each couple brings with it a degree of lexical-semantic information. The lexical-semantic information necessary to construct the NooJ grammar and highlight the contrasting pairs of words in our corpus is sentiment polarity.

The NooJ oxymoron grammar is based on the sentiment polarities for nouns, adjectives, and verbs in order to capture all the combinations of these linguistic categories (Fig. 2).

The NooJ oxymoron grammar presents a set of sub-graphs. In fact, to each node a sub-graph is assigned in which the lexical-semantic features of the words and the possible word distributions are stored. In particular, with the reference to the distribution of the syntactic categories formalized in the NooJ grammar (Fig. 2.), only one is the most productive, as it automatically identifies 21 examples of oxymorons, at least in our corpus: an adjective with negative polarity (**Adjective-Pos + Neg**) followed by a noun with positive (**Noun + Pos-Neg**) or neutral polarity (stored in the sub-graph). The other

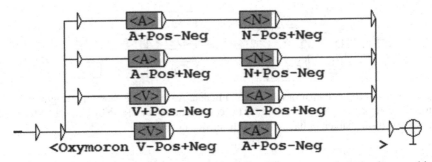

Fig. 2. The syntactic grammar of the oxymoron in Italian. The grammar includes four combinations of linguistic categories useful for the realization of the figure. Within the embedded graphs other possible lexical combinations are stored.

9 examples are recognized by the reverse construction: adjective with positive polarity and noun with negative polarity (stored in the sub-graph).

$$Un\ piacere\ ripugnante\quad \text{'A disgusting pleasure'}\qquad(8)$$

$$Una\ danza\ assurda\quad \text{'An absurd dance'}\qquad(9)$$

Therefore, as a result, above we show two examples of oxymorons identified by the NooJ grammar within our corpus. Both refer to the most productive path.

4.3 The Simple Metaphor Grammar

In various studies [6, 18, 28], metaphor is discussed as a way of transferring conceptual information from a given term to another one, or to put it differently, speaking of one thing in terms of another. Therefore, metaphors lay the foundation for relating different concepts to each other, structuring our way of thinking and our way of narrating [20] events and emotions.

Here, we focus our attention on building a NooJ grammar, structuring the simplest linguistic realization of the metaphor: the Simple Metaphor [33]. This structure is based on projecting the semantic-conceptual characteristics from one word to another related to the verb *essere* 'to be'. Our corpus contains 126 occurrences of simple metaphors. In order to relate words, specifically nouns, and highlight proximity and conceptual similarity in terms of metaphor, in this grammar we use the lexical-semantic information associated with abstract and concrete words [4]. In the way described up to now, we constructed the grammar of the simple metaphor shown in Fig. 3.

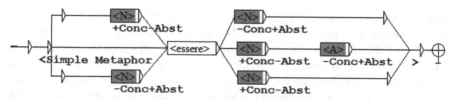

Fig. 3. The syntactic grammar of the simple metaphor in Italian. In the grammar we limit the linguistic categories to nouns and adjectives with the purpose of identifying the simplest distributional structure associated with metaphor. This simple and explicit linguistic realization hinges on the verb "to be" to establish the conceptual transfer of property from one word to another word.

As in the case of the oxymoron grammar, the simple metaphor grammar is implemented with sub-graphs in the main nodes of the grammar. The possible lexical combinations that nouns may have in the Italian grammar together with lexical-semantic information are stored in the sub-graphs.

$$La\ mia\ mente\ era\ una\ spiaggia \quad \text{'My mind was a beach'} \tag{10}$$

$$Era\ un\ topo\ perplesso \quad \text{'He/She was a perplexed mouse'} \tag{11}$$

$$Il\ mio\ anarchismo\ era\ ormai\ un\ rottame\ \text{'My anarchism was a wreck'} \tag{12}$$

As results, we present three simple metaphor examples identified by the NooJ grammar. In particular, each path followed by the machine generates results: 31 examples follow the realization **N + Conc** *essere* **N + Abst**; 19 examples follow the realization *essere* **N + Conc N + Abst;** and finally, the most productive path was **N + Abst** *essere* **N + Conc,** with 76 examples identified in our corpus.

4.4 Results and Analysis

The NooJ grammars developed for these specific phenomena are able to recognize 203 examples. In particular, all the paths of the constructed grammars are able to recognize linguistic phenomena previously controlled by a manual investigation of the corpus. However, some exceptions and errors also occurred during the grammar application phase. In fact, two paths in the simile grammar generates partial matches, namely (**Verb** *come* **DETerminer Noun** and **Adjective** *come* **DETerminer Noun** described in Fig. 1).

Being a preliminary research on the use of figurative language regarding the linguistic phenomena described, we are also aware of the limitations of the NooJ grammars proposed in this paper, since some linguistic markers are overlooked. For example, in the case of similes, some linguistic clues are not identified by the paths of our grammar, such as *così come*. This linguistic marker was present in our corpus but not tagged by the simile grammar.

5 Conclusions and Future Work

In this paper, we approach the study of figurative language to investigate a part of linguistic creativity and deepen the linguistic realization of metaphors, oxymorons and similes through the stylistic vehicle, in the particular context of dream narration. We describe, as a first attempt, how to automatically identify and annotate metaphors, oxymorons, and similes in an Italian corpus of dream descriptions using and exploiting the functionalities of the NooJ language environment. The main results of our research are as follows: the NooJ Italian dictionary composed of 11,865 entries enriched with semantic information and some semantic aspects related to the words of our domain of interest: dreams. In this way, we show how to project semantic information (sentiment polarity, abstractness/concreteness) contained in two lexical resources, developed and implemented in other projects, into the NooJ dictionary. The three different syntactic grammars take into account the stylistic features related to the linguistic realization of metaphors, similes, and oxymorons, at least for the Italian language. Through these grammars we are able to automatically identify and tag the linguistic realizations of the three types of language figures in addition to the support of stylometric features, at least for the case of simile.

Considering the limitations and complexity associated with figurative language processing, we will further explore aspects related to the three figures of language discussed in this paper, using other textual genres from, for example, literary studies, journalism, etc., and we will explore further lexical resources. Then, we will investigate further lexico-semantic features that can describe the behavior and linguistic realization of other types of figurative language in order to also expand the entries of the NooJ dictionary for Italian with additional semantic features capable of refining the identification techniques of figurative language figures.

Acknowledgments. This research was carried out within the framework of two Innovative Industrial PhD projects supported by the PON Ricerca e Innovazione 2014/20 and the POR Campania FSE 2014/2020 funds.

References

1. Aisenman, R.A.: Structure-mapping and the simile-metaphor preference. Metaphor Symbol **14**(1), 45–51 (1999)
2. Barrett, D.: Just how lucid are lucid dreams? Dreaming **2**(4), 221 (1992)
3. Bolognesi, M., Bichisecchi, R.: Metaphors in dreams: where cognitive linguistics meets psychoanalysis. Lang. Psychoanal. **3**(1), 4–22 (2014)
4. Casasanto, D.: When is a linguistic metaphor a conceptual metaphor. New directions in cognitive linguistics **24**, 127–145 (2009)
5. Crisp, P., Heywood, J., Steen, G.: Metaphor identification and analysis, classification and quantification. Lang. Lit. **11**(1), 55–69 (2002)
6. Deignan, A.: Metaphor and Corpus Linguistics, vol. 6. John Benjamins Publishing, Amsterdam (2005)
7. Domhoff, G.W.: Finding Meaning in Dreams: A Quantitative Approach. Springer, Heidelberg (1996). https://doi.org/10.1007/978-1-4899-0298-6
8. Domhoff, G.W., Schneider, A.: Studying dream content using the search engine and dream archive on dreambank. net. American Psychological Society, Chicago (2004)
9. Domhoff, G.W., Schneider, A.: Studying dream content using the archive and search engine on DreamBank. net. Conscious. Cogn. **17**(4), 1238–1247 (2008)
10. Flayih, M.: A linguistic study of oxymoron. J. Kerbala Univ. **3**, 30–40 (2009)

11. Frassinelli, D., Naumann, D., Utt, J., Walde, S.S.: Contextual characteristics of concrete and abstract words. In: 12th International Conference on Computational Semantics - Short papers. IWCS 2017 (2017)
12. Goatly, A.: The Language of Metaphors. Routledge, Abingdon (2011)
13. Hall, C.S.: The Meaning of Dreams. Harper, New York (1953)
14. Hall, C., Van de Castle, R.: The Content Analysis of Dreams. Appleton-Century-Crofts, New York (1966)
15. Hao, Y., Veale, T.: Support structures for linguistic creativity: a computational analysis of creative irony in similes. In: Proceedings of the Annual Meeting of the Cognitive Science Society, vol. 31, no. 31 (2009)
16. Hendrickx, I., et al.: Unraveling reported dreams with text analytics. Digit. Humanit. Q. **11** (2017)
17. Israel, M., Harding, J.R., Tobin, V.: On simile. In: Language, Culture, and Mind, p. 100 (2004)
18. Kittay, E.F.: Metaphor: Its Cognitive Force and Linguistic Structure. Oxford University Press, Oxford (1990)
19. LaBerge, S., Ornstein, S.: Lucid Dreaming. JP Tarcher, Los Angeles (1985)
20. Lakoff, G., Johnson, M.: Conceptual metaphor in everyday language. J. Philos. **77**(8), 453–486 (1980)
21. Lee, M. O.: Horace carm. 1. 23: simile and metaphor. Class. Philol. **60**(3), 185–186 (1965)
22. Ljubesic, N., Fiser, D., Peti-Stantic, A.: Predicting concreteness and imageability of words within and across languages via word embeddings. In: Proceedings of The Third Workshop on Representation Learning for NLP, pp. 217–222. Association for Computational Linguistics, Melbourne, Australia (2018)
23. Margolis, J.: Notes on the logic of simile, metaphor and analogy. Am. Speech **32**(3), 186–189 (1957)
24. Mkrtychian, N., Blagovechtchenski, E., Kurmakaeva, D., Gnedykh, D., Kostromina, S., Shtyrov, Y.Y.: Concrete vs. abstract semantics: from mental representations to functional brain mapping. Front. Hum. Neurosci. **13**, 267 (2019)
25. Page, R.E.: Stories and Social Media: Identities and Interaction. Routledge, Abingdon (2013)
26. Sam, G., Catrinel, H.: On the relation between metaphor and simile: when comparison fails. Mind Lang. **21**(3), 360–378 (2006)
27. Shen, Y.: On the structure and understanding of poetic oxymoron. Poetics Today **8**(1), 105–122 (1987)
28. Shutova, E.: Models of metaphor in NLP. In: Proceedings of the 48th Annual Meeting of the Association for Computational Linguistics, pp. 688–697, July 2010
29. Siclari, F., et al.: The neural correlates of dreaming. Nat. Neurosci. **20**(6), 872 (2017)
30. Silberztein, M.: NooJ's dictionaries. Proc. LTC **5**, 291–295 (2005)
31. Silberztein, M.: Syntactic parsing with NooJ (2009). hal-00498048
32. Silberztein, M.: Formalizing Natural Languages: The NooJ Approach. Wiley, Hoboken (2016)
33. Steen, G.J.: Finding Metaphor in Grammar and Usage. John Benjamins, Amsterdam/Philadelphia (2007)
34. Veale, T.: A computational exploration of creative similes. In: Metaphor in Use: Context, Culture, and Communication, 38, p. 329 (2012)
35. Vietri, S.: The Italian module for NooJ. The Italian module for NooJ, pp. 389–393 (2014)
36. Vuckovic, K., Tadic, M., Bekavac, B.: Croatian language resources for NooJ. J. Comput. Inf. Technol. **18**(4), 295–301 (2010)
37. Winson, J.: The meaning of dreams. Sci. Am. **263**(5), 86–97 (1990)

Paraphrasing Emotions in Portuguese

Cristina Mota[1,3] , Diana Santos[2,3(✉)], and Anabela Barreiro[1,3]

[1] INESC-ID, Lisbon, Portugal
cmota@ist.utl.pt, anabela.barreiro@inesc-id.pt
[2] ILOS-UiO, Oslo, Norway
d.s.m.santos@ilos.uio
[3] Linguateca, Aveiro, Portugal

Abstract. In this paper we describe the cooperation between the NooJ-based paraphrasing system eSPERTo and the broad-coverage emotion annotation of Linguateca's corpora, Emocionário, to develop strategies for analyzing the paraphrasing of emotions. We start by briefly introducing these two projects. Then, we describe how we selected five parallel texts in European and Brazilian Portuguese, automatically annotated them with Emocionário, and carefully revised the annotation, while paying special attention to multiword units and other phrases representing emotion paraphrastic units, and created a set of putative paraphrasing grammars in NooJ. We also comment on the translations and discuss disagreements on the annotation of emotions, as well as on formalization strategies used in the internal structure of the paraphrases.

Keywords: Emotions · Paraphrastic units · Paraphrase generation

1 Motivation

Emotions are described from several perspectives [9, 21] and, according to Wierzbicka [24, p. 276, 302–4], the variability in the forms of expression in language is very high.

This paper is the result of collaboration between two projects: **Emocionário**, which aims at organizing emotions in Portuguese and annotating them in corpora, and **eSPERTo**, the goal of which is to develop a large-scale paraphrasing system in which the NooJ linguistic engine, grammars, and lexicons are used together with other paraphrase acquisition techniques.

The aims of this collaboration were fivefold. From Emocionário's point of view, it would be particularly useful to have an emotion paraphraser to help identify more cases of emotions in corpora, while from eSPERTo's point of view, adding emotion paraphrases would considerably enhance its paraphrasing power. Thirdly, the application of the emotion classification to a hitherto unused application domain would be a good way to evaluate Emocionário's capabilities and shortcomings, and both projects would gain from learning more about real paraphrases of emotion in text. Finally, we examine the interesting question of how to assess the methodology employed to harvest emotion paraphrases from parallel text.

B. Bekavac et al. (Eds.): NooJ 2020, CCIS 1389, pp. 134–145, 2021.
https://doi.org/10.1007/978-3-030-70629-6_12

2 The Two Projects in a Nutshell

Emocionário[1] is a subproject of Linguateca [10, 16]. For more than twenty years, Linguateca has been making annotated corpora publicly available for Portuguese and has for fifteen years dealt with semantic annotation (of some domains) as well [19]. Linguateca's team started looking at emotions in 2014. Before the work described here, 24 emotion groups had been identified, covering more than 4,000 lexemes that can refer to an emotion in Portuguese (see [22] for the list of the groups present in a 20-million-word literary corpus in October 2019).

It is important to highlight the point that this project is concerned with references to – not expressions of – emotion. To clarify, an expression such as *Oh, my God!* expresses emotion but does not refer to it.

One of the goals of Emocionário is to understand what a reference to emotion in Portuguese is, and how to go about it systematically [15]. Also, we aim to gather arguments for the groupings suggested [17].

eSPERTo[2] is a project that aims at the development of a paraphrasing system using enhanced resources [11] developed within the NooJ [23] linguistic engine]. This system provides suggestions of semantically similar expressions for text (re)writing, and has been used, for example, in machine translation [1] and in the conversion of informal to formal language and vice-versa [4]. Within the eSPERTo project, we integrated and improved three lexicon-grammar tables which were already available for Portuguese. These linguistic resources resulted in (i) paraphrases of human intransitive adjectives (HIAs) [14]; (ii) paraphrases of support verb constructions (SVCs) with *fazer* [12]; and (iii) paraphrases of SVCs with *ser de* [13].

3 The Actual Study

In order to study the paraphrasing of emotions in Portuguese, we did the following:

(1) Automatically annotated parallel texts with emotions using Emocionário;
(2) Manually revised the result to guarantee the correctness of the conclusions and to assess the quality of the automatic annotation;
(3) Identified cases (a) in which emotions (in an emotion group) had been maintained but with other words, and (b) in which different emotions had been chosen;
(4) Coded them as paraphrastic resources in NooJ (Fig. 1).

---

[1] https://www.linguateca.pt/Emocionario/.
[2] https://esperto.hlt.inesc-id.pt/esperto/esperto/demo.pl.

eSPERTo - System for Paraphrasing in Editing and Revision of Text

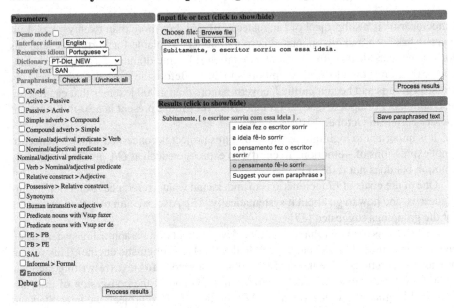

Fig. 1. Paraphrasing emotions in eSPERTo

3.1 The Material

It is not easy to obtain "parallel material" in the same language. In fact, most of the cases we could find came from different translations of an original book from another language. We had five texts, each published in two varieties of Portuguese (the one used in Portugal, or PP, and the one used in Brazil, or PB), already sentence-aligned in previous projects, namely, the COMPARA [7] and PANTERA [20] parallel corpora of Linguateca, and used in a contrastive study of language varieties [2, 5]:

(1) The independent translations of David Lodge's *Therapy* (DL1), translated by Maria do Carmo Figueira into PP and by Lídia Cavalcante-Luther into PB;
(2) The independent translations of Lodge's *Changing Places* (DL3), translated by Helena Cardoso into PP and by Lídia Cavalcante-Luther into PB;
(3) The independent translations of Jostein Gaarder's *Vita Brevis* (JG), translated by Pedro Maia Soares into PB and Maria Luísa Ringstad into PP;
(4) The independent translations of Karl Ove Knausgaard's *Min Kamp 1* (KOK) into PP by João Reis and into PB by Leonardo Pinto Silva;
(5) The adaptation of the book *Os livros que devoraram o meu pai* (AC) by Afonso Cruz, a Portuguese author, into PB.

Table 1. Quantitative overview: *alu* stands for alignment unit, *alu emo* means alignment unit with an emotion, *rev.* For revised

Text	No. of words	No. of alu	alu emo	emo rev.	Alu emo	rev. Emo
AC$_{PP}$	18,946	1,261	225	264	246	301
AC$_{PB}$	18,851		234	272	251	303
DL1$_{PP}$	17,132	652	221	290	230	311
DL1$_{PB}$	17,076		214	285	230	311
DL3$_{PP}$	10,891	417	139	203	147	227
DL3$_{PB}$	11,512		123	179	147	226
JG$_{PP}$	3,802	215	64	91	63	94
JG$_{PB}$	4,001		70	95	66	93
KOK$_{PP}$	7,026	309	57	83	64	101
KOK$_{PB}$	7,062		61	85	65	98
Total$_{PP}$	57,797	**2,854**	706	931	**748**	**1,042**
Total$_{PB}$	58,502		702	916	**760**	**1,031**

3.2   The Revision Process

The revision process showed clearly that agreement on what constitutes an emotion is not straightforward. In fact, the first human revision produced an annotation that added about 30% more emotion occurrences to the automatic one. However, a second revision, done by those responsible for the automatic revision, reduced the emotion surplus significantly. The main recommendations are reported here:

- in all cases where an MWU with the support verb *sentir* 'to feel' was employed, only one emotion (and not two) should be marked, and the same was true for *sentimento de X* or *sensação de X* when X was an emotion, corresponding respectively to *feeling* or *sensation* in English.
- the same should be the case when *sorriso* 'smile', *riso* 'laughter' or *choro* 'cry' were modified by an emotion word.
- words representing feelings used conventionally in other settings, like *sofrer* 'suffer', should not be marked as emotions.
- physical descriptions that are not conventionally used to refer to a feeling should not be marked as emotion. Still, some cases depend on the reader's interpretation, as in *tapou a cara com o jornal* 'she covered her face with the newspaper', which was interpreted as describing shyness.
- luck, bad luck, success, and failure should not be considered emotions (although there can be other opinions on that).

There were still a few cases of meaning differences that had to be decided in a third round. But, in general, if there was disagreement, we did not mark it as emotion. The only exceptions, because they were very frequent in the material, and which were classed in the OTHER emotion bin, were the many verbs that mean *make fun of* in Portuguese. One could consider this action as bringing shame to the patient and satisfaction to the agent, so one could argue that two emotions are actually involved.

The three previously described revisions looked independently at both sides of the corpora. Then we looked at the pairing and were able to find some instances of inconsistency across the collections, as well as cases that had been overlooked. It is the result of this fourth – and final – revision that is presented in this paper.

3.3 First Findings

Table 1 shows that we had at our disposal 2,854 alignment units (each of which corresponds to one sentence in the original text), and that 760 PB and 748 PP alignment units have at least a word referring to an emotion after revision. It also shows that, in the end, human revision added 12% of emotions compared to those found by the automatic system. (To be more precise, this is just the net result. Many cases of "automatic" emotions were removed, and therefore, many more emotions were actually added.)

There are some differences between the texts, with DL3 having the highest percentage of alignment units with at least one emotion (35.3%), and AC the lowest (19.5%), while for the average number of emotions per emotion-encoding alignment unit, the winner is KOK (1.58), with the lowest again being AC (1.23). It was surprising to observe that an original text in Portuguese had fewer emotions than any of the translations, but the sample is too small to generalize.

Another unexpected finding was the considerable number of cases in which the number of emotions referred to were not the same in the two halves, as can be seen in Table 2. Therefore, in 252 cases (out of 2,854, thus 9%) one translator referred to an emotion and the other did not. While some examples can be explained by different discursive strategies, most of them "say the same thing" in a different way, such as in example (1).

(1) PP - *e diz* **esperar** *que a viagem lhes tenha* **agradado** 'and he says he hopes that the trip has pleased them'
PB - *e ele* **desejava** *que tivessem tido uma boa viagem* 'and he wished that they had a good trip'
EN[3] - *and he* **hopes** *they have* **enjoyed** *the flight*

Table 2. Difference in number of emotions per alignment unit that featured at least one emotion

Difference	0	1	2	2	−2	3	−3
Number of alus	578	115	107	7	5	1	1

---

[3] EN is the original text.

After restricting our counts to the 578 cases in which the number of emotions were the same, we detected 483 alignment units (corresponding to 589 emotions) with the same group of emotions (84%). Of those, only 321 alignment units had exactly the same emotion words. After careful scrutiny, since several of the differences are due to trivial changes in person, tense, the presence of clitics, and even diathesis, we found out that, of all the cases expressed by the same emotion group, 195 involved different lexemes. This would suggest that this method is a good source of (at least) inspiration for paraphrasing.

In addition to the above-mentioned surprisingly frequent addition or removal of emotions in the alignment units, several (78) alignment units with different emotion groups were found, as example (2) illustrates.

(2) *PP - só teria confirmado os seus profundos* **receios**
PB - apenas confirmado suas **suspeitas** *mais profundas*
EN - merely confirmed his deepest **misgivings**

It should be noted that *misgivings* is a very difficult term to translate into Portuguese, and that the two translators produced satisfactory, albeit different, results, with *receios* 'fears' in PP and *suspeitas* 'suspicions' in PB.

Example (3) shows how difficult it is to delimit emotion groups: one could argue that *liberdade* 'freedom' is 'release from pressure', and therefore can be equivalent, in a way, to *alívio* 'relief'. However, we did not consider the two as belonging to the same group of emotions.

(3) *PP - Foi igualmente a expressão de um* **sentimento de liberdade** *porque, enfim, podíamos agir livremente num país longe de Mónica.* 'it was also the expression of a **sense of freedom** since we, at last, could act freely ...'
PB - Acho também que pode ter sido uma expressão de **alívio**, *porque final-mente podíamos nos mover com liberdade em uma terra distante de Mônica* 'I think it may have been an expression of **relief**, because we could finally ... '

3.4 Multiword Units

Another striking feature we noted was the need to add (or take into consideration) multiword units (MWUs). In fact, although multiword units are marked and dealt with in Linguateca's corpora (see, e.g., body annotation [8]), they are not extensively used for emotion. But, since MWUs are extremely relevant for paraphrasing, their presence was manually added in the human annotation, as examples (4) and (5) illustrate. Example (4) features the use of *fazer beicinho* 'pout', an MWU that expresses emotions of sadness, disappointment, and/or disagreement.

(4) *PP - Ela* **fez beicinho** *e disse: – É que eu tenho uma ideia fabulosa para uma série muito original, uma espécie de versão inglesa do Twin Peaks.*
PB - Ela **fez um beicinho** *e disse: – O negócio é que tive uma idéia sensacional para uma novela diferente, tipo Twin Peaks inglesa.*
EN - She **pouted** *a little and said, «It's just that I have this fabulous idea for an offbeat soap, a kind of English Twin Peaks.*

Example (5), involving three emotions on each side, is interesting for several reasons. First of all, it shows two cases in which there is an MWU on one side and one word on the other side of the aligned sentence. In Portuguese, the expressions *rogar* [] *pragas* and *dizer* [] *palavrões* are MWUs that express the emotion of anger and can be translated approximately as 'beg for plagues' and 'use curse words', respectively, and mean wishing for bad things to happen to someone. Then, it presents a case where the English formulation is so Germanic that it has no easy translation in Portuguese: *shock into silence*. Faced with this phrase, the two translators chose widely different solutions, which in fact refer to two different emotion groups: *chocar* 'shock' as a bad surprise, and *vociferação* 'cursing' as angry language. Finally, the example also illustrates a case in which one paraphrase only works in PB, since the verb *xingar* is only used in Brazil.

(5) PP - *Arranquei a venda e pus-me aos saltos na sala, a **rogar**antas **praga**se a*
     *dizertantos **palavrões**que acabei por ficar **chocado**e me calei.*
     PB - Arranquei a venda dos olhos e pulei de um lado para o outro ao redor da sala,
     ***xingando** e **blasfemando** coisas tão terríveis que finalmente minha **vociferação** me*
     fez silenciar
     *EN - I tore off the blindfold and hopped round the room **cursing** and **blaspheming***
     *so terribly I finally**shocked** myself into silence.*

All the emotion paraphrases were subsequently aligned with CLUE-Aligner [3], depicted in Fig. 2. This tool, developed in the context of eSPERTo, creates entries that can be included in NooJ dictionaries and/or grammars.

From this alignment task, we were able to obtain a list of 463 emotion paraphrases (out of ca. 1,300 paraphrastic units). After removing repetitions and creative or divergent translations, we selected 191, which are publicly available.[4]

Let us explain here what we considered a (real) emotion paraphrase (or "paraphrastic unit," as we call it, since it is not a full sentence). Basically, this is a different way of saying something that does not involve a crucial difference in the emotion expressed, restricted in this case to having more than one word in one of the sides. So, cases like *medo* ↔ *terror* 'fear', 'terror', which are one-word synonyms, and which were also obtained by our procedure, are not counted here, nor are different morphological features of the same lexeme (such as differences in person or in tense).

3.5 NooJ Resources

The last step was the enrichment of the paraphrastic resources of Port4NooJ, the Portuguese module of NooJ, with the emotion information gathered, and then the application of those resources to feed eSPERTo. Although at the time of writing this article, we have only been able to do a few tests to explore the best way of formalizing this knowledge within NooJ by creating or updating relevant dictionary entries and grammars, some of our ideas can be presented here.

We identified five main groups of pairs of paraphrastic units that, due to their specific properties, need to be formalized in different ways in NooJ:

---

[4] https://www.linguateca.pt/Gramateca/ExemplosParafrasesEmocao.html.

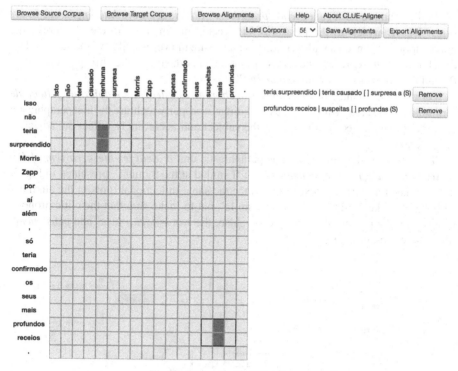

Fig. 2. Using the CLUE-Aligner

None of the Words of the Pair of Paraphrastic Units Varies. The words do not inflect, are not permutable with other words, and to a certain extent they are frozen (with a greater or lesser degree of idiomaticity). In this case, for each paraphrastic unit of the pair, we will create one dictionary entry that will be associated with the corresponding paraphrastic unit of the pair. Then, we need to create a grammar that identifies one paraphrastic unit and rewrites that unit with all other paraphrastic units in pairs that include it. For example, the pair *à beira de um ataque de nervos* ↔ *com os nervos à flor da pele* '(X's) nerves (BE) on edge' will originate the following two dictionary entries:

- à beira de um ataque de nervos, N + EMO:NERVOSO + PARA = com os nervos à flor da pele
- com os nervos à flor da pele, N + EMO:NERVOSO + PARA = à beira de um ataque de nervos

One or More Words of Either Paraphrastic Unit in the Pair Vary. Pairs of paraphrastic units in which at least one word of one of the units can inflect or may be permutable with more than one word will be represented with a grammar (and subgrammars), which may or may not need to represent a wider context to be able to inflect the words of the paraphrastic unit or to permute them.

In the example *entreguei-meaos prazeres* ↔ *direcionei a **minha**atenção aos inter-esses* 'I gave myself to the pleasures / I directed my interests to the pleasures', the grammar does not need a wider context to make sure the verbs will have the same inflectional traits, or to represent the correct pronoun on both sides – the clitic pronoun *me* in PP and the possessive pronoun *minha* in PB.

On the other hand, for the pair *a transbordar de alegria* ↔ *doido de felicidade* 'brimming over / crazy with happiness', in order to properly rephrase the first paraphrastic unit, the grammar needs to represent the subject and accordingly inflect the adjective *doido* 'crazy'.

The grammar that formalizes the paraphrastic unit *a ideia **fez-me**sorrir (emo:feliz)* ↔ *sorri(emo:feliz) com esse pensamento* 'I smiled at the thought', presented in Fig. 3, does not need a wider context to guarantee the same inflectional traits in the auxiliary verb *fazer* 'make' and the verb *sorrir* 'smile', but to make sure that the clitic pronoun agrees with the person of *sorrir*, it does. Also, the words *ideia* 'idea' and *pensamento* 'thought' are permutable.

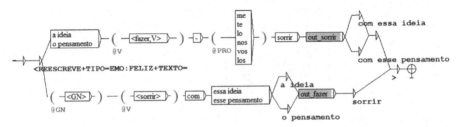

Fig. 3. Grammar to paraphrase the pair of paraphrastic units: *a ideia **fez-me**sorrir (emo:feliz)* ↔ *sorri(emo:feliz) com esse pensamento*

Several paraphrastic units include arguments which invert positions in the paraphrase. For example, the pairs *N0 achar N1 perturbante* ↔ *N1 deixar N0 desconcertado* 'N0 be disturbed with N1' and *N1 agradar minimamente a N0* ↔ *N0 estar razoavelmente satisfeito com N1* 'N0 be ADV pleased with N1' are symmetric.

Likewise, grammars can also be developed for constructions involving nouns related to body parts, fluids, or actions, such as *sorriso* 'smile', *riso* 'laugh', *olhos* 'eyes', *choro* 'cry', *ombros* 'shoulders - shrug', *sobrolho* 'eyebrows - frown', thus capitalizing from previous work on the interaction of body and emotion [16].

If one of the paraphrastic units in the pair involves a construction with a human intransitive adjective or nominal predicates supported by the verb *ser de* 'be of' or *fazer* 'do / make', already included and formalized in the corresponding lexicon-grammars integrated into Port4NooJ dictionaries, we will add the mark + EMO: subcategory to those entries in the dictionaries, which will make the grammar inherit the + EMO feature from the predicate and assign it to its paraphrases.

For example, in the pair *ficou muito envergonhada* ↔ *ficou muito constrangida* 'became very shy', the adjectives *envergonhada* and *constrangida* will add the emotion property + EMO: VERGONHA to the corresponding (simplified) dictionary entries:

- envergonhado, A + FLX = ALTO + AV + state + EN = bashful + DRV = AVDRV01:RAPIDAMENTE + EMO:VERGONHA + IH + Table = SEAHC3 + Nhum + Vcopser = ser [...]
- envergonhado, A + FLX = ALTO + PChappyType + EN = ashamed + DRV = AVDRV01:RAPIDAMENTE + EMO:VERGONHA + IH + Table = SEAHC3 + Nhum + Vcopser = ser[...] + UMNclas + UmModif + AdvQuant + Superlativo + NAdj + em-Vinf [...]
- constrangido, A + FLX = ALTO + IH + Table = EAHP3 + Nhum + Vcopestar = estar + Vcopandar = andar + Vcopficar = ficar + Vcopencontrarse + Vcopsentir-se + Vcopmostrarse + Vcoprevalarse + AdvQuant + Superlativo + NAdj + DRV = A2N1:ANO + DRV = A2V2:DIRIGIR

In this way, the grammar that handles the alternation of the copulative verbs will generate paraphrases where Vcop will be *ser/estar/ficar/andar/permanecer/sentir-se/mostrar-se/revelar-se/tornar-se*. Finally, it will be necessary to develop new grammars not only to represent the pair of paraphrastic units, but also to extend the pair of paraphrastic units to other constructions involving that nominal or adjectival predicate. We should like to explain that, in our previous example, we want to be able to represent *ficou muito envergonhada* ↔ *ficou muito constrangida* as a pair of paraphrastic units, but also to demonstrate that we can alternate the copulative verbs in this pair of paraphrastic units and that, consequently, *estar muito envergonhada* ↔ *estar muito constrangida*, *sentiu-se muito envergonhada* ↔ *sentiu-se muito constrangida*, etc. are also pairs of paraphrastic units.

The Paraphrastic Units Are Variety-Dependent. When at least one of the paraphrastic units of the pair is mostly used in one of the Portuguese varieties, this needs to be marked with the Portuguese variety (PP or PB), thus enriching eSPERTo's paraphrastic resources across Portuguese from Brazil and from Portugal [18].

The Paraphrastic Units Are Approximate Paraphrases. The paraphrastic units are often not absolutely identical semantically [6], and present subtle or less subtle deviations of meaning that eSPERTo users need to be aware of to be able to decide whether to proceed with rewriting, and to choose the most suitable for the context or the most stylistically appealing to the user. For this reason, some paraphrastic pairs, such as *competir pela honra de* ↔ *competir pela oportunidade de* ('compete for the honour of' ↔ 'compete for the opportunity to') and *ter coragem para* ↔ *ter a cara de pau de* ('dare' ↔ 'have the courage to') should be marked with the feature + APROX.

4 Future Work and Conclusions

We intend to use the pilot study presented in this paper to further our research in the near future. One important task is to produce a more systematic analysis and annotation of MWUs and phrases expressing emotion in Emocionário's large corpora. Another is to design and build high coverage paraphrastic grammars in NooJ to deal with the following phenomena:

- **emotion-conveying idiomatic expressions**, which may correspond to a single word with identical meaning, e.g., *ter pena de* '(to) pity, *sentir falta de* '(to) miss', *encolher os ombros* '(to) shrug (one's) shoulders', *fazer beicinho* '(to) pout', *(falar) com o coração nas mãos* '(to) speak with (one's) heart in (one's) hands', *de cabelos em pé* 'hair raising';
- **emotion quantification**, e.g., *gostar muito*, paraphrase of *amar* 'like a lot = love'; *não gostar nada*, paraphrase of *detestar* 'do not like at all = hate', also using **opposite emotions;**
- **combination of different emotions**, e.g., *sorriso triste* 'sad smile'; *amor violento* 'violent love'.

From the point of view of each of the initial projects, namely eSPERTo and Emocionário, the cooperation was very productive. For eSPERTo, a new set of paraphrases expressing emotions was collected and can be of use in language learning applications, for example. For Emocionário, it provided an independent evaluation of its procedures and of several new candidates, especially MWUs expressing emotion.

Acknowledgments. This work was partially supported by Portuguese national funds through FCT, Fundação para a Ciência e a Tecnologia, under project UIDB/50021/2020. We also thank UNINETT Sigma2 – the National Infrastructure for High Performance Computing and Data Storage in Norway – for use of their computational resources, as well as FCCN for hosting Linguateca in their servers. We thank Belinda Maia for having read a previous version and suggested considerable improvements in style and content.

References

1. Barreiro, A.: Make it simple with paraphrases: automated paraphrasing for authoring aids and machine translation. Ph.D. thesis, Universidade do Porto, Porto, Portugal (2009)
2. Barreiro, A., Mota, C.: Paraphrastic variance between European and Brazilian Portuguese. In: Zampieri, M., Nakov, P., Ljubei, N., Tiedemann, J., Malmasi, S., Ali, A. (eds.) Proceedings of the Fifth Workshop on NLP for Similar Languages, Varieties and Dialects (VarDial). COLING 2018, pp. 111–121. Association for Computational Linguistics (2018)
3. Barreiro, A., Raposo, F., Luís, T.: CLUE-aligner: an alignment tool to annotate Pairs of paraphrastic and translation units. In: Proceedings of the 10th Edition of the Language Resources and Evaluation Conference. LREC 2016, pp. 7–13. European Language Resources Association (2016)
4. Barreiro, A., Rebelo-Arnold, I., Baptista, J., Mota, C.: Parafraseamento automático de registo informal em registo formal na Língua portuguesa. Linguamática **10**(2), 53–61 (2018)
5. Barreiro, A., Rebelo-Arnold, I., Batista, F., Garcez, I., Kuhn, T.Z.: One book, two language varieties. In: Quaresma, P., Vieira, R., Aluísio, S., Moniz, H., Batista, F., Gonçalves, T. (eds.) PROPOR 2020. LNCS (LNAI), vol. 12037, pp. 379–389. Springer, Cham (2020). https://doi.org/10.1007/978-3-030-41505-1_36
6. Barzilay, R., McKeown, K.: Extracting paraphrases from a parallel corpus. In: Proceedings of the ACL/EACL (Toulouse, 2001), pp 50–57 (2001)
7. Frankenberg-Garcia, A., Santos, D.: Introducing COMPARA: the Portuguese-English parallel corpus. In: Zanettin, F., Bernardini, S., Stewart, D. (eds.) Corpora in Translator Education, pp. 71–87. JSt Jerome, Manchester (2003)

8. Freitas, C., Santos, D., Carriço, B., Mota, C., Jansen, H.: O léxico do corpo e anotação de sentidos em grandes corpora – o projeto Esqueleto. Revista de Estudos da Linguagem **23**(3), 641–680 (2015)
9. Maia, B., Santos, D.: Language, Emotion, and the emotions: multi-disciplinary and linguistic background. Lang. Linguist. Compass **12**(5) (2018). https://doi.org/10.1111/lnc3.12280
10. Mota, C., Santos, D.: Emotions in natural language: a broad-coverage perspective. Technical report, Linguateca (2015). https://www.linguateca.pt/acesso/EmotionsBC.pdf
11. Mota, C., Carvalho, P., Barreiro, A.: Port4NooJ v3.0: integrated linguistic resources for Portuguese NLP. In: Proceedings of the Tenth International Conference on Language Resources and Evaluation LREC 2016. LREC 2016, pp. 1264–1269 (2016)
12. Mota, C., Chacoto, L., Barreiro, A.: Integrating the lexicon-grammar of predicate nouns with support verb fazer into Port4NooJ. In: Mourchid, M., Silberztein, M. (eds.) Mbarki S, pp. 29–39. Formalizing Natural Languages with NooJ and Its Natural Language Processing Applications, Springer (2017)
13. Mota, C., Baptista, J., Barreiro, A.: The lexicon-grammar of predicate nouns with ser de. In: Port4NooJ: 12th International Conference, NooJ 2018, Palermo, Italy, 20–22 June 2018, Revised Selected Papers, pp. 124–137 (2019)
14. Mota, C., Carvalho, P., Raposo, F., Barreiro, A.: Generating paraphrases of human intransitive adjective constructions with Port4NooJ. In: Okrut, T., Hetsevich, Y., Silberztein, M., Stanislavenka, H. (eds.) NooJ 2015. CCIS, vol. 607, pp. 107–122. Springer, Cham (2016). https://doi.org/10.1007/978-3-319-42471-2_10
15. Ramos, B., Freitas, C.: "Sentimento de quê?" uma lista de sentimentos para a Análise de Sentimentos. In: STIL - Symposium in Information and Human Language Technology, Salvador, BA, 15–18 October, 2019, pp. 38–47 (2019)
16. Ramos, B., Santos, D., Freitas, C.: Looking at body expressions to enrich emotion clusters. In: Finatto, M.J.B., Luz, S., Pollak, S., Vieira, R. (eds.) 2020 Proceedings of the Digital Humanities and Natural Language Processing Workshop at the 14th International Conference on the Computational Processing of Portuguese Language, pp. 57–62 (2020)
17. Ramos, B.C.: Leitura Distante e categorização de sentimentos represen-tados pelo corpo humano na Literatura (2019). https://www.linguateca.pt/ELD/aprELDBarbaraRamos.pdf
18. Rebelo-Arnold, I., Barreiro, A., Quaresma, P., Mota, C.: EP–BP Alinhamentos Parafrásticos PE–PB de Construções de Predicados Verbais com o Pronome Clítico 'lhe.' Linguamática **10**(2), 3–11 (2018)
19. Santos, D.: Corpora at Linguateca: vision and roads taken. In: Berber Sardinha, T., de Lurdes Sao Bento Ferreira, T. (eds.) Working with Portuguese Corpora, Bloomsbury, pp. 219–236 (2014)
20. Santos, D.: PANTERA: a parallel corpus to study translation between Portuguese and Norwegian. BELLS **10**(1), 1–13 (2019)
21. Santos, D., Maia, B.: Language, emotion and emotions: a computational overview. Linguist. Lang. Compass **12**(5) (2018). https://doi.org/10.1111/lnc3.12279
22. Santos, D., Simões, A.: Towards a computational environment for studying literature in Portuguese (2019). https://www.linguateca.pt/Diana/download/PresentationBudapestSantosSimoes.pdf
23. Silberztein, M.: Formalizing Natural Languages: The NooJ Approach. Wiley, Hoboken (2016)
24. Wierzbicka, A.: Emotions Across Languages and Cultures: Diversity and Universals. Cambridge University Press, Cambridge (1999)

Preparing the NooJ German Module
for the Analysis of a Learner Spoken Corpus

Mirela Landsman Vinković[1]([⊠]) and Kristina Kocijan[2] [iD]

[1] Department of German Language and Literature, Faculty of Humanities and Social Sciences,
University of Zagreb, Zagreb, Croatia
mlandsma@ffzg.hr

[2] Department of Information and Communication Sciences, Faculty of Humanities and Social
Sciences, University of Zagreb, Zagreb, Croatia
krkocijan@ffzg.hr

Abstract. This project merges the knowledge of a foreign language teaching specialist and a language processing specialist to detect and classify different types of errors found in the spoken classroom discourse of Croatian learners of German as a foreign language. The role of NooJ in this project is to detect and annotate different types of errors in order to facilitate the analysis of such data. The preliminary corpus consists of 5 different classroom interactions of Croatian master's level students of teaching German as a foreign language that were recorded during their regular classes. The recordings have been faithfully transcribed, keeping the mistakes originally introduced by the student-speakers.

In order to evaluate the student-speakers' linguistic, lexicosemantic, and pragmatic competences, the rated criteria fall into the areas of general linguistics, vocabulary, vocabulary control, grammatical accuracy, coherence, and pragmatic appropriateness. This classification conforms to the recommendations by the Common European Framework of Reference for Languages. The project uses the existing NooJ resources for German that had been enhanced with new dictionary entries, an additional morphological grammar constructed to recognize misspellings, and syntactic grammars introduced to find and annotate errors at the higher levels of syntactic analysis.

Keywords: Student learner corpus · Detecting errors · German language · Dictionary · Morphology · Syntax · NooJ

1 Introduction

The term *classroom language* describes "the type of language used in classroom situations" with its "particular social roles students and teachers have in classrooms and the kinds of activities they usually carry out there" [25: 79].[1] Hence, it consists of general language as well as of specific classroom phraseology and pragmatic features.

---

[1] Richards and Schmidt (2010) equate the term *classroom language* with the term *classroom discourse*.

© Springer Nature Switzerland AG 2021
B. Bekavac et al. (Eds.): NooJ 2020, CCIS 1389, pp. 146–158, 2021.
https://doi.org/10.1007/978-3-030-70629-6_13

Since it is predominantly oral in nature, classroom language is quite often referred to as *classroom talk,* which comprises *teacher talk* and *student talk.* The relation between *teacher* and *student talking time* is the most frequently analyzed part of classroom language. The fact that *teacher talking time* constitutes as much as 75% of a foreign language lesson shows the importance of this type of language input [cf. 3, 5, 14, 18, 32]. And exactly this input, this *teacher talk,* has been found to be problematic in many error analysis studies of classroom English in German schools [cf. 6, 27], which leads us to the conclusion that students who are to become foreign language teachers should be taught classroom language during their studies, in order to use it properly in the foreign language classroom [cf. 2, 35].

But future language teachers are not excluded from making mistakes that may be turned into a rewarding learning tool. In order to prepare an easy-to-use environment that would automatically detect and classify their errors, a thorough analysis of such errors was needed. The aim of the analysis was to produce criteria ranging from general linguistic, vocabulary control, and grammatical accuracy to coherence and pragmatic appropriateness that will help evaluate the student-speaker linguistic, lexicosemantic, and pragmatic competences as is recommended within the CEFR - Common European Framework of Reference for Languages [4].

Thus, errors found in the spoken classroom language of Croatian learners of German as a foreign language, i.e., future teachers of German in Croatian primary and secondary schools, are at the center of this research. NooJ is used to automatically detect and annotate different types of errors in a prepared written corpus, in such a manner as to facilitate the easier analysis of data via a simple error-dashboard. Before this process is thoroughly explained and exemplified in Sect. 5, a short theoretical overview of classroom discourse is given in Sect. 2, followed by the descriptions of the corpus and error classification in Sects. 3 and 4, respectively. The paper concludes with an outline of future work.

2 Theoretical Overview

According to Tsui [33], the study of classroom discourse is mainly focused on the following three aspects: language input, language output, and interaction. On the one hand, there is so-called comprehensible input (for the input hypothesis, cf. [16, 17]) of the teacher with all its linguistic modifications and simplifications cf. [3, 11, 30] which are known in the literature as "foreigner talk" cf. [12] or "caretaker talk" [12], and on the other hand, there is the language output of the student (for the output hypothesis, cf. [29]). The interaction between the two makes up the third component of classroom discourse.

One of the first analyses of language classroom interaction was conducted by Sinclair and Coulthard [28], who documented the most typical pattern of classroom communication controlled by the teacher known as the "IRF model" (initiation – reply – feedback). This and many other classroom interaction analyses and models [cf., for instance, 22] led to Long's interaction hypothesis [19] in second language acquisition, which stresses the importance of (comprehensible) interactive input where learners "negotiate for meaning" [20].

Although the study of foreign language classroom discourse was very intensive in the 1980s, interest in this subject field has always been present and is currently experiencing a revival (the theses on teacher talk by Deters-Philipp and teacher-and-student talk by Dörr in 2018 [cf. 6, 7]; and the conference dedicated to classroom language held in 2018 at the University of Cologne in Germany,[2] to name just a few).

Two names which stand out in the study of classroom discourse in Croatia are those of Yvonne Vrhovac and Sanja Čurković-Kalebić [9, 10, 34]. Some recent research in Croatia which focused on the error analysis of classroom English [24] and classroom German [21, 31] of students and trainee teachers used either observation sheets or diagnostic tests, partially turning a blind eye to the oral nature of classroom language.

Numerous examples show NooJ as a tool of choice for educational applications. Frigiere and Fuentes [13] found NooJ to be very helpful as a language reflection tool for future teachers of French as a foreign language. Bououd and Fafi [1] used it to interactively correct dictations during French classes by looking not only for spelling mistakes, but also incorrect agreement between verb and subject as well as for other disagreements on a sentence level. Rodrigo et al. [26] have successfully used NooJ as a tool for teaching Spanish as a foreign language to Portuguese speakers with a specific interest in discourse connectors. In the following sections, we will show how it can be used in detecting several types of errors in foreign language classroom discourse.

3 On the Corpus

The thesis research titled *The Impact of Classroom Language Teaching in German Language Teacher Education*[3] – which was conducted on master's students of German studies before and after the explicit learning of classroom German and young teachers of German who were not exposed to this input – included audio recorded materials as part of the research, shifting the focus towards spoken production.[4] For the purpose of this research, the audio recordings of 11 Croatian master's students of teaching German as a foreign language were analyzed in order to detect and classify different types of errors found in them, by using the German module for NooJ, "Module German v2.0", developed by Ralph Müller in 2010 and modified in 2014 [23]. Since the German module was introduced to analyze primarily literary texts and was not meant to detect errors, significant changes were necessary to adjust the module to meet the needs of this study.

---

[2] https://sprachfoerderprojekt.phil-fak.uni-koeln.de/veranstaltungen/tagung-sprache-im-unterr icht-der-zukunftsstrategie-lehrerinnenbildung-zus.

[3] The analyzed spoken corpus *ClassLang-Ge-S* is part of the thesis of this article's first author written for her PhD degree within the Doctoral Programme in Foreign Language Education at the Faculty of Humanities and Social Sciences, University of Zagreb, Croatia.

[4] Apart from the audio recorded spoken discourse of Croatian master's students and young teachers of German as a foreign language, the research instruments included a general language proficiency test (according to CERF), a written test on classroom language, and a semi-structured interview. The results of the thesis research should prove the efficiency of the systematic teaching of classroom language.

The spoken corpus [ClassLang-Ge-S[5]] used in this research was recorded and transcribed for the purpose of the afore mentioned thesis. The preliminary text corpus [ClassLang-Ge-T] was manually built by transcribing 5 different classroom interactions of Croatian master's students of teaching German as a foreign language at the Faculty of Humanities and Social Sciences at the University of Zagreb. Each student pair (or in one case a group consisting of 3 students) had one microteaching session that was approximately 6–12 min long. The topics they covered in the classroom were predefined by the school curriculum. The sessions were recorded and faithfully transcribed, keeping the mistakes originally introduced by the student-speaker. This resulted in a text of 4,852 tokens (but also 11,667 annotations).

Except for the student-speaker gender, mother tongue, and years of language learning, no other personal data about the speakers was registered. Each student was assigned a marker (two letters, a number accompanied by the letter f or m, e.g., LP1f and LP6m, where LP stands for German *Lehrperson*, f for a female and m for a male teacher) to disambiguate him/her during the analysis. Although small in number, the microteaching sessions encompass almost the entire generation of students at the beginning of the first year of their master's studies (11 out of 13 students).

Before we could commence with the search for errors, we needed to prepare the audio data and transcribe it to the written text but still keeping all the original mistakes made by the speakers. Several pragmalinguistic elements were used in the transcribed text to specify the following:

- didascalies[6] were put into square brackets, and students' replies into round brackets;
- three dots were put into round brackets if students' replies were considered irrelevant for the further development of the lesson, while three hyphens were used to annotate incomprehensible word or utterances;
- a short pause of up to 3 s was expressed with one vertical line; a longer pause of 3–6 s, with two vertical lines; and a very long pause, with three vertical lines;
- if a vowel in a word is pronounced longer than in its standard version [8], its length was marked by a colon.

Additional steps included the preparation of all the main language resources on the linguistic level. Upon preparing the test corpus [*ClassLang-Ge-T*], we applied the existing German resources [23], that is, the main German dictionary and two additional resources to recognize alternative orthographies and composite nouns in particular.

However, these resources did not prove sufficient for our purposes, so we introduced an additional dictionary that covered the remaining unknown words and a new dictionary with prepositions. The reason behind this new preposition dictionary was to enhance the existing data with the case markers of the nouns that each particular preposition has to

---

[5] This particular spoken corpus will further be referred to as ClassLang-Ge-S and will denote a corpus of Classroom Language (ClassLang) for German as a foreign language (Ge) where the S stands for the speech section of the corpus as distinguished from its textual version, marked with a final T.

[6] The term is used to describe what is going on in the classroom, e.g. *the teacher is writing on the board*; *everybody is laughing*, etc.

match with. This information was used in a disambiguation grammar that helped us to remove some extra annotations from the text. Thus, if we take, for example, the German noun *Paar*, which has the same form in nominative, dative, and accusative singular, the basic lexical analysis will add 3 tags to this noun: one for nominative singular, one for dative singular and one for accusative singular. The presence of the article (*das*) will further help us disambiguate that the noun is not in the dative (the article *dem* would be used in such a case). However, we still want to know which of the two remaining tags is the correct one, that is, whether the noun *Paar* is being used in the nominative or accusative singular. If there is a preposition characteristic of the accusative form found prior to the nominal phrase (e.g., *für*), it will help us make this disambiguation (e.g., in the phrase *für das Paar*), leaving the noun with only one annotation – accusative singular.

All of the words in the German dictionary are written in lowercase letters in order to allow for compound-noun formation. However, this does not agree with the standard practice of capitalizing nouns in German texts. In order to disambiguate between the nouns and other POS annotations for capitalized words, we have used the existing *UppercaseNouns* syntactic grammar [23], which only removes the *noun* annotation, i.e., if the word is written in lowercase, the *noun* marker is deleted. But we also wanted to remove the extra annotations if the word is capitalized, keeping only the *noun* annotations. Thus, we added another syntactic grammar that found such words, considering that they were not found at the beginning of a sentence. These two grammars reduced 505 extra annotations from the text.

Next, we introduced the syntactic grammar that was designed to disambiguate the extra annotations within the noun phrases and prepositional phrases, which removed an additional 1,950 annotations. This grammar took into account the gender, case, and number of a noun and matched it to a preceding adjective, article, and preposition, removing those annotations that did not match.

The removing of erroneous annotations was of extreme importance for this project, since we only wanted to mark the mistakes that the student makes, and not to catch all the possible mistakes enabled by the ambiguous markers. Thus, these additional grammars were necessary prior to the deployment of error-catching algorithms.

4   Challenges in Error Classification

The classification of errors applied in this study depends mainly on the classification according to linguistic levels of language suggested by Karin Kleppin [15]. She differentiates between phonetic/phonological errors (i.e., pronunciation and orthography), morphosyntactic, lexico-semantic, pragmatic, and finally, content errors.

Each and every linguistic level mounted a challenge and aroused a question, such as how to treat wrongly pronounced words as lexical entries; how to annotate the length of vowels, which gives additional meaning to the standard unmarked version; or how to deal with an inflation of modal particles. The fact that the German NooJ model does not recognize articles as a special word class, but puts them into the same category as pronouns, caused another problem with word annotation.

However, the most challenging part of using NooJ as a tool for detecting and classifying errors seemed to be the extension of its domain to the semantic, pragmatic, or even content level. Having in mind the nature of classroom discourse, certain communication strategies were included in the research and are used in error classification, above all the so-called compensation strategies which include describing, non-verbal communication, using the mother tongue or another foreign language, as well as strategies of avoidance, above all the strategy of omission. Whereas the strategy of omission is undoubtedly considered an error, compensation strategies cannot so easily be classified as belonging to this category.

Teacher talk is sometimes explanatory and sometimes encouraging which results in many unfinished sentences or even words. The use of the mother tongue in a foreign language classroom has always been an arguable point and it is sometimes not easy to decide whether its use was justified or not. The same goes for another foreign language, laughter or pauses which can sometimes be seen as a positive device in the hands of a teacher, but sometimes they only mark their perplexity.

5   Building the Grammars

Two types of grammars were built for this project: a morphological grammar and a syntax grammar. The morphological grammar was introduced in order to prepare the needed markers that later on could be used in the syntax grammar for the detection of errors falling into the pronunciation category. Syntax grammars were built around different types of errors that were found in the ClassLang-Ge-T corpus. For this preliminary research, we have introduced six main categories with category specific sub-types:

A. Pronounciation
B. Articles and Pronouns
C. Verbs
D. Sentence Word Order
E. Question Words vs Connectors
F. Didascalies and Additional Notes

Each category has a category specific sub-type described in the following sections. The category represented by letter F (Didascalies and Additional Notes) is provided only for statistical purposes and to get some input about the classroom interaction. Since this topic is not within the scope of this paper, it will not be further discussed here.

5.1   What is that Word?

In this project, it was important to annotate words that either are unrecognizable to the German language, or are mispronounced – regarding the long or short vowel pronunciation that results in a double or single vowel appearance in the word used. For the latter, we have used a single morphological grammar that checks if the word exists in the dictionary in the case where the double consonant is replaced with only one, and vice versa. These words were marked as FW (*false word*) with an additional attribute + VL (*vowel length*) (Fig. 1.) in order to recognize them in our syntactic grammar under the pronunciation category of errors.

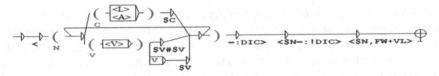

Fig. 1. Morphological grammar for detecting wrong vowel length pronunciation

It is also important to note that this morphological grammar has a lower priority level and is applied to the text after all the other resources have been applied. In this way, only unrecognized words will be subjected to this grammar.

The transcription of the student speech was performed in a way to keep the original errors in pronunciation introduced by the student-speaker. Thus, the words were written down not as they should appear in an error-free text, but rather to mimic the error. These words, as expected, were not recognized by NooJ, since NooJ does not have a dictionary of erroneous words. Still, we wanted to be able to count these errors as well and to annotate them where possible.

Three distinctive sub-types of errors, marked as ClassA errors, were detected in this category. A student mispronouncing a word resulting in a non-German word (sentence 1) was thus marked as an *errUnknown* subtype of ClassA error. This word was recognized by NooJ if it was missing from any of available dictionaries.

(1)   *Also jetzt* **zeiche** *ich äh euch etwas.*

If the student-speaker pronounces the long vowel as a short one (or vice versa), this scenario may result either in an unknown word, or a word with another meaning (sentences 2 and 3). In the latter case, it would be classified as an error subtype *errVowLength*. We have found one such word that was repeated on multiple occasions by two student-speakers.

(2)   *Aber jedes Land hat diese* **Statssymbole***.*
(3)   *Ja, also generelle* **Statssymbole***.*

The last subtype of pronunciation error is that of using a word or words belonging to another language marked as *errDifLang*. In our examples, Croatian was the choice for other-language usage, as expected, since that is the mother tongue of our student-speakers. To detect these occurrences, a Croatian dictionary was made available at the lowest priority level.

5.2   Articles and Pronouns

The second class of errors, marked *ClassB,* deals with false agreement in gender, number, or case within a noun phrase. We have defined three separate subtypes that we were able to find and annotate with the power of NooJ syntactic grammars.

Article-Noun Mismatch. Unlike Croatian, the German nouns may have an article. Both noun and article agree in gender, number, and case. Mistakes fall mostly in the category of gender disagreement – in the form of direct negative transfer of a Croatian noun's gender.

Contrary to the disambiguation grammar, which is aimed at finding the matching gender, number, and case in article + noun phrases, this grammar has a different role: to detect and annotate article-noun phrases that do not match in at least one of the arguments ([1] gender, [2] number, [3] case). Regardless of which argument (or arguments) the mismatching concerns, at least one mismatch needs to be detected to annotate the error. So any of the seven scenarios found in Table 1 is valid for our grammar.

Table 1. Possible mismatch paths for article-noun phrases

	Gender	Number	Case
Path 1	Match	match	**Mismatch**
Path 2	Match	**mismatch**	Match
Path 3	Match	**mismatch**	**mismatch**
Path 4	**mismatch**	match	Match
Path 5	**mismatch**	match	**mismatch**
Path 6	**mismatch**	**mismatch**	Match
Path 7	**mismatch**	**mismatch**	**mismatch**

This table can be replicated as a graph (Fig. 2.), thus allowing us to trace any type of a valid mismatch. Clearly, there is only one path that should not be recognized, namely, the one with all three matches, and it is not included in the graph.

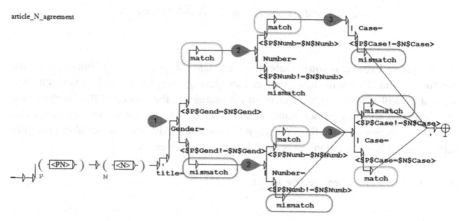

Fig. 2. Local grammar for article-noun disagreement

First, we check for agreement (or the lack of it) in gender; then in number; and finally, in case. This order was arbitrarily chosen, since the final result does not depend on the order of constraints. We have given this type of an error a ClassB marker with sub-type errArticle. The algoritham visualized in Fig. 3. Detected erroneous usage of an article with the noun as in the following sentence:

(4) *Danach haben wir **die** Nationalfeiertag.*

Preposition-NP Matching. Prepositions followed by an NP in German require that the NP be in a specific case, depending on the preposition. If this constraint is not met, we mark it as a ***Type A*** error of the class ***errPreposition***. It usually consists of a preposition followed by an NP (either noun alone, or a noun preceded by an article).

The logic behind this error detection is the same as in the Article-Noun matching, except that the number of checks is reduced down to only a case marker. However, we need to check the case form of both the noun and the article, since either one of these two mismatches is what we want to detect (Fig. 3.), as in the following example, in which the preposition *mit*, which requires an NP in the dative case, is followed by the article *ein* that is not in a dative form:

(5) *Und jetzt machen wir weiter **mit ein Bingo**.*

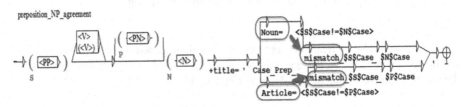

Fig. 3. Local grammar for preposition–NP disagreement

Interrogative Pronoun-Noun Matching. The last subtype in this category is the error **errNoun_InterrPro**, a mismatch between an interrogative pronoun and a noun (sentence 6). Just as with the first type of error in this category, the noun and the interrogative pronoun must agree in gender, number, and case. In the ClassLang-Ge-T corpus, there was one occurrence where this constraint was not met. Although the speaker promptly self-corrected herself, the initial phrase did not match in gender.

(6) *Und könnt ihr sagen, **welche Vogel**.*

5.3 Verbs

This section deals with different errors that involve verbs. These are marked as TypeC errors, and we will start with the class ***errImperative*** as the easiest one to detect.

Imperative. German grammar prescribes that the 2nd person imperative does not take a personal pronoun.

(7)   *Jetzt **bilde du** zwei Sätze.*

Thus, if a student uses it (sentence 7), as it would be customary for the German 3rd person plural imperative, the so-called *Imperative mit Sie*, we want to mark this intra-lingual error using the proper class for the reference. The section of NooJ grammar describing such occurrences is straightforward. It looks for the verb marked as imperative 2nd person <V+IP+2> followed by the 2nd person personal pronoun <PN+Perspron+2> (Fig. 4.).

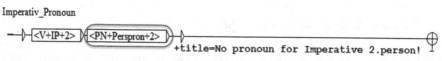

Fig. 4. Local grammar for imperative followed by a pronoun

Modal Verbs. Another common mistake among Croatian students of German is to place the preposition before the final infinitive when the infinitive is found with a modal verb in a sentence. This type of error is marked as ***errModalVerb*** and is also categorized under the rubric of ***Type C*** errors. The algorithm that finds and annotates this error is shown in Fig. 5, and it can match a modal verb (*darf|muss|kann|soll|will|mag*) followed immediately by a preposition and an infinitive, or followed by other part(s) of speech (*noun|numeral|adjective...*) before the final preposition and an infinitive.

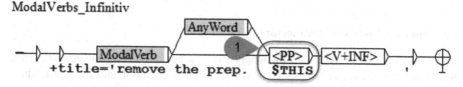

Fig. 5. Local grammar for detecting a preposition before infinitive

Non-reflexive Verbs. There are reflexive verbs in the Croatian language. However, they do not always match the reflexive verbs in German. Thus, it is not uncommon that students make a negative transfer and use German non-reflexive verbs as if they were reflexive, i.e. with a reflexive pronoun. Such examples are detected in sentences with the non-reflexive German verb *spielen,* the Croatian equivalent of which is reflexive:

(8) *Heute werden wir **uns** ein bisschen **spielen**.*

5.4 Sentence-Level Errors

At the sentence level, we have managed to detect three types of errors regarding irregular sentence word order in dependent clauses (***errZSR***), the position of verbs in the vicinity of question words (***errQwordsVerbs***), and verb conjugation (***errUnConjVerb***).

WO in Dependent Clauses. In German, a conjugated verb in a dependent clause must be found at the end of the sentence. Connectors like *dass* and *weil* give us a hint that we are dealing with a dependent clause, and if an algorithm does not find a verb at the end, it will mark the expression as erroneous.

(9) *Und könnt ihr sagen, welcher Vogel **ist** das?*

Question Words. In both declarative sentences and interrogative sentences starting with a question word, the conjugated verb is found in the second position, while the non-conjugated verb comes at the sentence end. The algorithm will mark as erroneous anything that does not conform to these specifications.

(10) *Was soll es **stehen** unter i?*

Un-conjugated Verbs. Just as in the previous sub-category, all declarative sentences expect a non-conjugated verb at its end in order for the algorithm not to mark it as an erroneous sentence.

(11) *Jemand hat **gesagt** also tippen.*

5.5 Question Words vs. Connectors

A special type of error, type E, is the inappropriate usage of the words *wann* and *wenn*. Although both words carry the same meaning ('when'), *wann* is a question word, while *wenn* is a connector of time used in complex dependent clauses. The algorithm detects an error if *wenn* is found in an interrogative sentence like in the following two examples:

(12) *Kennt ihr, wenn es, **wenn** der Nationaltag in Kroatien ist?*
(13) *Und **wenn** ist der Nationalfeiertag Deutschlands?*

6 Conclusion and Future Work

Students tend to repeat the same language-dependent types of mistakes over and over again. These are mostly cases of negative transfer from the mother tongue to the foreign language. Thus, the model of an algorithm we propose may not show the same consistency in the number of mistakes for all language combinations.

The main problems we encountered that influenced the performance of the algorithm can be categorized into the following five domains: pronunciation, article and pronoun mismatch, errors including verbs, sentence word order, and differentiating between question words and connectors. However, this categorization does not cover all errors, which also include self-correction and separable prefixes, or pragmatic and content-level errors. These will be addressed in our future work.

References

1. Bououd, I., Fafi, R.: Using serious games to correct French dictations: proposal for a new Unity3D/NooJ connector. In: Proceedings of the Linguistic Resources for Automatic Natural Language Generation – LiRA@NLO 2017, pp. 49–52 (2017). https://www.aclweb.org/anthology/W17-3808.pdf
2. Butzkamm, W.: Unterrichtssprache Deutsch. Wörter und Wendungen für Lehrer und Schüler. 2., aktualisierte Auflage. Hueber, Ismaning (2007)
3. Chaudron, C.: Second Language Classrooms. Cambridge University Press, Cambridge (1988)
4. Council of Europe: Common European Framework of Reference for Languages: Learning, Teaching, Assessment. Cambridge University Press, Cambridge (2001). https://www.coe.int/en/web/common-european-framework-reference-languages/home
5. Cook, V.: Second Language Learning and Language Teaching, 4th edn. Routledge, New York (2013)
6. Deters-Philipp, A.-C.: Lehrersprache im Englischunterricht an deutschen Grundschulen. Waxmann Verlag GmbH (2018)
7. Dörr, S.: Lehrer- und Schülersprache im Englischunterricht der bayerischen Mittelschulen. Waxmann Verlag GmbH (2018)
8. Duden On-line Dictionary. Bibliographisches Institut GmbH (2020). www.duden.de
9. Čurković-Kalebić, S.: Jezik i društvena situacija – istraživanje govora u nastavi. Školska knjiga, Zagreb (2003)
10. Čurković-Kalebić, S.: Teacher Talk in Foreign Language Teaching. Redak, Split (2008)
11. Ellis, R.: Task Based Language Learning and Teaching. Oxford University Press, Oxford (2003)
12. Ellis, R.: The Study of Second Language Acquisition. Oxford University Press, Oxford (2003)
13. Frigiere, J., Fuentes, S.: Pedagogical use of NooJ dealing with French as a foreign language. In: Monti, J., Silberztein, M., Monteleone, M., di Buono, M.P. (des.) Formalising Natural Languages with NooJ 2014: Selected papers from the NooJ 2014 International Conference, pp. 186–197. Cambridge Scholars Publishing (2015)
14. Helmke, T., Helmke, A., Schrader, F.-W., Wagner, W., Nold, G., Schröder, K.: Die videostudie des englischunterrichts. DESI-Konsortium, Hg.: Unterricht und Kompetenzerwerb in Deutsch und Englisch. Ergebnisse der DESI-Studie. Weinheim u.a: Beltz, pp. 345–363 (2008)
15. Kleppin, K.: Fehler und Fehlerkorrektur. Fernstudieneinheit 19. Langenscheidt, München (1998)
16. Krashen, S.: Principles and Practice in Second Language Acquisition. Internet Edition (1982). https://www.sdkrashen.com/content/books/principles_and_practice.pdf
17. Krashen, S.: The Input Hypothesis: Issues and Implications. Longman, Harlow (1985)
18. Legarreta, D.: Language choice in bilingual classrooms. TESOL Q. 1, 9–16 (1977)
19. Long, M.H.: Input, interaction, and second-language acquisition. Ann. N. Y. Acad. Sci. 379, 259–278 (1981). https://doi.org/10.1111/j.1749-6632.1981.tb42014.x
20. Long, M.H.: The role of linguistic environment in second language acquisition. In: Ritchie, W., Bhatia, T.K. (eds.) Handbook of Second Language Acquisition, pp. 413–468. Academic Press, San Diego (1996)

21. Lütze-Miculinić, M., LandsmanVinković, M.: Wie gut beherrschen Germanistik studenten und Deutschlehrer in Kroatien die Unterrichtssprache Deutsch? Eine Erhebung der aktuellen Sachlage. Zagreber germanistischeBeiträge: Jahrbuch für Literatur- und Sprachwissenschaft **26**(1), 277–302 (2017). https://doi.org/10.17234/ZGB.26.15

22. Moskowitz, G.: The classroom interaction of outstanding foreign language teachers. Foreign Lang. Ann. **9**(2), 135–143 (1976)

23. Müller, R.: NooJ as a concordancer in computer-assisted textual analysis. The case of the German module. In: Koeva, S., Mesfar, S., Silberztein, M. (eds.) Formalising Natural Languages with NooJ 2013: Selected Papers from the NooJ 2013 International Conference, pp. 197–208. Cambridge Scholars Publishing, Newcastle (2014)

24. Patekar, J.: Common challenges in delivering successful foreign language lesson. Strani jezici: časopis za unapređenje nastave stranih jezika **46**(1–2), 101–118 (2017)

25. Richards, J.C., Schmidt, R.: Longman Dictionary of Language Teaching and Applied Linguistics, 4th edn., pp. 79–80. Longman. Pearson Education Limited, Great Britain (2010)

26. Rodrigo, A., Reyes, S., Mota, C., Barreiro, A.: Causal discourse connectors in the teaching of Spanish as a foreign language (SLF) for Portuguese learners using NooJ. In: Fehri, H., Mesfar, S., Silberztein, M. (eds.) NooJ 2019. CCIS, vol. 1153, pp. 161–172. Springer, Cham (2020). https://doi.org/10.1007/978-3-030-38833-1_14

27. Schröder, K.: Problematischer input. Der Classroom Discourse wird im Englischunterricht häufig vernachlässigt. Praxis Englisch **2**, 46–48 (2010)

28. Sinclair, J., Coulthard, M.: Towards an Analysis of Discourse: The English Used by Teachers and Pupils. Oxford University Press, London (1975)

29. Swain, M.: The output hypothesis and beyond: mediating acquisition through collaborative dialogue. In: Lantolf, J. (ed.) Sociocultural Theory and Second Language Learning, pp. 97–114 (2000)

30. Thaler, E.: Englisch unterrichten: Grundlagen, Kompetenzen, Methoden. Cornelsen, Berlin (2012)

31. Truck Biljan, N.: Unterrichtssprache als Fachsprache für künftige kroatische Fremdspracgenlehrkräfte. Scripta Manent, the journal of the Slovene Association of LSP Teachers **12**(2), 168–190 (2018)

32. Tsui, A.B.M.: Analyzing input and interaction in second language classrooms. RELC J. **16**(1), 8–32 (1985). https://doi.org/10.1177/003368828501600102

33. Tsui, A.B.M.: Classroom interaction. In: Carter, R., Nunan, D. (eds.) The Cambridge Guide to Teaching English to Speakers of Other Languages, pp. 120–125. Cambridge University Press, Cambridge (2001). https://doi.org/10.1017/CBO9780511667206.018

34. Vrhovac, Y.: Govorna komunikacija i interakcija na satu stranoga jezika. Naklada Ljevak, Zagreb (2001)

35. Wulf, H.: Communicative teacher talk. Vorschläge zu einer effektiven Unterrichtssprache. Hueber, Ismaning (2001)

Automatic Treatment of Causal, Consecutive, and Counterargumentative Discourse Connectors in Spanish
A Pedagogical Application of NooJ

Andrea Rodrigo[1]([⊠]), Silvia Reyes[1], and María Andrea Fernández Gallino[2]

[1] Facultad de Humanidades y Artes, Universidad Nacional de Rosario, Rosario, Argentina
andreafrodrigo@yahoo.com.ar, sisureyes@gmail.com
[2] Facultad Regional Rosario, Universidad Tecnológica Nacional, Rosario, Argentina
mandrea.fernandezg@gmail.com

Abstract. Our intention, within the framework of the pedagogical application of NooJ to Spanish teaching undertaken by the research team Argentina (Centro de Estudios de Tecnología Educativa y Herramientas Informáticas, UNR), is to continue to apply discourse tags, as we have done in previous work dealing with causal discourse connectors in Spanish. We added counterargumentative and consecutive discourse connectors to our dictionary, taking into consideration a specific population of Spanish learners whose mother tongue is Spanish, but who sometimes face the same difficulties as those experienced by learners of Spanish as a foreign language (SFL). The corpus comprises stories for kids written by students of two tertiary colleges for primary education teachers. The corpus texts show enormous deficits. One of the main deficiencies lies in the lack of resources enabling metalinguistic reflection, which in turn, in our teaching experience, is the motor of linguistic knowledge. Another difficulty tangentially lies in a lack of clarity concerning the correction and self-correction of texts, since there is a belief that writing is the result of inspiration and that it is done in a flash. NooJ can give at least a partial answer to these issues, because dictionaries and grammars contribute to the formalization of linguistic knowledge. Our idea is to show some syntactic grammars created with the NooJ platform in order to analyse corpus phrases and make visible the use of causal, consecutive, or counterargumentative connectors.

Keywords: NLP · Pedagogy · Causal connectors · Consecutive connectors · Counterargumentative connectors · Spanish language · NooJ

1 Introduction

1.1 The Purpose of Our Paper

Within the framework of the pedagogical application of NooJ to Spanish teaching undertaken by the research team Argentina (Centro de Estudios de Tecnología Educativa y

B. Bekavac et al. (Eds.): NooJ 2020, CCIS 1389, pp. 159–169, 2021.
https://doi.org/10.1007/978-3-030-70629-6_14

Herramientas Informáticas, UNR, Argentina), we first focused on working with grammatical categories such as nouns, adjectives, and adverbs. However, some difficulties in learning were noted in native speakers of Spanish, since linguistic terminology is not always fully understood by them and on occasions it may become an obstacle in itself. Sometimes these difficulties arise because linguistic knowledge acquired by them long ago in language classes has been forgotten. Consequently, we turned our attention to discourse tags because the relations of cause, consequence, and counter argumentation are universal, and thus it is easier to have recourse to that knowledge.

In line with these ideas, we made progress towards causal discourse connector tags, thinking of learners whose mother tongue is Portuguese [6]. On this basis, we inserted this type of connector in our NooJ dictionaries. Our intention in this paper has been to continue with the introduction of discourse tags by adding counterargumentative and consecutive connectors to our dictionary. Unlike previous papers, in this opportunity we take as reference a population of students of two tertiary colleges for primary education teachers whose average age ranges from 18 to 25 years. They constitute a heterogeneous group of low socioeconomic status who in fact study with a view to finding a job after graduation. These students generally completed their secondary studies with interruptions, or even started other careers which they had to abandon due to financial or family problems. We chose this specific population because we considered it ideal for us to enrich our research with a new perspective. Although these learners are native speakers whose mother tongue is Spanish, they sometimes face the same difficulties as those experienced by learners of Spanish as a foreign language (SFL). Disjointed sentences and decidedly complex syntax are a constant. For this reason, our contribution using NooJ is relevant for addressing discourse connectors.

1.2   The Research Subject Matter: Discourse Connectors

To conceptualize connectors we relied on Martín Zorraquino and Portolés, who define a connector as *"a discourse marker that semantically and pragmatically relates a discourse member with another discourse member"* [1 p. 4093]. The assembly effect resulting from the presence of discourse connectors precisely explains the fact that we do not have the feeling that we are reading disconnected phrases. Otherwise, if there are no discourse connectors, the understanding of the relationship between phrases is left to the reader, who must deduce the cohesion between them.

In this paper, we particularly address three types of connectors: causal, counterargumentative, and consecutive connectors. It is interesting to highlight what Montolío [2] states about causal connectors, for they imply *"a kind of instruction given to the interlocutor, of the type 'what follows constitutes the cause of what has been said before' (meant, for example, by porque"*, or how she describes consecutive connectors: *"what follows is the conclusion that is deduced from previous information"* [2 p. 29]. Finally, with respect to counterargumentative connectors, Quintero Ramírez [4] defines them as those that *"establish a relationship in which what is represented in the second textual segment contrasts or limits what is expressed in the first segment"* [4 p. 51]. As an additional detail, it is worth noting that one of the most common counterargumentative connectors in Spanish is *pero* 'but', whose main function is to divert *"the argumentative line of the previous sentence"* [2 p. 23].

1.3 The Corpus

The writing of children's tales was undoubtedly a major challenge for our tertiary students because of the difficulties we have already stated above, which are centred on sometimes discontinuous or fragmented secondary education training. However, the aim of the *Workshop on Text Comprehension and Production* was to bring into play essential textual skills for their future work as primary education teachers.[1] In this respect, after doing revision of the basic notions of syntax and semantics in Spanish, students were asked to write a tale. The only requirement was that the story should be addressed to children who are eight to twelve years old. Fortunately, students voluntarily signed a consent form so that their texts could be analysed anonymously by our research team.

Generally speaking, the texts show enormous deficits. One of the main deficiencies is the lack of resources enabling metalinguistic reflection, which in turn, in our teaching experience, is the motor of linguistic knowledge. Another difficulty tangentially lies in a certain lack of clarity concerning the correction and self-correction of texts, as there is a belief that writing is the result of inspiration and that it is done in a flash.

The corpus of short stories comprises 49,462 characters and 8,927 words. As regards orthography, many of these words present spelling difficulties, and it would be possible to create new dictionaries to include those words. As a general rule, the writing lacks accents, punctuation marks, capitalization, and proper spelling. For example, in one instance, the word *nietos* 'grandchildren' was misspelt as *ñetos*. We are aware that the sample we are analysing only constitutes a small part and that we cannot jump to major conclusions until the sample is enlarged. However, we are in a position to offer a useful appreciation of the situation. In our opinion, the reasons for this carelessness in writing have to do, more often than not, with mobile phone textspeak and chats, whose immediacy hinders the correction of errors. What Odrowąż-Coates [3] states about the English language can apply to other languages such as Spanish:

> The popularity of English is reinforced online not only by software makers, but also by Internet users who embrace a new spelling code for English deemed as cool and hip [cut]. It has no formal corpus and is orthographically flexible. It grew in popularity due to netspeak or chat speak, which is an interaction with the use of live text online. The IT-mediated code used by users in electronic mailing, instant messaging, SMS, or chat, known as textese or textism is also based on English. [3 p.85]

---

[1] These students are being trained to become primary education teachers at two tertiary colleges: *Escuela Normal Superior* N°35 "*J. M. Gutiérrez*" and *Escuela Normal Superior* N°36, "*M. Moreno*". We acknowledge Camila Ferramondo for compiling the corpus.

As we all can see, we are witnessing changes in writing which are the result of the irruption of information technology into everyday life. In our view, there is no point in making judgements about these changes because they should be understood in a more profound sense and not only "standardized". This is the fundamental premise that forms the basis of our work.

2 Working with NooJ

2.1 Why NooJ?

The tool developed by Silberztein [7, 8] constitutes a useful instrument to analyse the reference corpus, since it allows us to validate whether our linguistic descriptions are accurate or not. The pedagogical application of NooJ is founded on the metalinguistic reflection that arises during the process.

> When linguistic descriptions have been entered into a computer, a computer can apply them to very large texts in order to extract from these texts examples or counterexamples that validate (or not) these descriptions [cut]. Finally, the description of certain linguistic phenomena makes it possible to construct NLP software applications. [8 p. 6]

NooJ has indeed the advantage of not being a black box, and accordingly, new linguistic information can always be entered into the dictionaries and grammars created by researchers in order to process and systematize students' written texts as regards, for example, accentuation, punctuation, capitalization, and spelling, which are the aspects that attracted our attention in the previous section.

2.2 The Dictionary of Discourse Connectors

With the purpose of formalizing the Spanish expressions containing discourse connectors, new tags were introduced into the Spanish Module Argentina dictionaries [9]. In a previous study, we introduced a new tag into the Properties´ Definition file by incorporating a new category to name discourse connectors, Connector [C]. And within this category, the tag [+caus] was added to name the subclass of causal discourse connectors: [C+caus] [6]. In the present study, we added two new subclasses of discourse connectors [C+consec] and [C+contrarg], which refer to consecutive and counterargumentative discourse connectors, respectively.

Today, our dictionary includes some of the most usual causal, consecutive, and counterargumentative discourse connectors (Fig. 1).

```
# Special Characters: '\' '"' ' ' ',' '+' '-' '#'
#

porque,C+caus
gracias a,C+caus
gracias al,C+caus
ya que,C+caus
a causa de,C+caus
por eso,C+caus
pues,C+caus
puesto que,C+caus
dado que,C+caus
por el hecho de que,C+caus
en virtud de,C+caus
por tanto,C+consec
en consecuencia,C+consec
por consiguiente,C+consec
de ahí,C+consec
así pues,C+consec
pero,C+contrarg
en cambio,C+contrarg
por el contrario,C+contrarg
sin embargo,C+contrarg
no obstante,C+contrarg
con todo,C+contrarg
ahora bien,C+contrarg
```

Fig. 1. Excerpt from the dictionary of connectors in Spanish

The next step was to collect information about the connectors in our corpus. To do so, we first apply **TEXT > Locate** to search for discourse connectors <C> in the texts, and finally, in order to know the frequency of connectors, **CONCORDANCE > Statistical Analyses** is applied. The statistical analysis of connectors is displayed in Fig. 2.

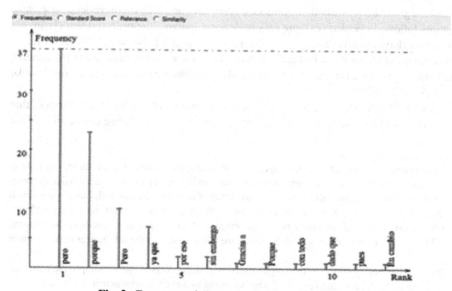

Fig. 2. Frequency of discourse connectors in the corpus

This statistical analysis shows that the counterargumentative discourse connector *pero* 'but' ranks first as the most frequent connector, and in the second place stands the causal discourse connector *porque* 'because'. Thus, our analysis with **TEXT > Locate** finds 36 occurrences of causal discourse connectors and 51 occurrences of counterargumentative discourse connectors, showing a clear tendency. And conversely, it does not find any occurrence of consecutive discourse connectors. Our interpretation of this lack of consecutive discourse connectors is related to the fact that orality prevails over writing, as we have already indicated in the previous section.[2]

The low frequency of consecutive discourse connectors, as for example, *ya que* 'since', is quite striking and points out the need to reinforce the use of this type of discourse connectors among students. However, we will not indicate here how to increase their use, and leave this challenge to future work.

3 Our NooJ Grammars. Analysis of Sentences Containing Discourse Connectors

At this point, we are interested in addressing certain phrases containing discourse connectors with our NooJ syntactic grammars. Thus, we will analyse three sentences of our corpus.

- Sentence 1:
  - pero la verdad (es)[3] que no soy de tener amigos prefiero estar solo.
  - 'but the truth (is) that (I) am not inclined to have friends (I) prefer to be alone.'

This sentence shows significant complexity, since it begins with the extrasentential counterargumentative discourse connector *pero* 'but', and then two asyndetic coordinate clauses follow: *la verdad* (es) *que no soy de tener amigos* 'the truth (is) that (I) am not inclined to have friends', and *prefiero estar solo* '(I) prefer to be alone'. The coordinator has been omitted, but it can be easily deduced from the sentence structure or the context. A syntactic grammar is created with NooJ, which includes embedded graphs for the sake of clarity (Fig. 3).[4]

An additional detail is that the first person pronoun subject has been dropped, that is, there is a PRO_DROP null or implicit subject in the subordinate clause of the first

---

[2] Some occurrences are not, properly speaking, discourse connectors. For example, *con todo el corazón*, "with all the heart", where *todo* is the first modifier of the noun *corazón* inside the noun phrase following the preposition *con*, is an adverbial of manner, whereas in the sentence *no tenía dinero pero con todo pagó el taxi*, "(she/he/it) didn't have money but all the same (she/he/it) paid the taxi," *con todo* certainly is a counterargumentative discourse connector which means "all the same". However, for reasons of space, we will not analyse the differences between these phrases.

[3] The verb has been omitted in the original sentence of the corpus, but we supply the expected third person singular of the verb *ser* 'to be' so as not to make the grammar more complex.

[4] In this particular grammar, we had no difficulty in creating embedded graphs inside embedded graphs up to three levels.

pero la verdad es que no soy de tener amigos prefiero estar solo

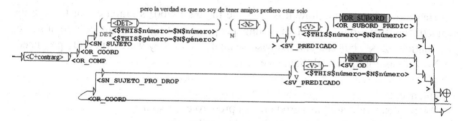

Fig. 3. Main grammar of Sentence 1

coordinate sentence: *que no soy de tener amigos* '(I) am not inclined to have friends' and also in the second coordinate clause *prefiero estar solo* '(I) prefer to be alone'.[5]

The first embedded graph (OR_SUBORD), corresponding to the subordinate clause, which also has an embedded graph inside it, is displayed in Fig. 4. For reasons of space, we do not include here the graph of the verb phrase SV.

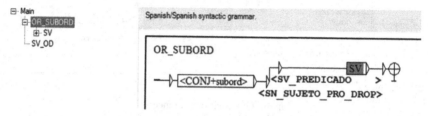

Fig. 4. Graph of OR_SUBORD embedded into the main grammar of Sentence 1

Next, the graph corresponding to the prepositional phrase SP is displayed in Fig. 5 in order to show how it is possible to embed graphs recursively. We do not include here the graph (SV_OD) inside the second coordinate clause, which is the direct object of the main verb *prefiero*, because we have already shown the syntactic richness of the first sentence by displaying the previous figures.

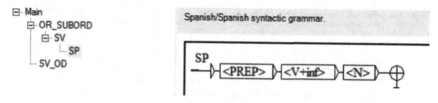

Fig. 5. Graph of SP embedded into the embedded graph SV

---

[5] Here, we again take up the advancements we achieved in previous work [6] in the processing of sentences with an empty element.

These grammars show how it is possible to adapt NooJ's graph editor to describe syntactic constructions typical of young people's writing, without coordinators, or punctuation marks, but that can likewise be analysed as they were originally produced.

Now let us continue with Sentence 2.

- Sentence 2:
  - pues yo si tengo amigas pero también prefiero estar sola.
  - 'well yes I have friends but (I) also prefer to be alone.'

This second sentence begins with the extrasentential causal discourse connector *pues* 'well' and has a predicate with two nucleus verb phrases, *tengo* 'have' and *prefiero* 'prefer', coordinated by the intrasentential counterargumenative discourse connector *pero* 'but'. Its grammar is displayed in Fig. 6.

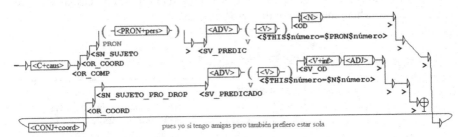

Fig. 6. Grammar of Sentence 2

After applying **Show Debug** in order to check if the grammar works, we perform Generation (Fig. 7) to see the structure of this second sentence.

```
# Dictionary
#
# Language is: sp
#
# Alphabetical order is not required.
#
# Use inflectional & derivational paradigms' description files (.nof), e.g.:
# Special Command: #use paradigms.nof
#
# Special Features: +NW (non-word) +FXC (frozen expression component) +UNAMB (unambiguous lexical entry)
#                   +FLX= (inflectional paradigm) +DRV= (derivational paradigm)
#
# Special Characters: '\' '"' ' ' ',' '+' '-' '#'
#
#
# Dictionary generated automatically
#

<C+caus> <PRON+pers> <ADV> <V> <N> <CONJ+coord> <ADV> <V> <V+inf>

<ADJ>,OR_COMP#<OR_COORD#<SN_SUJETO>#<SV_PREDIC<$THIS$número=$PRON$número><OD>#>#>

<OR_COORD#<SN_SUJETO_PRO_DROP>#<SV_PREDICADO<$THIS$número=$N$número><SV_OD>#>#>#
```

Fig. 7. Performing *Generation* in the grammar of Sentence 2

- Sentence 3:
  - A Pablo le encantaba ir al parque pero había un problema.
  - 'For Paul (it) was enjoyable for him to go to the park but (there) was a problem.'

There is further complexity in this sentence that includes two clauses coordinated by the intrasentential counterargumentative discourse connector *pero* 'but'. The subject of the first coordinate clause is the subordinate clause *ir al parque* 'to go to the park', whereas the second coordinate clause, *había un problema* '(there) was a problem', is impersonal and has no subject at all. The grammar of Sentence 3 is shown in Fig. 8.

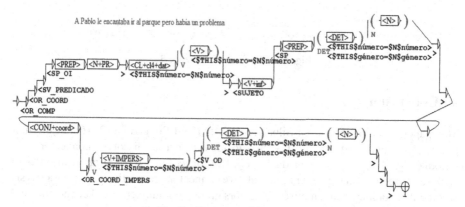

Fig. 8. Grammar of Sentence 3

To check that this grammar suits Sentence 3 we perform *TEXT > Linguistic Analysis* (Fig. 9 and Fig. 10).

*A Pablo le encantaba ir al parque pero*había un problema.

*A Pablo le encantaba ir al parque **pero** había un problema.*

Finally, as our check is successful, we apply *Locate* and then *Outputs*, so that its structure is shown (Fig. 11).

OR									
SV					SUJETO				
SP			le,CL+cl4+3era+sg+dat	encantar,V+pi+ind+1a+sg	ir,V+inf	SP			pero,C+contrarg
a.PREP	Pablo,N+PR			encantar,V+pi+ind+3a+sg		a.PREP	el,DET+artdet+masc+sg	parque,N+masc+sg	pero,CONJ+coord
									pero,N+masc+sg

Fig. 9. First clause of Sentence 3

This last figure displays the complexity of the third sentence by highlighting the possibility of including an impersonal construction in a NooJ grammar.

Fig. 10. Second clause of Sentence 3

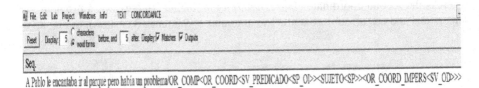

Fig. 11. Structure of Sentence 3

4   Conclusions

This paper is mainly based on Silberztein (2015) and Silberztein (2016). In the first place, as we only had the tag [C+caus] to identify causal discourse connectors, we introduced two new tags in our dictionary, [C+consec] and [C+contrarg], in order to analyse consecutive and counterargumentative connectors, respectively. Corpus analysis showed that counterargumentative connectors greatly outnumber causal connectors and that there is almost a striking absence of consecutive connectors.

In the second place, we analysed certain sentences of the corpus. This analysis gave us an interesting view of the degree of plasticity of NooJ's graph editor, since it allowed us to account for various sentences and clauses: coordinate clauses, subordinate clauses inside coordinate clauses, clauses with null subject, and predicates with more than one nucleus verb phrase. We not only analysed different sentences, but we were also able to apply Generation, among other resources, in order to validate our initial linguistic description. All this work relied on our research project on the pedagogical application of NooJ [5].

Metalinguistic reflection as the generator of learning provides support for our research. In our study, we show how it is possible to process with NooJ the texts produced by tertiary students who will become primary education teachers. We checked how chat or textspeak writing licence (deviating from conventions) stands at the same level of expressions that are close to orality and make syntactic structure extremely rich. The analysis of this corpus leads us to consider our role as teachers in terms of how necessary it is to intervene in the learning process, what aspects may be changed, and what aspects should be maintained and fostered.

References

1. Martín Zorraquino, M.A., Portolés Lázaro, J.: Los marcadores del discurso. In: Bosque, I., Demonte, V. (eds.) Gramática descriptiva de la lengua Española, pp. 4051–4213. Espasa-Calpe, Madrid, España (1999)

2. Montolío, E.: Conectores de la lengua escrita. Ariel Letras. Barcelona, España (2015)
3. Odrowąż-Coates, A.: Socio-Educational Factors and the Soft Power of Language: The Deluge of English in Poland and Portugal. Rowman & Littlefield, Maryland (2019)
4. Ramírez, S.Q.: Identificación de los conectores discursivos de más alta frecuencia en notas periodísticas deportivas. RLA. Revista de lingüística teórica y aplicada, **53**(2), 47–71 (2015). https://scielo.conicyt.cl/pdf/rla/v53n2/art_03.pdf
5. Rodrigo, A., Bonino, R.: Aprendo con NooJ. Editorial Ciudad Gótica, Rosario (2019)
6. Rodrigo, A., Reyes, S., Mota, C., Barreiro, A.: Causal Discourse Connectors in the Teaching of Spanish as a Foreign Language (SFL) for Portuguese Learners Using NooJ. In: Fehri, H., Mesfar, S., Silberztein, M. (eds.) NooJ 2010. CCIS, vol. 1153, pp. 161–172. Springer, Cham (2019). https://doi.org/10.1007/978-3-030-38833-1_14 ISBN 9783030388324
7. Silberztein, M.: La formalization des langues, l´approche de NooJ. ISTE Editions, London (2015)
8. Silberztein, M.: Formalizing Natural Languages: The NooJ Approach. Wiley, London (2016)
9. Spanish Module Argentina. https://www.noojassociation.org/resources.html. Accessed 10 Apr 2020

Natural Language Processing Applications

NooJ for Artificial Intelligence: An Anthropic Approach

Mario Monteleone[✉]

Dipartimento di Scienze Politiche e della Comunicazione, Università degli Studi di Salerno, Fisciano, Italy
mmonteleone@unisa.it

Abstract. Today, Artificial Intelligence (AI) appears as a topic widely referred to for commercial purposes, while from a technical-scientific point of view, it remains of niche interest. Unfortunately, commercial purposes often lead to confusion in defining the functionalities of human-machine interfaces (HMIs), whereas such AI tools should have to efficiently imitate or replace human beings and body parts in specific cognitive tasks. Instead, AI is often defined too vaguely, that is, not from an anthropic point of view, and therefore, it remains quite distant from the human activities it tries to imitate. Today, AI is categorized among the cognitive sciences, i.e., those sciences that call upon computational neuro-biology (particularly neural networks), mathematical logic (as a part of mathematics and philosophy), and computer science.

Keywords: NooJ · NooJ local grammars · NooJ FSA/FSTs · Artificial Intelligence · Natural Language Processing · Lexicon-Grammar · Machine Learning · Question-answering systems · Formal Semantics · Fuzzy Logic · Ontologies

1 Artificial Intelligence: A State of the Art

Today, Artificial Intelligence (AI) appears a topic widely referred to for commercial purposes, while from a technical-scientific point of view, it remains of niche interest. Unfortunately, commercial purposes often lead to confusion in defining the functionalities of human-machine interfaces (HMIs), whereas such AI tools should have to efficiently imitate or replace human beings and body parts in specific cognitive tasks. Instead, AI is often defined too vaguely, that is, not from an anthropic point of view, and therefore, it remains quite distant from the human activities it tries to imitate.

Today, AI is categorized among cognitive sciences, i.e. those sciences that call upon computational neuro-biology (particularly neural networks), mathematical logic (as a part of mathematics and philosophy), and computer science. Similarly, it copes with stochastic-based problem-solving methods with high logical or algorithmic complexity. However, in current AI systems, the functional and applicative analysis of Natural Language (NL) and Natural Language Processing (NLP) is scarcely considered, despite

© Springer Nature Switzerland AG 2021
B. Bekavac et al. (Eds.): NooJ 2020, CCIS 1389, pp. 173–184, 2021.
https://doi.org/10.1007/978-3-030-70629-6_15

language being the most specific and peculiar among human attributes and characteristics. Consequently, AI today seems rather uninterested in the inclusion of studies in General Linguistics (GL), Rule-Based Computational Linguistics (RBCL), Morphosyntactic Formalization (MSF) (such as those produced by Lexicon-Grammar (LG) [1–4] and NooJ [5, 6]), Formal Semantics (FS), NLP and Natural Language Understanding (NLU).

Starting from these premises, the aims of this study will be to outline a brief state of the art of contemporary AI tools (or so defined), focusing specifically on those that require speech recognition and interfacing with Web search engines. In addition, we will try to verify the consistency of the information produced on AI issues by subjects with high communicative and commercial impact, such as Google.

In such cases, our attention will focus on topics related to linguistic automatisms, such as Automatic Translation (AT), Question-Answering (QA) and Problem-Solving (PS). Furthermore, we will try to highlight the current methodological limits of AI, while mentioning some scientific theories and technological innovations appropriate for supporting an anthropic development of AI, such as ontologies, Fuzzy Logic, and quantum computers.

Finally, yet importantly, we will stress how the NLP tools offered by NooJ [5, 6] may be more than useful for the correct and effective structuring of AI machines. To this end, we will build a set of finite-state grammars / transducers specific for Fuzzy-type problem solving, in which having "yes" and "no" as the outer points of the whole interval, or answer orientation, will also include relative[1] intermediate values of negation and affirmation. In addition, by means of specific Sentiment Analysis (SA) settings and procedures, we will use NooJ tools and procedures to rank and tag different sample types of answers.

2   Attempting a Comprehensive Definition of Artificial Intelligence

As deriving directly from the concept of *human intelligence*, the concept of AI is not easy to comprehend or delineate once for all. A rather all-inclusive definition sees AI as a set of theories and techniques used to create machines capable of simulating human intelligence. More precisely, AI aims to study the "tactics" by which specifically built devices can reproduce the most complex processes of the human mind [7].

A slightly minimalist but widely accepted definition sees AI as a set of theories and techniques used to create computer programs, calculation models, and algorithms that enable machines to reproduce *a form of intelligence*. This definition makes AI fall within the same category as Machine Learning (ML), that is, a procedure based on computational models and algorithms used for the purposes of classification, partitioning, regression, and dimensionality reduction [8]. Thanks to this perspective, AI programming differs from conventional programming because it mimics some level of human intelligence, while non-AI programs carry out defined sequences of instructions.

AI research develops along two complementary paths: on the one hand, it tries to bring the functioning of computers closer to the capabilities of human intelligence; on

---

[1] Here the word *relative* is used in its narrowest dialogical sense.

the other hand, it uses computer simulations to make hypotheses about the mechanisms of the human mind [7].

From all these premises, it ensues that AI cannot be considered a self-contained discipline. Rather, it tries to bring together concepts and technologies of different origins, using them in a way that is functional to its purposes.

Nonetheless, and inevitably, an uncertain AI definition leads to difficulties in classifying (and accepting) AI results. Up to today, and even not so recently, there have been examples of pure AI that have caused great expectations. Two such examples are Deep Blue[2] and AlphaGo.[3] However, as we will see in the following pages, today the progress of AI seems to have run aground before a question that is both philosophical and physiological. Through the formal and computational models available today, is it possible to replicate those mechanisms of the human mind that are, among other factors, also the result of a very long and complex evolutionary path?

In this regard, and with a pessimistic tone, Kevin Wang stresses that the most powerful supercomputer in the world, Summit,[4] occupies the space of two whole tennis courts, consumes up to 15 megawatts, and has worked on hard problems such as the simulation of earthquakes in urban environments and the explosion of supernovae. In stark contrast, the brain weighs about three pounds, consumes only about 20 watts, and has worked on (arguably) harder problems like the creation of such supercomputers. Computers today have many limitations: [they] are not energy-efficient compared to the brain. The average computer consumes up to 300 watts of energy. Computers are deterministic machines and thus do not handle uncertainty well. They need tons of data, processors, and power to handle ambiguous, probabilistic situations like autonomous driving or image classification. Computers cannot even learn. Most of the machine learning and artificial intelligence today can be broken down into basic curve-fitting. This is not learning, it is just statistics. But the brain possesses all of these capabilities [9].

Therefore, we may state that the purposes and sometimes the developments of AI have always aroused many concrete expectations, as well as interpretations, fantasies, or concerns, expressed both in science fiction narratives[5] or films and in philosophical essays. However, reality still seems to keep AI away from the tangible performances of living people. Perhaps this is the reason why, in France, the CNIL[6] has defined AI as the great myth of our time.

3   Contemporary Artificial Intelligence Tools and Procedures

Today, there are mainly four different kinds of AI (or presumedly AI) tools and procedures:

(1)   Intelligent Personal Assistants (IPAs);
(2)   Software tools and ML algorithms;

---

[2] See https://en.wikipedia.org/wiki/Deep_Blue_(chess_computer).

[3] See https://en.wikipedia.org/wiki/AlphaGo.

[4] See https://en.wikipedia.org/wiki/Summit_(supercomputer).

[5] As, for example, in Isaac Asimov's Robot series.

[6] *Commission Nationale de l'Informatique et des Libertés.*

(3) Hardware components;
(4) Screening aids for learning disability and recovery of essential body functions.

1. An *IPA*, also called a virtual or digital assistant, even if often commercialized as an IA tool[7] is actually a man-machine interface that achieves tasks with a slightly higher level of automation. Basically, by means of a speech-recognition routine, it decodes natural language voice commands by users to complete tasks such as (so-called) automatic translation, taking dictation, reading text or email messages aloud, looking up phone numbers, scheduling, placing phone calls and appointment reminding. Popular virtual assistants currently are Amazon Alexa, Apple's Siri, Google Assistant, and Microsoft's Cortana.

2. The typology of *IA software tools* [10] and *ML algorithms* [11] is quite vast. Based on Computational Statistics (CS), they can mainly be subdivided into four categories:

- *Supervised Machine Learning Algorithms (SMLAs)*;
- *Unsupervised Machine Learning Algorithms (UMLAs)*;
- *Semi-Supervised Machine Learning Algorithms (SSMLAs)*;
- *Reinforcement Machine Learning Algorithms (RMLAs)*.

SMLAs can analyze new data using what they have been "learning" during previous applications (i.e., labeled examples) to predict future events.

UMLAs apply when the information used to train is neither classified nor labeled[8].

SSMLAs use both labeled and unlabeled data for training, typically employing a small amount of labeled data and a large amount of unlabeled data.

RMLAs interact with their environments by producing actions and discovering errors or rewards (trial and error search and delayed reward).

3. *IA hardware components* are built with the intent to accelerate computing power for specific operations [12, 13], such as image recognition tasks,[9] machine learning, or algorithmic management of complex systems.

---

[7] Actually, IPAs are not IA tools, since they do not present any of the hardware or algorithmic characteristics peculiar to AI tools. In this case, it is worth noting that the commercial strategies adopted for these devices nullify the technical-scientific and functional differences that exist between man-machine interfaces and AI tools. This nullification brings in noteworthy cultural issues. Among other damages, from a cultural and sociological point of view, selling a man-machine interface as if it were or contained an AI tool (such as new generation smartphone cameras) induces in buyers both a false expectation towards the purchased object and a misperception of the concept and functionalities of AI.

[8] Unsupervised learning studies how systems can infer a function to describe a hidden structure from unlabeled data. The system does not figure out the right output; rather, it explores the data and can draw inferences from datasets.

[9] However, as for the new and very powerful AI chips (see https://www.nextbigfuture.com/2020/08/eight-nvidia-a100-next-generation-tensor-chips-for-5-petaflops-at-200000.html),   which can perform image recognition tasks in nanoseconds, it is worth stressing that very often they cannot deal with much more than blocky 3×3 images, which results in an ineffective cost-benefit ratio.

4. *IA screening aids for learning disability and the recovery of essential body functions* deal mainly with brain implants.[10] These implants aim to address blindness with next-generation neuroprosthetics; address vision restoration with cortical visual neuroprostheses; decode and regulate mental functions through digital twins and machine learning; and decode motor skills for restoring communication and muscle control (as, for instance, in Parkinson's Disease) [14, 15].

4 Artificial Intelligence and Robotics

Only a small part of robotics involves AI, which means that most industrial robots are non-intelligent. Besides, a large part of AI programs are almost never used to control robots, and even when this happens, AI algorithms are only a part of the larger robotic system, which also includes sensors, actuators, and non-AI programming.

There exist artificially intelligent robots [16], which are controlled by AI programs, and for which AI algorithms are necessary to allow the robot to perform more complex tasks. However, most artificially intelligent robots only use AI in one particular aspect of their operation. Examples of artificially intelligent robots are warehousing robots (using path-finding algorithms to navigate around a warehouse); drones (using for instance autonomous navigation to return home when battery is running out); and self-driving car (using a combination of AI algorithms to detect and avoid potential hazards on the road).

5 Artificial Intelligence Current Challenges and Problems

In addition to the aforementioned problems concerning ineffective cost-benefit ratios, ethics, and possible personal freedom limitations, AI current challenges seem to derive also from an excessively random approach to unpredictability, especially as regards the simulation of human behavior and choices. In this sense, the massive use of statistic ML procedures and tools does not seem to help. Besides, the fact that AI does not seem likely to rely on rule-based NLP tends to complicate noticeably the scenario.

Incidentally, AI based on (also neural) ML seems to work better with those small-world networks[11] in which all the possible links, tasks, and interactions between elements are predictable because they are governed by specific rules, as is the case with the game of chess or quizzes with non-argumentative answers. On the contrary, when facing more unpredictable complex network systems, as for instance two or more ontologically interconnected domains, AI/ML analyses and procedures seem not to be completely effective.[12]

---

[10] Still, these are very controversial procedures, involving ethical questions as well as problems related to the limitation of personal freedoms, since those who undergo a brain implant subsequently have no control over its functions.

[11] See https://en.wikipedia.org/wiki/Small-world_network.

[12] As for this issue, witty and funny explanations can be found in the cartoons on ML and AI published by kdnuggets.com (https://www.kdnuggets.com/2018/06/cartoon-fifa-world-cup-football-machine-learning.html).

However, today there are contemporary research and tools capable of bringing AI closer to a more correct management of unpredictability. For instance, Fuzzy Logic (FL), which is a versatile logic where the truth-values of variables, instead of being true or false, are reals between 0 and 1. FL tries to go beyond the fixity of binary calculation, and extends classic Boolean logic with partial truth-values. Therefore, taking into account various numerical factors to arrive at a decision that we wish to accept, a formalized FL could help making AI/ML analyses less "rigid" and AI/ML procedures more dependent on the interaction intermediate stages occurring between stimulus and response.

This possible interfacing between FL and AI could be even more feasible if achieved by means of quantum computing and quantum computers/processors. *Quantum computing*[13] [17] uses quantum-mechanical phenomena, such as superposition and entanglement, to perform computation. *Quantum computers/processors* are substantially supposed to be able to solve certain computational problems faster than classical computers, such as for instance integer factorization (which underlies Rivest–Shamir–Adleman encryption). Today, one of the most advanced quantum computers is Baidu,[14] which has released a quantum machine learning toolkit on GitHub, "enabling developers to build and train quantum neural network models, and includes quantum computing applications."

Unfortunately, with regard to AI and quantum computing, a competition is currently underway to achieve, and therefore to advertise, only apparently revolutionary results, and above all to demonstrate one's technological superiority over competitors. This is clearly unrelated to the possible advantages that quantum computing can bring to all research areas, and it seems to be nothing more than a market strategy. In this sense, Google has recently been publishing various news items which, in the eyes of many experts, appeared questionable if not fairly bizarre. Such news includes the launch of BERT,[15] or an AI procedure supposed to decode "broken Greek texts better than humans."[16] Finally, Google has also claimed to have reached quantum supremacy.[17] Due to this, it is therefore providentially helpful that elsewhere, in more scientifically

---

[13] The study of quantum computing is a subfield of quantum information science. There are several models of quantum computing: the quantum circuit model, the quantum Turing machine, the adiabatic quantum computer, and the one-way quantum computer, as well as various quantum cellular automata. Quantum circuits (the most widely used) are based on the quantum bit, or "qubit", which can be in a 1 or 0 quantum state, or in a superposition of the 1 and 0 states. When qubits are measured, the result is always either a 0 or a 1; the probabilities of these two outcomes depend on the quantum state that the qubits were in immediately prior to measurement. Computation is performed by manipulating qubits with quantum logic gates, which are somewhat analogous to classical logic gates.

[14] See https://www-zdnet-com.cdn.ampproject.org/c/s/www.zdnet.com/google-amp/article/baidu-releases-quantum-machine-learning-toolkit-on-github/?fbclid=IwAR2j7jp5YPgkdFQ-uw2MtjTRNKdu-0ek4tEgD538FHIfFLku6tbDOvO01YQ.

[15] See "BERT - Understanding searches better than ever before" at https://www.blog.google/products/search/search-language-understanding-bert/.

[16] See https://www.ancient-origins.net/news-history-archaeology/greek-texts-0012762.

[17] See https://www.ft.com/content/b9bb4e54-dbc1-11e9-8f9b-77216ebe1f17.

based research fields, the true state of the art on quantum computing is honestly high-lighted, that is, a near quantum computing future is actually unlikely, due to random hardware errors.[18]

6 Rule-Based Natural-Language Processing and Artificial Intelligence

As stated previously, rule-based NLP does not seem to be crucial for/within AI programs and research. We therefore believe this context to be the most appropriate for some questions, such as the following:

(1) What scientific and methodological relationship exists between AI and NLP?
(2) What AI projects and/or functionalities do make use of structural and trans-formational linguistics studies, or rules-based computational linguistics rou-tines/environments?
(3) In the design and actualization of current statistically based AI procedures, what weight has human supervision?

A concrete answer to all these questions seems to come from Judith Spitz,[19] who confirms that, when it comes to Natural Language, NLP/AI systems have yet to live up to their promise in customer service in large part, because the challenge has been defined as either full automation or failure to automate. As starting from the outside, trying to 'deflect' as much traffic/call volume as they can and punting to live serve reps when they fail. The result of this has been hundreds of millions of dollars spent on lowering the cost of customer contact – lots of 'claimed success' in terms of deflection rates – and no change in the cost of customer contact or improved customer service. How could this be? The very essence of 'conversations' cannot be replicated by a chat bot with a programmable set of rules: If the customer says this – the bot says that and so on. That is not how any but the most simplistic of conversations go. *Conversations are inherently probabilistic* – they involve turn taking which includes disambiguation, successive approximation, backing up and starting over, summarization, clarification and so on.

For Spitz, the future of AI will be built on AI native platforms enabling a powerful collaboration between people and machines. Therefore, this perspective seems to open the possibility of interfacing rule-based NLP (closer to the dynamics of human-being linguistic production) with AI as a whole.

---

[18] See https://theconversation.com/a-quantum-computing-future-is-unlikely-due-to-random-har dware-errors-126503?fbclid=IwAR2YbQNuXOkiAkjX01_Dx4qt4AUUh9GkshVyvDwonhK 7YFLtravE7xUJpmE.

[19] See https://www.asapp.com/blog/collaboration-in-the-digital-age-the-value-proposition-at-the-intersection-of-people-and-machines/.

7   NooJ Local Grammars for a Fuzzy-Logic Question-Answering System

Together with PS, QA is most likely the system by which, in a not yet decipherable future, we imagine ourselves talking to an AI machine as if we were talking to a human being, expecting to receive answers very similar to those that a human would give, that is, unpredictable and logically covering vast ranges of topics. This AI scenario, often proposed by science fiction books and films, postulates that the machine simulates a total understanding of human language, meant as transformation of sound waves not only into executive commands, but also and above all into semantically meaningful requests leading to coherent and semantically complex answers.[20]

This is undoubtedly a very futuristic scenario, which however does not seem feasible without a profound NL morphosyntactic formalization, therefore without an equally detailed FL and well-structured Knowledge Management Systems (KMSs). This NL coding-decoding procedure requires a fine-grained morphosyntactic formalization, based on a universal method such as LG [1–4], capable of relating the syntactic forms of sentences and utterances to their semantic contents. Besides, only a highly performing and dynamic NLP environment such as NooJ [5, 6] can offer the specific tools and routines necessary to achieve a coherent "fusion" between FL and AI.

Therefore, starting from these premises, we have developed a sample and rough FL question-answering system (Fig. 1), equipped with a light SA parser to use for reply weighting and calibration. In our system, each node of each NooJ local grammar may connect to one or more specific and interconnected (domain and/or goal) ontologies providing detailed choices in terms of subdomains and facets. This type of system does not currently need any quantum calculations, although it could certainly benefit from them. This indirectly demonstrates that an IA procedure, embedded in a well-structured rule-based NLP environment, can use classical computing architecture.

To complete our example, the following Fig. 2 shows the different debugging of a NooJ local grammar which, to a specific given question, can respond positively, doubtfully, or negatively, using seven different sentiment "intensities," ranging from "absolutely yes" (*SÌ+*) to "absolutely no" (*NO+*) and passing through three different types of "perhaps" (*FORSE-, FORSE, FORSE+*).

Due to the limit of pages to observe here, we created this NooJ Finite-State Transducer (FST) combining seven other different grammars, each of which performs its own specific debugging of a given single answer. To facilitate the reading and understanding of this grammar, we have numbered the searched expressions, together with their corresponding results in the (reconstructed) debugging window.

As we can see, the NooJ debug window correctly tags the answer:

(1)   *ne sono fermamente convinto* (I am firmly convinced of this) with *SÌ+* (YES+);
(2)   *ben inteso* (this is clear) with *SI*;
(3)   *sono molto pessimista* (I am very pessimistic) with *NO+*;
(4)   *per niente* (not at all) with *NO*;

---

[20] For example, a question Alexa or Siri would not be able to answer today is, "What are the religious and philosophical differences between Judaism, Catholicism, and Islam?".

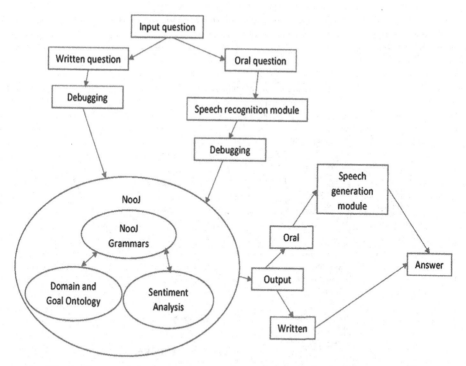

Fig. 1. Structure of a NooJ-Based Fuzzy-Logic Question-Answering System[21]

(5) *non del tutto* (not completely) with ***FORSE*** (PERHAPS)
(6) *probabilmente sì* (probably yes) with ***FORSE+***;
(7) *probabilmente no* (probably no) with ***FORSE-***.

Therefore, from a computational point of view, this grammar transforms binary calculus into responses that include intermediate states between zero (NO+) and one (YES+), as required by Fuzzy Logic.

We are aware of the fact that this is only a demonstrative grammar, which however can aim to the production of more complex answers[22], an aspect attainable straightforwardly with NooJ and LG. Indeed, the effectiveness of the answers provided depends mainly

---

[21] We are aware of the fact that the speech recognition module of this scheme is the most complex element to create. Due to page limits, also in this case we will not analyze further this topic, even if it might seem to be strictly necessary and useful.

[22] In particular, we are fully aware of the fact that it is very difficult to precisely compute the various shades of meaning that separate, for example, an answer likely to be tagged with "SÌ" from one to be tagged with "FORSE-" or even "FORSE +". This appears even more evident in cases where, as we are doing here, the exemplary grammar presented is both morphosyntactically and semantically decontextualized. However, in this regard, we believe it is important to underline that often these subtle differences in intensity are difficult to "interpret" even for human beings, while in our case it is more important to focus on the effectiveness of the result obtained automatically, i.e., the answer intensity degrees obtained in the application of a NooJ FST.

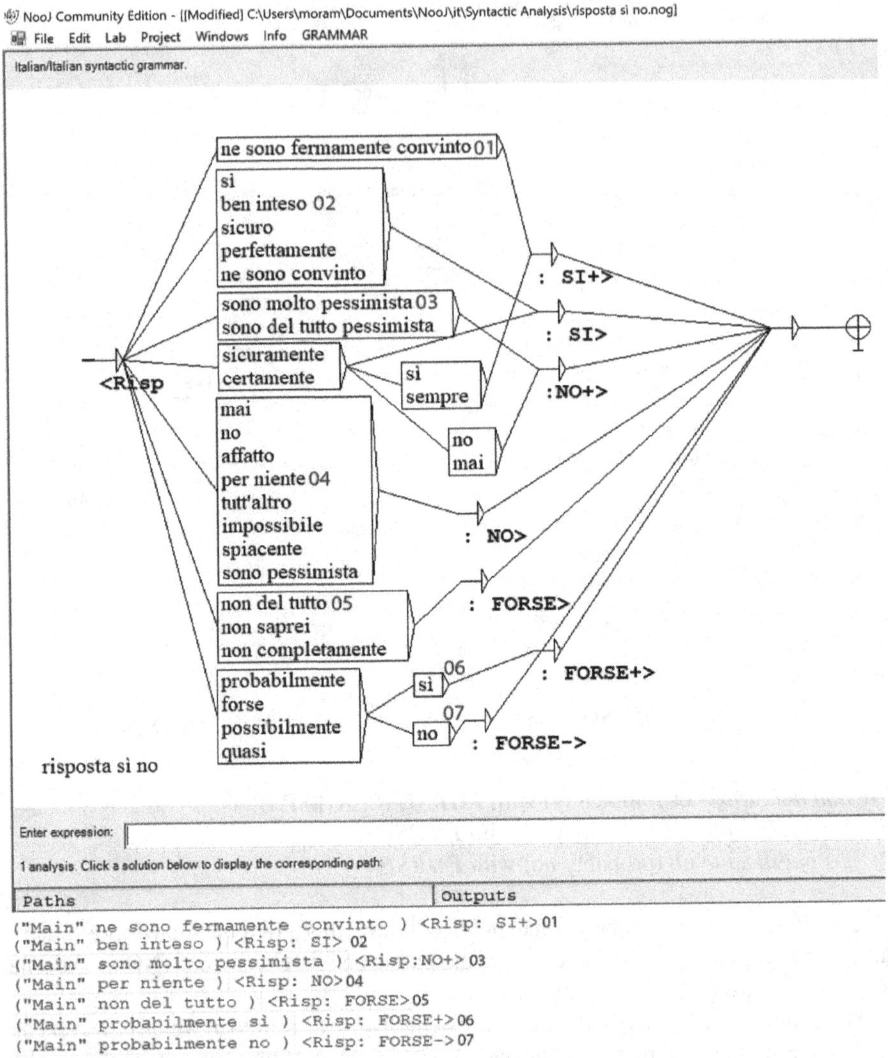

Fig. 2. NooJ Local Grammar for the Fuzzy-Logic Question-Answering System

on the ontological complexity of the KMS embedded inside the system: embedding the KMS also in an AI machine would allow linking phraseologically complex questions and answers (such as human ones) to more detailed sentiment analysis labels, thus allowing the machine itself to better "simulate" both question interpretation and human dialogues.

8 Conclusion

The structuring and revision of the NooJ local grammar shown in Fig. 2 required a very limited time in relation to the results produced, thus establishing a quite valuable cost-benefit ratio.

As already indicated elsewhere [18], we can also see that, in structuring a Fuzzy-Logic Question-Answering grammar, the most crucial syntactic and sentiment analysis task to accomplish is the creation and formalization of a fine-grained Italian negation grammar, to which in this case we also added an uncertainty grammar. Formalizing Italian negations/uncertainties may represent a complex but not impossible task, which, by the way, could also lead us to adding other positive/negative sentiment "intensities," if we were to discover that seven of them are not sufficient to correctly cope with a rule-based AI dialoguing system.

Furthermore, to simulate a systematic reasoning for such a system, one could build NooJ local grammars semantically contiguous to each other, then appropriately recalling and cascading them when necessary.

Another possibility would be to create a network of tagged local grammars, based on the ontologies to exploit and consult, applying all grammars in a single passage, therefore allowing the machine itself to "choose" them based on the topic or topics dealt with by the questions.

Regarding an AI machine, perfecting a similar procedure would therefore allow the effective simulation of human reasoning, using rule-based NLP as shown by NooJ and LG, therefore establishing a so-called "anthropic approach to Artificial Intelligence."

References

1. Gross, M.: Méthodes en syntaxe: régime des constructions complétives. Hermann, Paris (1975)
2. Gross, M.: Les bases empiriques de la notion de prédicat sémantique, Paris, Langages, 63 (1981)
3. Gross, M.: Grammaire transformationnelle du français: Tome 1, Syntaxe du verbe, Paris, Larousse, (1968)
4. Gross, M.: Grammaire transformationnelle du français : Tome 2, Syntaxe du nom, Paris, Cantilène, (1996)
5. Silberztein, M.: The NooJ Manual (2003). https://www.nooj-association.org.
6. Silberztein, M.: Formalizing Natural Languages: The NooJ Approach. Wiley, London (2016)
7. Enciclopedia Treccani On-line page. https://www.treccani.it/enciclopedia/intelligenza-artifi ciale/. (translation by the author)
8. Plasseraud page. https://www.plass.com/en/articles/Patentability_simulation_methods_IA
9. The Startup page. https://medium.com/swlh/neuromorphic-computing-spiking-neural-net works-d8c5755b78e3. Accessed 11 Jan 2021
10. Edureka page. https://www.edureka.co/blog/top-12-artificial-intelligence-tools/. Accessed 11 Jan 2021
11. ExpertAI page. https://expertsystem.com/machine-learning-definition/. Accessed 11 Jan 2021
12. NextBigFuture page. https://www.nextbigfuture.com/2020/08/eight-nvidia-a100-next-gen eration-tensor-chips-for-5-petaflops-at-200000.html. Accessed 11 Jan 2021

13. MIT Technology Review page. https://www-technologyreview-com.cdn.ampproject.org/c/s/www.technologyreview.com/2020/03/04/916701/ai-chip-low-power-image-recognition-nanoseconds/amp/?fbclid=IwAR0Sim6tamwj9gNgYBePogvR-dHsbzfHzjC7UGpRdEFW_uwMChcj934R_wg. Accessed 11 Jan 2021

14. Innovation Origins page. https://innovationorigins.com/artificial-intelligence-for-the-recovery-of-essential-body-functions/?fbclid=IwAR0PgEPv-s1-oe0DtBQfsQ0wH_qIEPZ3z9PSanlhOks9USbMclgRY8wuRwY. Accessed 11 Jan 2021

15. My Great Learning page. https://www.mygreatlearning.com/blog/artificial-intelligence-to-aid-screening-for-learning-disability-and-recovery-of-essential-body-functions/. Accessed 11 Jan 2021

16. Analytic Insight page. https://www.analyticsinsight.net/eleos-robotics-revolutionizing-agriculture-with-artificially-intelligent-robots/. Accessed 11 Jan 2021

17. Wikipedia page. https://en.wikipedia.org/wiki/Quantum_computing. Accessed 11 Jan 2021

18. Monteleone, M.: NooJ grammars and ethical algorithms: tackling on-line hate speech. In: Mauro Mirto, I., Monteleone, M., Silberztein, M. (eds.) NooJ 2018. CCIS, vol. 987, pp. 180–191. Springer, Cham (2019). https://doi.org/10.1007/978-3-030-10868-7_16

Answering Arabic Complex Questions

Sondes Dardour[✉], Héla Fehri, and Kais Haddar

MIRACL Laboratory, University of Sfax, Sfax, Tunisia
dardour.sondes@yahoo.com, hela.fehri@yahoo.fr,
kais.haddar@yahoo.fr

Abstract. Factoid questions and definitional questions are commonly used in recent works in Question Answering (QA). These questions can be answered by a Named Entity (NE) or a short sentence. However, a more challenging and less common question to deal with is the complex question, or why-question. This issue motivated us to develop a new question-answer system for answering Arabic complex questions in the medical domain. Our system uses Natural Language Processing (NLP) and Information Retrieval (IR) techniques. Using the NooJ platform, we construct dictionaries and transducers to analyze complex questions and to extract causal sentences which represent the answers of why-questions. Experimentations of our Arabic medical question answering system show interesting results.

Keywords: Question answering · Complex question · Natural Language Processing · Arabic language

1 Introduction

Nowadays, due to the continuous exponential growth of information produced in the medical domain, and due to the important impact of such information upon research and upon real world applications, there is a particularly great and growing demand for Question Answering systems that can effectively and efficiently aid users in their medical information search [1].

QA system takes a question posted in natural language instead of a set of keywords, analyzes and understands the meaning of the question, and then provides the exact answer from a set of knowledge resources [2]. The QA system consists of three main processing modules, namely, question processing, passages retrieval processing, and answer processing.

To our knowledge, proposed Arabic medical QA systems are so limited either in terms of their performance as well as in terms of the types of questions they are designed to answer. Moreover, the most attention in Arabic has been paid to answering factoid and definitional questions, in which the answer is a single word or a short phrase [3]. However, why-questions are less common because they are more complex and harder to answer.

The aim of this paper is to propose a new approach to handling Arabic complex questions (why-questions) in the medical field. Our proposal is based on four components: a study of the corpora, question analysis, documents/passages retrieval, and

© Springer Nature Switzerland AG 2021
B. Bekavac et al. (Eds.): NooJ 2020, CCIS 1389, pp. 185–195, 2021.
https://doi.org/10.1007/978-3-030-70629-6_16

answer extraction. We use dictionaries and transducers to answer any complex medical question in the Arabic language using NooJ platform. The experimentations of our Arabic medical QA system show interesting results.

The remainder of this paper is structured as follows. Section 2 presents related works. Arabic-specific difficulties are presented in Sect. 3. Section 4 describes our proposed method. Section 5 deals with the experimentation carried out to evaluate the efficiency of our question-answering system. Finally, Sect. 6 draws the main contributions and proposes further perspectives.

2 Related Works

The problem of answering questions formulated in natural language has been studied in the field of Information Retrieval (IR) since the mid-1990s [4]. However, unlike IR, a QA system returns a simple and precise answer to a natural language question instead of a large number of documents [5, 6]. As we mentioned, a QA system is composed of three modules: question analysis, passage or document retrieval, and answer extraction. Different QA systems may use different implementations for each module [7, 8].

Until now, very little effort has been directed toward the development of a QA system that answers Arabic complex questions for the medical domain, in comparison with other languages such as French and English. This is mainly attributed to the particularities of the medical domain and the Arabic language (see Sect. 3). This situation is further aggravated by the lack of linguistic resources and Natural Language Processing (NLP) tools available for Arabic [9, 10].

Most of the research in the area of question answering has focused on answering definitional and factoid questions. The system DefArabicQA is proposed by [6] for definition questions. DefArabicQA identifies the answer using manual lexical patterns of sequences of letters, words, and punctuation symbols, as well as heuristic rules deduced from a set of correct and incorrect definitions.

AQuASys [11] is an Arabic QA system which is composed of three modules: a question analysis module, a sentence filtering module, and an answer extraction module. AQuASys segments a question into an interrogative noun, the question's verb, and keywords. Experiments have been showing that, for test data of 80 questions, AQuASys obtained as recall of 97.5, 66.25% as precision, and 78.89% as F-measure.

The system of [12] describes QARAB, which is based on a set of rules for each question type with the exception of why- and how-questions. QARAB utilizes well-known techniques from IR to extract the relevant documents by processing the question as a query. Then, the system applies a keyword-matching strategy.

The Arabic QA System proposed in [13] handles factoid and definition questions using linguistics resources building with the NooJ platform, as described in [14]. Experiments have shown satisfactory results.

The Japanese QA system NAZEQA handles why-questions. This system uses sentiment analysis and semantic word classes. This method improves the QA system on a large-scale web corpus, as described in [15]. In another study [16], the authors explored the utility of intrasentential and intersentential causal relations to rank the candidate answers to a why-question. This increased their precision by 4.4% over the work of [15].

LEMAZA is an Arabic QA system for why-questions [3]. This system uses Rhetorical Structure Theory (RST) to answer why-questions in Arabic. If several candidate answers correspond to different rhetorical relations, then LEMAZA returns the answer whose RST relation has the highest priority.

We can confirm from this study that most QA systems designed for Arabic can handle definitional and factoid questions. However, few studies have addressed the problem of answering complex questions, which makes the development of a new Arabic QA system crucial.

3 Arabic-Specific Difficulties

Arabic-specific difficulties consist in the language's richness, which needs special processing, which makes regular NLP systems designed for other languages unable to process it. One of the Arabic-specific difficulties is the lack of diacritics (i.e., kasra, fatha, damma), which leads to more ambiguous situations than in any other language. This issue can be explained through the question "لماذا يولد الرضيع مشوهاً؟" (Why is a baby born with a deformity?).

The lack of diacritics in the verb يولد 'to be born' presents at least two possibilities for the question's processing:

- يُولَد (yuladu), which means that the question is "Why is a baby born with a deformity?", so يولد in this question means born.
- يُولِد (yuwal ~ idu), which means that the question is "Why is a baby generate with a deformity?", so يولد in this question gives the wrong meaning 'generate'.

Arabic language morphology is challenging when compared to other languages. This is because Arabic is a highly agglutinative and derivational language in which a word token can replace a whole sentence in other languages. For example, for the sentence فبارتفاعها 'and with its rise', which includes the stem ارتفاع 'rise', the proclitic ف 'and', the prefix ب 'with', and the pronoun ها 'its'. Therefore, extracting keywords from an Arabic question will be more complex than any other language. Furthermore, in a question like لماذا منحا الطبيبان جائزة نوبل في الطب؟ 'Why did two scientists win the Nobel Prize in medicine?, the user looks for the cause of the win of the two scientists (NOT one). In English, the system catches this user requirement through the word *two*. In Arabic QA, this keyword is embedded in the word الطبيبان *Alt ~ abiybaAni* 'two scientists' thanks to the suffix ان *(Ani)*. Actually, the question above is just an example; the morphology of an Arabic word may contain multiple information (basic POS, number, gender, etc.) which are important for each module of Arabic QA.

Unlike English and most Latin-based languages, Arabic does not have capital letters, which makes Named Entity Recognition (NER) harder [17].

4 Proposed Method

The challenges discussed in the previous section make clear the need for a new method to deal with Arabic medical QA. In addition, most of the previous studies are based on factoid questions (i.e., where, when, how much/many, who, and what). In our proposal, we focus on complex questions (why-questions). Figure 1 shows the proposed QA system based on four modules: a study of the corpora, question analysis, document/passage retrieval, and answer extraction. In the following, we detail each module.

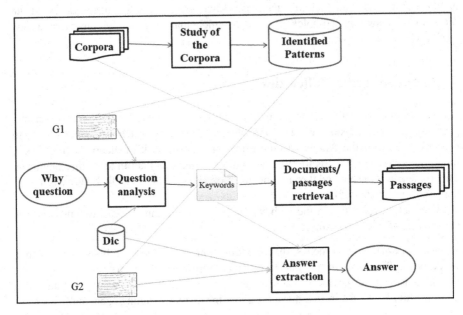

Fig. 1. Overall architecture of the proposed QA system

4.1   Study of the Corpora

The need to have an Arabic corpus is a necessity for processing Arabic QA systems. Indeed, the questions are gathered from several sources, namely, discussion forums, frequently asked questions (FAQ), and some questions translated from the Text REtrieval Conference (TREC). Currently, we gathered 145 why-questions, and for each question, we collected texts from the internet. The questions were then subjected to an analysis step.

4.2   Question Analysis

The question analysis module allows the processing of complex questions to extract some useful keywords representing the user's need. This module uses transducers and dictionaries to analyze complex questions. In Arabic, complex questions starting with لماذا (limaA *aA) and ماسبب (maA sababu) are both defined in the patterns of the question analysis module. In the following, we cite an example of a question asking in two forms.

لماذا ينخفض ضغط الدم ؟ (1)

'Why does blood pressure drop?'
P(1): **[N: Disease] [V]** لماذا

ما سبب انخفاض ضغط الدم ؟ (2)

'What is the cause of low blood pressure?'
P(2): **[N: Disease] [N]** ما سبب

P(1) was constructed from question (1), specifying that the word following لماذا (*limaA*aA*) describes a verb (V) which is followed by a disease noun (N). When we pose the same question using ماسبب (*maA sababu*), question (2), the structure of the question will change, as shown in P(2). Indeed, the word following ماسبب (*maA sababu*), انخفاض 'low', is the noun of the verb ينخفض 'to drop'. This noun is followed by ضغط الدم 'blood pressure', which is a disease noun. Therefore, there are two main patterns for complex questions, the first is لماذا (*limaA*aA*) followed by a verbal phrase and the second is ماسبب (*maA sababu*) followed by a noun phrase (See Fig. 2).

Fig. 2. Main graph

The transducer of Fig. 2 describes the different paths allowing the processing of complex questions. For instance, the path that can process the question ماذا يقود شلل الأطفال إلى الوفاة لماذا 'Why does poliovirus lead to death?' is the sub-graph "VP" because the question begins with لماذا (*limaA*aA*). Figure 3 shows the sub-graph "VP".

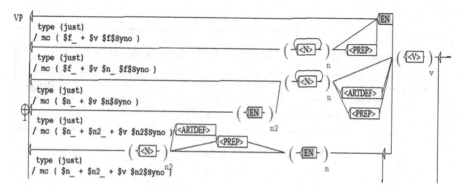

Fig. 3. Segment of the sub-graph "VP"

The transducer in Fig. 3 analyzes the rest of the question. It can recognize verbs and Named Entities represented in sub-graph "EN" (see Fig. 4). The outputs of this transducer are the following:

- keywords of the questions and their synonyms (if they exist)
- expected type of answer.

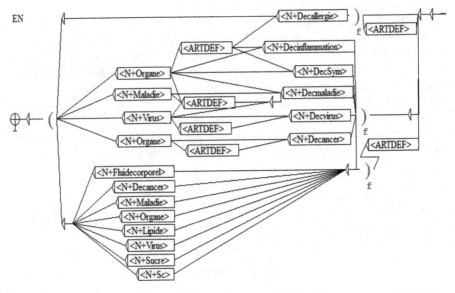

Fig. 4. The sub-graph "EN"

Figure 4 shows that the transducer allows recognizing Named Entities such as diseases, Organ, Virus.

Continuing with the same example, the analysis result of the question لماذا يقود شلل الاطفال إلى الوفاة 'Why does poliovirus lead to death?' is illustrated in Fig. 5.

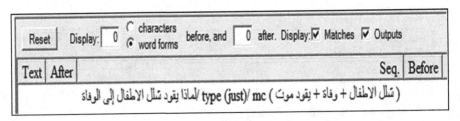

Fig. 5. The result of a question analysis

The keywords extracted from the question لماذا يقود شلل الاطفال إلى الوفاة 'Why does poliovirus lead to death?', as shown in Fig. 5, are شلل الاطفال 'poliovirus', يقود 'lead', وفاة 'death', and the synonym of وفاة 'death', which is موت.

4.3   Document/Passage Retrieval

This module uses keywords extracted by the earlier module, question analysis, to retrieve a ranked list of candidate passages. In our proposal, we take advantage of Lucene Apache for developing such a PR module for complex questions in the Arabic language. There are several reasons for this decision. First, due to specific difficulties of Arabic, as we mentioned in Sect. 3, it is very relevant to have the ability to customize Lucene by adding lexical analyzers for multiple languages including Arabic. In addition, our QA system is entirely implemented on the Java platform, and Lucene is an open source library written in Java, as well.

Table 1. List of candidate passages

Score	Passages
7.6	... يتسبب في الإصابة بالشلل وقد يؤدي أحيانًا إلى الوفاة بسبب إصابة العضلات المسؤولة عن التنفس بالشلل وقد يقتل هذا الفيروس الكثير ممن أصيبوا به قبل ظهور اللقاح...
7.0	... يجرى تشخيص شلل الضفيرة العضدية في حجرة نوم الاطفال عند الولادة. على أطباء العناية الاولية تعيين وإحالة المريض فريق معالجة الضفيرة العضدية المؤلف من اختصاصيين من حقول العلوم والتطبيق الطبي ...
6.5	... في بعض الحالات قد يؤدي إلى الموت ويكون عادة نتيجة قصور عمل الرئتين. ...

Table 1 shows an example of a ranked list of candidate passages according to the keywords: شلل الاطفال 'poliovirus', يقود 'lead', وفاة 'death', and موت 'death'.

4.4   Answer Extraction

Once candidate passages are retrieved, they are further transferred to the answer extraction module to return the relevant answer.

To answer Arabic complex questions, we identified four causal relation types, which are justification, interpretation, explanation, and result as shown in Fig. 6. In addition, we defined patterns for each type. Table 2 shows some examples.

Table 2. Examples of patterns

	Pattern
Justification	[Cause] بسبب [Effect]
Interpretation	[Effect] معنى ذلك [Cause]
Explanation	[Effect] اما [Cause]
Result	[Effect] نتيجة [Cause]

The extracted patterns are transformed into transducers as shown in Fig. 7.

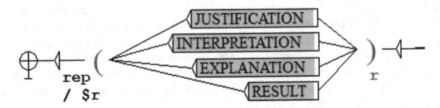

Fig. 6. Main graph of Answer extraction

The transducer in Fig. 6 describes the causal relation. The inputs of this transducer are the retrieved candidate passages. Then, this transducer will extract the causal relation that answers the user's question. For example, the sub-graph "Justification" as shown in Fig. 7 extracts the following answer for the question 'Why does poliovirus lead to death?': لماذا يقود شلل الاطفال إلى الوفاة

- Answer:... وقد يؤدي أحيانًا إلى الوفاة بسبب إصابة العضلات المسؤولة عن التنفس بالشلل...

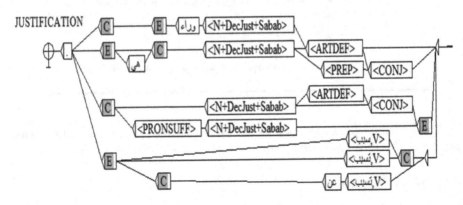

Fig. 7. The sub-graph "Justification"

In the case that the transducer extracts more than one answer, we apply the Jaro Winkler distance to extract the relevant answer.

5   Experimental Evaluation

We implemented a prototype of the proposed Arabic QA system that exclusively handles complex questions in the medical domain. In this prototype, transducers, and dictionaries were built with the linguistic platform NooJ. Figure 8 shows an extract from a dictionary. We conducted a set of experimentations to evaluate our proposal efficiency. Therefore, we exploited the test corpus OSAC.

After testing 130 complex questions on the test corpus, we obtained the results illustrated in Table 3.

Table 3. Summarizing the measured values

	Results
Precision	83%
Recall	78%
F-Measure	80%

As shown in Table 3, our proposed Arabic QA system achieves satisfactory results. Errors often occurred due to problems in writing some Arabic letters, such as the letter ا (a), which can also be written as أ or > or إ or ! or < . For example, in some questions, we can find the word 'inflammation' written as التهاب (AltihaAb) or إلتهاب (< iltihaAb). To resolve this problem, we need to rewrite the question by unifying all variants of a letter into a single form. Furthermore, the presented errors are due to poor coverage by the dictionaries, which must be improved, and the complexity of some questions that require special handling techniques.

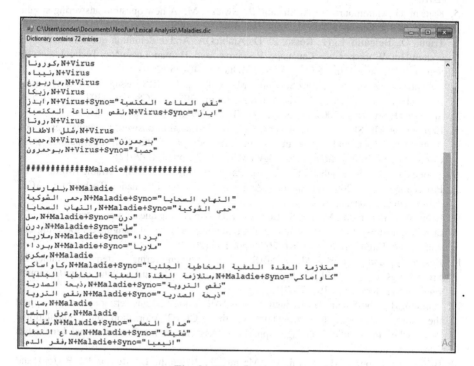

Fig. 8. Dictionary extract

6 Conclusion

In the present paper, we have developed a question answering system to analyze Arabic medical why-questions. Our QA system is mainly concerned with four modules: a study of the corpora, question analysis, document/passage retrieval, and answer extraction. Our proposed method achieves satisfactory results.

In our future work, we seek to add a pre-processing step to normalize the complex question. We also seek to improve our linguistic resources by adding new terms in the dictionaries and new causal relations.

References

1. Athenikos, S.J., Han, H.: Biomedical question answering: a survey. Comput. Methods Programs Biomed. **99**(1), 1–24 (2010)
2. Hammo, B., Abuleil, S., Lytinen, S., Evens, M.: Experimenting with a question answering system for the Arabic language. Comput. Hum. **38**(4), 397–415 (2004)
3. Azmi, A.M., Alshenaifi, N.A.: Lemaza: an Arabic why-question answering system. Nat. Lang. Eng. **23**(6), 877–903 (2017)
4. Verberne, S.: In Search of the Why. Ph.D. Thesis, University of Nijmegen, The Netherlands (2010)
5. Kanaan, G., Hammouri, A., Al-Shalabi, R., Swalha, M.: A new question answering system for the Arabic language. Am. J. Appl. Sci. **6**(4), 97 (2009)
6. Trigui, O., Belguith, L. H., Rosso, P.: DefArabicQA: Arabic definition question answering system. In: Workshop on Language Resources and Human Language Technologies for Semitic Languages, 7th LREC, Valletta, Malta, pp. 40–45 (2010)
7. Benajiba, Y., Rosso, P., Gómez Soriano, J.M.: Adapting the JIRS passage retrieval system to the Arabic language. In: Gelbukh, A. (ed.) CICLing 2007. LNCS, vol. 4394, pp. 530–541. Springer, Heidelberg (2007). https://doi.org/10.1007/978-3-540-70939-8_47
8. Ezzeldin, A.M., Shaheen, M.: A survey of Arabic question answering: challenges, tasks, approaches, tools, and future trends. In: Proceedings of the 13th International Arab Conference on Information Technology (ACIT 2012), pp. 1–8 (2012)
9. Abouenour, L., Bouzoubaa, K., Rosso, P.: Improving Q/A using Arabic wordnet. In: Proceedings of the 2008 International Arab Conference on Information Technology (ACIT 2008), Tunisia, December 2008
10. Brini, W., Ellouze, M., Mesfar, S., Belguith, L.H.: An Arabic question-answering system for factoid questions. In: IEEE International Conference on Natural Language Processing and Knowledge Engineering, NLP-KE 2009, pp. 1–7 (2009)
11. Bekhti, S., and Al-Harbi, M.: AQuASys: a question-answering system for Arabic. In: Proceedings of the WSEAS International Conference. Recent Advances in Computer Engineering Series, pp. 19–27 (2013)
12. Hammo, B., Abu-Salem, H., Lytinen, S.: QARAB: a question answering system to support the Arabic language. In Proceedings of the ACL-02 Workshop on Computational Approaches to Semitic Languages, pp. 1–11. Association for Computational Linguistics (2002)
13. Brini, W., Ellouze, M., Trigui, O., Mesfar, S., Belguith, L., Rosso, P.: Factoid and definitional Arabic question answering system. In: Post-Proceedings of the NOOJ-2009, Tozeur, Tunisia, pp. 8–10 (2009)

14. Silberztein, M.: Using linguistic resources to evaluate the quality of annotated corpora. In Proceedings of the First Workshop on Linguistic Resources for Natural Language Processing, pp. 2–11 (2018)
15. Oh, J.H., Kawada, T., De Saeger, S., Kazama, J., Wang, Y.: Why question answering using sentiment analysis and word classes. In: Proceedings of the 2012 Joint Conference on Empirical Methods in Natural Language Processing and Computational Natural Language Learning, pp. 368–378. Association for Computational Linguistics (2012)
16. Oh, J., Torisawa, K., Hashimoto, C., Sano, M., De Saeger, S., Ohtake, K.: Why-question answering using intra- and intersentential causal relations. In: Proceedings of the 51st Annual Meeting of the Association for Computational Linguistics, pp. 1733–1743 (2013)
17. Shaheen, M., Ezzeldin, A.M.: Arabic question answering: systems, resources, tools, and future trends. Arab. J. Sci. Eng. **39**(6), 4541–4564 (2014). https://doi.org/10.1007/s13369-014-1062-2

The Optimization of Portuguese Named-Entity Recognition and Classification by Combining Local Grammars and Conditional Random Fields Trained with a Parsed Corpus

Diego Alves(✉), Božo Bekavac, and Marko Tadić

Faculty of Humanities and Social Sciences, University of Zagreb, Zagreb, Croatia
{dfvalio,bbekavac,marko.tadic}@ffzg.hr

Abstract. This article presents the results of a study concerning named-entity recognition and classification for Portuguese focusing on temporal expressions. We have used the Conditional Random Fields (CRF) probabilistic method and features coming from an automatically annotated parsed corpus and local grammars. We were able to notice that Part-of-Speech (PoS) tags are the most relevant information coming from a parsed corpus to be used as a feature for this task. No positive synergy emerges from the association of these tags with other linguistic information from the parsed corpus. A NooJ local grammar, created to recognize "Time" category entities (without detailing types and subtypes), provides information that surpasses PoS tags as a feature for CRF training in terms of precision and recall. The combination of PoS and NooJ annotations does not bring any advantage.

Keywords: Named entity · Conditional Random Field · Portuguese

1 Introduction

Named-Entity Recognition and Classification (NERC) involves recognizing information units such as person, organization, location (sometimes), time expressions, and others present inside unstructured texts. This information extraction task is crucial for many natural language processing (NLP) applications such as question and answering systems and entity-oriented search [4]. The awareness of NERC evaluation started with the Message Understanding Conferences (MUC), more precisely MUC-6 [3], and since then, many different evaluation campaigns have been developed worldwide.

For the Portuguese language (both native and Brazilian), the HAREM evaluation campaigns [1] (Avaliação de Reconhecedores de Entidades Mencionadas)[1] established a complex, and therefore, ample set of tags for this task and evaluated several NERC systems based on either machine learning approaches or hand-coded rules in combination with dictionaries, gazetteers, and ontologies. HAREM hierarchy is composed of

---

[1] Translation: "Evaluation of Recognizers of Mentioned Entities".

© Springer Nature Switzerland AG 2021
B. Bekavac et al. (Eds.): NooJ 2020, CCIS 1389, pp. 196–205, 2021.
https://doi.org/10.1007/978-3-030-70629-6_17

three levels: the first one consisting of ten categories ("Person," "Place," "Organization," "Time," "Work," "Thing," "Event," "Miscellaneous," "Abstraction," and "Value"), the second level having 36 types and the third one with 21 sub-types.

A rule-based model for Portuguese NERC has been proposed inside Port4NooJ v3.0 [8]; however, the evaluation of this tool has not been provided and the module is not fully available. Pirovani and De Oliveira proposed in their article [9] the association of local grammars with the Conditional Random Fields (CRF) probabilistic method based on a training set containing Part-of-Speech (PoS) tags achieving better results than previous works concerning HAREM. In this study, the authors considered only the following HAREM named-entity categories: "Person," "Place," "Organization," "Time," and "Value." Types and sub-types of these categories (corresponding to the second and third levels of the HAREM hierarchy) were not taken into consideration by them. Precise evaluation of the deeper structure of HAREM was not provided in previous studies, like in the proposed method using Stencil and NooJ [7], which considers only "Date," "Hour," and "Period" types.

Conditional Random Fields [6] is a machine learning method which has been widely used in several types of NLP tasks, including NERC. This task is treated as a sequence labelling problem, and a conditional model is built from a training set to predict which is the most appropriate labelling sequence given an input sentence.

Local Grammars correspond to the representation of contextual rules. They are finite-state grammars or finite-state automata that represent sets of utterances of a natural language [2]. NooJ software allows the development of formalized descriptions of natural languages in terms of electronic dictionaries and grammars represented by organized sets of graphs [12].

The IOB format, proposed by Ramshaw and Marcus [11], which allows a more detailed analysis of the boundary identification of the entities, was chosen for our study following the work of Pirovani and De Oliveira [9].

Our proposal is to focus on the "Tempo" ("Time") annotation. Our hypothesis is that, by combining linguistic information coming from a parsed corpus with pre-annotations in terms of Named-Entity Recognition provided by NooJ local grammars, we can improve precision and recall considering the whole complexity of the "Time" category described in HAREM. By understanding and identifying possible synergies between different features to be used in CRF model training, these findings can be used in any other NERC CRF system to enhance the final evaluation metrics of this task.

This paper is organized in six sections. Section 2 details the HAREM dataset used in our study, then Sect. 3 presents the third-step methodology adopted in this work. The obtained results are presented in Sect. 4 and discussed in Sect. 5. Section 6 presents conclusions and perspectives for future work.

2 Data Description

The golden collection used in our study (xml file) was created for the second edition of the HAREM evaluation campaign for Portuguese,[2] addressing named-entity recognition

---

[2] The corpus file is called "CDSegundoHAREMReRelEM" and is available at the website https: www.linguateca.pt.

[1]. It consists of 129 documents from different domains: news, didactic, opinion, blog, questions, interview, legal, literary, promotional, and private manuscripts. The corpus was manually annotated according to specific guidelines and contains 4,053 sentences and 89,634 tokens. The HAREM named-entity hierarchy has 3 levels:

- First level: 10 categories.
- Second level: 36 types.
- Third level: 21 sub-types.

As previously mentioned, our focus is on the "Time" category, which is described in Table 1.

Table 1. Description of "Time" category from the HAREM named-entity hierarchy in terms of types, sub-types and number of occurrences in the golden collection.

Type	Sub-type	Number of occurrences
TIME CALENDAR	*DATE*	873
	HOUR	37
	INTERVAL	63
DURATION	–	56
FREQUENCY	–	71
GENERIC	–	89

In total, there are 1,189 occurrences of "Time" entities in the selected corpus, 73% correspond to the type "TIME CALENDAR" and sub-type "HOUR". This golden collection was pre-processed by two python scripts:

- Format change: from inline XML Schema to IOB format.
- Random selection of sentences to compose training and test sets concerning the ratio 70/30.

Therefore, we have established a training set composed of 2,842 sentences, 63,032 tokens, and 808 named-entities, and a test set containing 1,211 sentences, 26,602 tokens, and 352 entities.

3 Three-Step Experimental Design

We have developed a three-step methodology to analyze the influence of different features and their synergy when training CRF models for the task of named-entity recognition and classification. The first step consisted in training CRF models using part-of-speech, morphological and dependency parsing tags as features. In the second step, NooJ software was used to generate a local grammar to identify and annotate named-entities of the "Time" category. In the last step, we merged features coming from steps 1 and 2 to analyze their combined influence when training CRF models. Each step will be detailed in the following sub-sections.

3.1 Step 1: CRF Trained with Parsed Corpus

As mentioned above, in this step, linguistic information coming from a parsed corpus is used as features to train CRF models. The objective was to identify the best combination that allows the enhancement of metrics results (precision, recall and F1-measure) for the NERC task.

The golden collection provided by HAREM does not contain any linguistic information besides the identification of named entities. Therefore, to provide additional features, we have parsed the training and test sets using UDpipe tool v.1.2.0 [14] with an available Portuguese model (BOSQUE v.2.4), which was developed using the Bosque Treebank [10].

We have used the sklearn-crsuite v.0.3.6 python library (with Python 3.6.2) [5], which allows the implementation of CRF models [15] for labelling sequential data. The basic features that were used in all our CRF tests and which comprise our baseline (the simplest model, with fewer features) are the following:

- Lower case: if the token is composed only of lower-case characters.
- Upper case: if the token is composed only of capital letters.
- Title: if the token starts with a capital letter followed only by lower characters.
- Digit: if the token is composed only of digits.

Each token (n) also receives information concerning the previous (n − 1) and following (n + 1) tokens. The following combinations of features (Table 2) have been tested:

Table 2. Different combinations of features from a parsed corpus used to train CRF models.

Test number	Features
1	Basic Features (baseline)
2	Basic Features + Part-of-Speech tags
3	Basic Features + Dependency Parsing labels
4	Basic Features + Morphosyntactic tags
5	Basic Features + Part-of-Speech + Dependency Parsing
6	Basic Features + Part-of-Speech + Morphosyntactic
7	Basic Features + Part-of-Speech + Morphosyntactic + Dependency Parsing

3.2 Step 2: The Development of Local Grammar to Identify "Time" Entities

The main idea behind this step is to develop a local grammar with NooJ software v.6.1 [12] and the general dictionary provided by the Port4NooJ resource [8] to identify "Time" expressions in the training and test sets. Our aim is to give this additional information as a feature when training CRF models.

The local grammar that has been created is composed of 22 graphs and allowed us to recognize and annotate entities concerning the category level. We have not considered all the types and sub-types of "Time" in this step. NooJ xml tags have been transformed into IOB format using a python script.

3.3 Step 3: Combination of Features Coming from the Parsed Corpus and Local Grammar

In this final step, we combined the features identified in the first step, providing the best results in terms of named-entity recognition and classification with the pre-annotations performed by the local grammar generated using NooJ software (Table 3).

Table 3. Different combination of features coming from the parsed corpus and NooJ local grammar to train CRF models.

Test number	Features
8	Basic Features + NooJ local grammar "Time" tags
9	Basic Features + Part-of-Speech + NooJ local grammar "Time" tags

4   Results

4.1   Step 1: CRF Trained with the Parsed Corpus

In Table 4, we present the results of the tests that were conducted using CRF models trained with linguistic information coming from the HAREM golden set corpus parsed with the UDpipe tool.

The best results in terms of precision, recall, and F1-measure were obtained using the basic features associated with Part-of-Speech information, with an increase in these metrics compared to the baseline. Dependency parsing labels provided an improvement in terms of recall but not of precision compared to the baseline. Morphosyntactic tags used as a feature increase precision but have no effect in terms of recall. The association of Part-of-Speech tags with the other linguistic data coming from the parsed corpus (tests 5, 6, and 7) does not have any positive impact in the metrics compared to the results obtained using Part-of-Speech alone.

4.2   Step 2: Development of Local Grammar to Identify "Time" Entities

A local grammar composed of 22 graphs was created to identify entities concerning the "Time" category. Each token from the training and test sets was annotated with one of the following tags: "B-Time," "I-Time," or "O".

Table 4. Results of different combinations of features coming from the parsed corpus used to train CRF models in terms of Precision (P), Recall (R) and F1-measure (F1).

Test number	Features	P	R	F1
1	Basic Features (baseline)	0.809	0.636	0.700
2	Basic Features + PoS	**0.838**	**0.671**	**0.735**
3	Basic Features + Dep. Parsing	0.805	0.664	0.723
4	Basic Features + Morphosyntactic	0.823	0.634	0.708
5	Basic Features + PoS + Dep. Parsing	0.807	0.670	0.727
6	Basic Features + PoS + Morpho	0.830	0.658	0.727
7	Basic Features + PoS + Morpho + Dep. Parsing	0.823	0.655	0.721

Table 5. Evaluation of annotations from the NooJ local grammar in terms of Precision (P), Recall (R), and F1-measure (F1).

Data-set	P	R	F1
Training	**0.870**	**0.661**	**0.751**
Test	0.847	0.660	0.741

The accuracy of the annotations provided in this step is presented in Table 5. We examined both the training and test sets.

Precision and recall values for the training and test sets are relatively similar. These results show that the local grammar has been built favouring precision over recall. This local grammar can be improved by increasing the complexity of "Time" expressions that it can identify and by the creation of disambiguation grammars that would allow better identification of entities containing ambiguous words such as era, which in Portuguese can correspond to era as in English and also the past tense of the verb ser 'to be'.

4.3 Step 3: Combination of Features Coming from the Parsed Corpus and Local Grammar

In this final step, we have analyzed the combination of the best model coming from the training of CRF models using parsed data with the annotations provided by NooJ as an additional feature. Our results are presented in Table 6.

It is possible to notice that the combination of NooJ annotations as a feature with the basic ones enables the CRF model to achieve better results than the best model obtained in the first step (using part-of-speech tags). NooJ "Time" expression identification allows us to increase precision by approximately 6 points while recall is increased by almost 9 points. When NooJ information is combined with part-of-speech tags, precision is close to the value obtained using only the basic features (baseline), and there is only a small increase in recall. Therefore, combining basic features with NooJ annotations provides

Table 6. Results of the combination of features coming from the parsed corpus and NooJ annotations to train CRF models in terms of Precision (P), Recall (R), and F1-measure (F1).

Test number	Features	P	R	F1
1	Basic Features (baseline)	0.809	0.636	0.700
2	Basic Features + PoS	0.838	0.671	0.735
8	Basic Features + NooJ annotations	**0.867**	**0.725**	**0.757**
9	Basic Features + PoS + NooJ annotations	0.797	0.675	0.700

the best CRF model for the NERC of temporal expressions in Portuguese, using the HAREM golden set.

As presented in Table 1, HAREM proposes a classification of "Time" expressions composed by types and sub-types. For further understanding of how the best model works, it is important to analyze the results for each possible tag in detail (Table 7).

Table 7. Detailed results of the combination of features coming from parsed corpus and NooJ annotations to train CRF models in terms of Precision (P), Recall (R) and F1-measure (F1).

Test number	P	R	F1
B-DURATION	0.333	0.059	0.100
I-DURATION	0.333	0.089	0.140
B-FREQUENCY	**1.000**	0.545	0.706
I-FREQUENCY	**1.000**	0.516	0.681
B-GENERIC	0.500	0.138	0.700
I-GENERIC	0.800	0.082	0.148
B-TIME CALENDAR-DATE	0.841	0.821	0.831
I-TIME CALENDAR-DATE	0.828	**0.857**	**0.842**
B-TIME CALENDAR-HOUR	**1.000**	0.167	0.286
I-TIME CALENDAR-HOUR	0.750	0.194	0.308
B-TIME CALENDAR-INTERVAL	0.778	0.438	0.560
I-TIME CALENDAR-INTERVAL	0.778	0.404	0.532

The type "Duration" presents the worst values for both precision and recall. The tag "B-GENERIC" also has considerably lower values for these two metrics than the other tags. In general, recall results are much lower than precision, except for the type "Time Calendar," sub-type "Date," for which the values are similar.

These instances are the most numerous in the golden set, corresponding to 73% of all named-entity occurrences. Only the types "Time Calendar" subtype "Date," and "Frequency" have recall results higher than 0.500 concerning the "Time" category. Each token from the training and test sets were annotated with one of the following tags: "B-Time", "I-Time" or "O".

5 Discussion

By analyzing the results presented in the previous section, it is noticeable that, when using information from an annotated parsed corpus, the most relevant linguistic information to be used as a feature for CRF training is part of speech. When used alone, PoS increases the values of all metrics. The association with other information coming from the parsed corpus showed no further increase, and thus, no positive synergy has been identified. This observation corroborates what is usually seen in the literature concerning CRF for the NERC task, where, usually, only PoS is used as a feature [9].

We used the UDpipe tool (with the BOSQUE model) to annotate the HAREM golden set. As this task was carried out automatically, some bias was introduced into our study. According to the UDpipe official website, when evaluated with their test set, the BOSQUE model achieved part-of-speech and morphosyntactic tagging accuracy higher than 90%, with a dependency parsing tagging (LAS metric) of 85.65% [13].

Table 6 shows that, when using the CRF method for this specific task, generating a local grammar has better final results than using part-of-speech as a feature. Also, no positive impact has been observed when associating both PoS and NooJ annotations. We chose to focus on temporal expressions for this study, thus, it seemed pertinent to proceed with the same analysis for other main categories present in HAREM to validate these observations.

Therefore, the hypothesis that the best results for NERC can be achieved by the combination of linguistic features from the parsed corpus combined with annotations from local grammars was not confirmed. No positive synergy has been observed between them. However, it was possible notice that, using only the local grammars, annotations as a feature for CRF training considerably increases the overall results for this task.

The evaluation of the local grammar showed that it can still be improved, especially in terms of recall, which would probably lead to an enhancement of the CRF model. Other possible improvements would be detailing, in this grammar, the types and sub-types of HAREM, focusing on the cases with low recall values. It is possible to see in Table 7 that entities corresponding to type "Time Calendar", sub-type "Date" are the ones with highest value of recall, which is probably influenced by the number of occurrences in the golden set (much higher compared to other entities). Thus, it is important for the further development of the local grammar to focus on what is least represented in HAREM.

Pirovani and De Oliveira [9] also used local grammar and PoS annotations associated with CRF models for the NERC task. However, no proof of the synergy between these two types of features was demonstrated. Also, the highest F1 measure obtained by the proposed system (for all HAREM categories, not considering second and third levels of the hierarchy) was 60.4%, while our system achieves 75.7% for the "Time" category considering all its types and sub-types. Additionally, the best NERC system identified during the second HAREM evaluation campaign [1] presents an F1 measure slightly inferior to 60%. Our system composed only of annotations from the local grammar and basic CRF features seems, therefore, a great improvement for this task. Nevertheless, as mentioned above, since our focus was on the recognition and identification of the detailed "Time" category structure only, further analysis considering the whole HAREM structure must be conducted.

6 Conclusions and Future Work

We have presented a detailed study with the aim to analyze the influence of different features when training CRF models to perform the task of named-entity recognition and classification for Portuguese. Our focus was on temporal expressions, using the hierarchy established by the HAREM initiative [1].

First, we have identified that, among all possible features that can be used from a parsed corpus, the most relevant one for this specific task is part-of-speech tags used alone. Associating different features did not provide better results compared to the model trained only with PoS.

Second, we have built a local grammar capable of identifying "Time" category entities using NooJ software to use this information as a feature for CRF training. The evaluation of this grammar showed that it has room for improvement, especially in terms of recall.

In the final step, we observed that NooJ annotations used as a feature enabled us to create the best CRF model in terms of precision and recall. No positive synergy has been observed when NooJ annotations were combined with PoS tags. Thus, it seems more pertinent to generate local grammars that recognize entities and their boundaries than to use an automatic tool to parse the corpus. Compared to previous works, it is possible to observe that the overall metrics of our system, even though focusing only on the "Time" category, are better.

Therefore, we can conclude that the combination of local grammar information with linguistic annotations as CRF features does not necessarily improve the overall results. Previous studies did not evaluate this synergy. Local grammars alone provide sufficient information to increase precision and recall for the NERC task.

As our next step, it would be interesting to proceed with the improvement of the local grammar, increasing the recall and introducing the whole complexity of "Time" expressions as described in the HAREM guidelines, considering all types and sub-types. Also, it would be relevant to test other machine-learning methods to verify whether the lack of synergy observed here is due to the algorithm tested. And, finally, it seems pertinent to complete this study by considering the whole HAREM hierarchy to be able to compare precisely the overall results of our system with those proposed in the literature.

Acknowledgments. The work presented in this paper has received funding from the European Union's Horizon 2020 research and innovation program under Marie Skłodowska-Curie grant agreement no. 812997 and under the name CLEOPATRA (Cross-lingual Event-centric Open Analytics Research Academy).

References

1. Freitas, C., Carvalho, P., Gonçalo Oliveira, H., Mota, C., Santos, D.: SecondHAREM: advancing the state of the art of named entity recognition in Portuguese. In: Calzolari, N., et al. (eds.) Proceedings of the International Conference on Language Resources and Evaluation (LREC 2010) (Valletta 17–23 May de 2010) European Language Resources Association. European Language Resources Association (2010)
2. Gross, M.: A bootstrap method for constructing local grammars. In: Bokan, N. (ed.) Proceedings of the Symposium on Contemporary Mathematics, pp. 229–250 (1999)
3. Hirschman, L.: The evolution of evaluation: lessons from the message understanding conference. Comput. Speech Lang. **12**, 208–305 (1998)
4. Jiang, J.: Information extraction from text. In: Aggarwal, C., Zhai, C. (eds.) Mining Text Data, pp. 11–47. Springer, Boston (2012). https://doi.org/10.1007/978-1-4614-3223-4_2
5. Korobov, M.: sklearn-crfsuite 0.3 (2015). https://sklearncrfsuite.readthedocs.io/en/latest/index.html. Accessed 20 May 2020
6. Lafferty, J., McCallum, A., Pereira, F.: Conditional random fields: probabilistic models for segmenting and labelling sequence data. In: Proceedings of the 18th International Conference on Machine Learning, pp. 282–289. Morgan Kaufmann, San Francisco (2001). citeseer.ist.psu.edu/lafferty01conditional.html
7. Mota, C., Silberztein, M.: Em busca da máxima precisão sem almanaques: O stencil/nooj no harem. In: Diana Santos, N.C. (ed.) Reconhecimento de entidades mencionadas em português: Documentação e actas do HAREM, a primeira avaliação conjunta na área, pp. 191–208 (2007)
8. Mota, C., Carvalho, P., Barreiro, A.: Port4NooJ v3.0: integrated linguistic resources for Portuguese NLP. In: Proceedings of the Tenth International Conference on Language Resources and Evaluation (LREC 2016), pp. 1264–1269. European Language Resources Association (ELRA), Portorož (2016). https://www.aclweb.org/anthology/L16-1201
9. Pirovani, J., Oliveira, E.: Portuguese named entity recognition using conditional random fields and local grammars. In: Proceedings of the Eleventh International Conference on Language Resources and Evaluation (LREC 2018). European Language Resources Association (ELRA), Miyazaki (2018). https://www.aclweb.org/anthology/L18-1705
10. Rademaker, A., Chalub, F., Real, L., Freitas, C., Bick, E., de Paiva, V.: Universal dependencies for Portuguese. In: Proceedings of the Fourth International Conference on Dependency Linguistics (Depling), Pisa, Italy, pp. 197–206 (2017). https://aclweb.org/anthology/W17-6523
11. Ramshaw, L., Marcus, M.: Text chunking using transformation-based learning. In: Third Workshop on Very Large Corpora (1995). https://www.aclweb.org/anthology/W95-0107
12. Silberztein, M.: NooJ Manual (2003)
13. Straka, M.: UDPipe 2.0 prototype at CoNLL 2018 UD shared task. In: Proceedings of the CoNLL 2018 Shared Task: Multilingual Parsing from Raw Text to Universal Dependencies, pp. 197–207. Association for Computational Linguistics, Brussels, October 2018. https://doi.org/10.18653/v1/K18-2020. https://www.aclweb.org/anthology/K18-2020
14. Straka, M., Straková, J.: Tokenizing, pos tagging, lemmatizing and parsing UD 2.0 with UDPipe. In: Proceedings of the CoNLL 2017 Shared Task: Multilingual Parsing from Raw Text to Universal Dependencies, pp. 88–99. Association for Computational Linguistics, Vancouver (2017). https://www.aclweb.org/anthology/K/K17/K17-3009.pdf
15. Wijffels, J., Okazaki, N.: CRFsuite: conditional random fields for labelling sequential data in natural language processing based on crfsuite: a fast implementation of conditional random fields (CRFs) (2007–2018). https://github.com/bnosac/crfsuite. R package version 0.1

The Automatic Recognition and Translation of Tunisian Dialect Named Entities into Modern Standard Arabic

Roua Torjmen[1(✉)] and Kais Haddar[2]

[1] Faculty of Economic Sciences and Management of Sfax, Miracl Laboratory,
University of Sfax, Sfax, Tunisia
rouatorjmen@gmail.com
[2] Faculty of Sciences of Sfax, Miracl Laboratory, University of Sfax, Sfax, Tunisia
kais.haddar@yahoo.fr

Abstract. Developing an automatic named-entity recognition system accompanied by a translation system has become an important task in Natural Language Processing applications. In this context, we are interested in building a named-entity recognition system for Tunisian dialect by providing their translation into modern standard Arabic. In fact, Tunisian dialect is a variant of Arabic, as much as it differs from modern standard Arabic. Still, it is difficult to understand for non-Tunisian Arabic speakers. To develop our system, we studied many Tunisian dialect corpora to identify and look into various structures for different named entity types. The proposed method is based on a bilingual dictionary extracted from the study corpus and an elaborated set of local grammars. In addition, local grammars were transformed into finite-state transducers using recent technologies of the NooJ linguistic platform. To test and evaluate the designed system, we applied it to a Tunisian dialect test corpus containing around 20,000 words. The obtained results are ambitious.

Keywords: Named-entity recognition · Translation · Finite transducer · Tunisian dialect

1 Introduction

Named entities (NEs) are enormously widespread in different corpora. The Tunisian Dialect (TD) corpus is no exclusion and also contains a huge number of NEs. Moreover, non-Tunisian Arabs find TD difficult to understand. These incentives prompted us to build a tool to recognize NEs in a TD corpus and to translate them into Modern Standard Arabic (MSA). Furthermore, this tool offers the possibility of tackling other fields such as information retrieval, automatic indexing, clustering, and classification of documents.

Among the encountered problems, TD has no standard spelling. This dialect also contains words of different origins, such as Arabic, Amazigh, French, Maltese, Spanish, and Turkish. It also differs from one region to another. Furthermore, TD proper nouns can be written in different ways. In addition, there are no capital letters at the beginning of a

© Springer Nature Switzerland AG 2021
B. Bekavac et al. (Eds.): NooJ 2020, CCIS 1389, pp. 206–217, 2021.
https://doi.org/10.1007/978-3-030-70629-6_18

word to indicate the presence of a TD proper noun. Sharing the same problems as MSA, the absence of diacritical marks and the presence of the phonemenon of agglutination aggravate the situation and produce homographs which, in turn, can create ambiguities.

The main objective of this paper was to build a system able to recognize and translate TD named entities into MSA using the NooJ linguistic platform. To manage this, we started by reusing a bilingual TD-MSA dictionary. Then, we established a set of syntactic grammars that offer NE recognition and their translation from TD into MSA. Indeed, our tool is realized using finite-state transducers implemented in the NooJ linguistic platform. Moreover, we can experiment with our tool, thanks to previously designed resources (the bilingual TD-MSA dictionary and inflectional, derivational, and morphological grammars).

The paper is structured into six sections. In the second section, we present previous works dealing with named-entity recognition in MSA and Arabic dialects. In the third section, we carry out a linguistic study on the different types of NEs and their translations. In the fourth section, we propose a method for our automatic named-entity recognition (ANER) system. In the fifth section, we experiment and evaluate our system by applying it to the TD test corpus. Finally, the paper ends with a conclusion and some perspectives.

2   Related Work

The number of studies on the Arabic NER system for MSA is large. Nevertheless, when it comes to Arabic dialects, the researchers are non-existent with the exception of Egyptian dialect. In this section, we cite some works dealing with ANER based on linguistic, statistical, and hybrid approaches.

Mesfar [8] has built an Arabic NER system based on the linguistic approach. The designed system recognizes person, location, organization, numerical, and temporal NEs. The Arabic NER process focuses on three sequential modules, namely, a NooJ tokenizer, a morphological analyzer, and an ANER. The morphological analyzer and the ANER use finite-state technologies, trigger words, and gazetteers. The test corpus is collected from the Arabic version of the newspaper *Le Monde Diplomatique*. The average of the results obtained for all NE types is as follows: Precision, 91.6%; Recall, 83.4%; and F-measure, 87.3%. Another work is devoted to the Arabic NER using a linguistic approach and the NooJ platform [10]. This NER system [5] is designed for sports fields and recognizes locations and players. It allows the translation of recognized NEs into French. The test corpus is collected from Newspaper texts. As results, the system obtains 98%, 90%, and 94% as Precision, Recall, and F-measure, respectively.

Many research projects have adopted the supervised Arabic NER. The majority of these NER systems have used classical features. For lexical features such as prefixes, suffixes, character n-grams, word length, and punctuation, we cite [1, 9]. For contextual features such as word n-grams and rule-based features, we cite [3, 9]. For morphological features such as part of speech, number, gender, person, or aspect, we cite [2, 7]. For other features, such as gazetteers, lexical trigger words, and nationality information, we cite [2, 3]. Benajiba and his teams [2, 3] have suggested an NER system dedicated to microblogs. Their language-independent system relies on a set of features that are equivalent to [1]. Their dataset contains dialectal data which is collected from Twitter. It also contains

English and MSA. The obtained results are 76.7%, 55.6%, and 55.8% for location, organization, and person, respectively. Zirikly and Diab [13, 14] have constructed an NER system dedicated to Egyptian dialect, especially in social media. Their system is based on a machine-learning approach using the CRF approach. It recognizes person and location NEs. Zirikly and Diab have included Brown Clustering as a new feature among the NER features, adding to lexical, contextual, and morphological features and gazetteers. As results, they have gotten 91.429% and 49.18% for locations and person names using the F-measure. This work is inspired by the work of [4].

Finally, some other studies in Arabic NER are based on the hybrid approach such as [9] and [6]. The authors of [9] have obtained a 90% F-measure, while the authors of [6] have obtained 81.9%.

Research on the TD ANER system is absent. Noting that the linguistic approach gives ambitious results, we decided to opt for this approach by using the new technologies of the NooJ platform.

3   Linguistic Study

Named entities are classified into three different types: ENAMEX for proper names, TIMEX for temporal expressions, and NUMEX for numerical expressions. In this linguistic study, we seek to understand the NE composition in TD. We also want to compare NEs between MSA and TD. In the following subsections, we detail the structure rules of each type.

3.1   ENAMEX

In our linguistic study, ENAMEX NEs include persons, organizations, and locations. Starting with person NEs, three categories – name, profession, and nationality – could present it. Table 1 presents some structural rules of each category.

Table 1. Some structural rules of person NEs

Person NE category	Structure rule
Name	(Pronoun| name_trigger suffix | civility_noun)? first_name last_name?
Profession	(Profession_noun definite_noun? first_name last_name?) | (profession_trigger_verb Profession_noun definite_noun?)
Nationality	((pronoun?) first_name last_name? nationality_noun) | (nationality_noun first_name last_name?)

Comparing person NE categories in TD with those of MSA, we notice that they are similar. Thus, in this case, we have to use word-for-word translation. For example, in profession NE, the TD NE نخدم رئيس تحرير (*nikhdim ra'Is tahrIr*) 'I work as Chief Editor' is translated into MSA NE أشتغل رئيس تحرير (*achtaghil ra'Issa tahrIrin*).

Table 2. Some structure rules of location NEs

Location NE category	Structure rule
Country	(Country_trigger suffix)? Country_name
City	(City_trigger)? City_name (city trigger)?
Nature	Nature_trigger City_name
Address	Adress_trigger road_name (كل digit)l Address_trigger definite noun

Location NEs encompass four categories: country, city, nature, and address. Table 2 shows structure rules for each category.

Comparing location NE category in TD with those of MSA, we notice that these are similar, as well. Thus, in this case, we have to use word-for-word translation. For example, the TD country NE بلادي تونس (*blAdI tUnis*) 'My country Tunisia' is translated word-for-word into بلادي تونس(*bilAdI tUnissa*) in MSA.

Organization NEs include public establishments and societies. Table 3 presents some structure rules.

Table 3. Some structure rules of organization NEs

Organization NE category	Structure rule
Public establishment	Public_establishment_trigger ((Address_trigger? (first_name? Last_name) definite noun) date l road_name l city_name)
Society	Company_trigger (first_name? last_name l company_name) preposition definite_noun))

Comparing organization NE categories in TD with those of MSA, we notice that they are similar. Thus, in this case, we again have to use word-for-word translation. For instance, using word-for-word translation into MSA, the TD public establishment NE ستاد 20 مارس 1956(*stAd 20 mAris 1956*) '20th of March 1956 Stadium' becomes ملعب 20 مارس 1956(*mal'abu 20 mAris 1956*).

In conclusion, TD ENAMEX NE can be translated into MSA using word-for-word translation. However, we must take into account that some TD single nouns could transform into composite nouns. For example, the noun كولاج(*kUlAj*) 'middle school' becomes in MSA مدرسة إعدادية(*madrassatun i'dAdIyatun*).

3.2 TIMEX

Comparing the two different NE types, we notice that TIMEX NEs are smaller and simpler than ENAMEX NEs. TIMEX NEs have only four categories, without subcategories. These are period, hour, date, and age. Table 4 shows structure rules for each TIMEX NE category.

Table 4. Some structure rules of TIMEX NEs

TIMEX NE category	Structure rule
Period	(prep suffix I indefinite_noun)? (number I digit$^+$)* time_unit
Hour	((indefinite_noun day_name)? (prep)? (number I digit$^+$) (prep part_day)?) I (noun part_day)
Date	((noun_time? (numberIdigit$^+$) month_name?) I saison_name (noun_time? (numberIdigit$^+$))) I numeral_adj noun_time prep (month_name I saison_name Inoun_time)
Age	(Age_trigger_verb IAge_trigger suffix? (numberIdigit$^+$) time_unit

Comparing the TIMEX NE category in TD with those of MSA, we notice that the translation keeps the same syntax structure for TIMEX NEs except for hours. Hence, in this case, we have to use word-for-word translation for all cases, except the readjustment translation for hour NEs.

Exhibiting some example for TIMEX NE, the TD date NE أول نهار من رمضان(*awil nhAr min ramdhAn*) 'The first day of Ramadan' is converted, using word-to-word translation, into MSA أول يوم من رمضان(*awallu yawmin min ramdhAnin*). However, the TD hour NE غدوة الصباح(*ghodwah ilsbAh*) 'tomorrow morning' is converted, using readjustment translation, into MSA غدا صباحا(*ghadan saba7an*). In this case, we use inversion and we delete the definite article. Other cases of TD hour NEs need readjustment translation, as is evident in the example التسعة متاع الصباح(*iltes'ah mtA' ilsbAh*) 'at 9 am' becomes التاسعة صباحا(*altAssi'atu sabAhAn*). In this case, we have to delete the preposition متاع(*mtA'*).

3.3 NUMEX

According to our study, NUMEX NEs are restricted to four categories, which are percentage, weight, measure, and money. Table 5 presents the structure rules for all four NUMEX NE categories.

Table 5. Structure rules of NUMEX NEs

NUMEX NE category	Structure rule
Percentage	(number I digit$^+$) (preposition definite_noun I %)
Weight	(number I digit$^+$) weight_unit
Measure	(number I digit$^+$) indefinite_noun
Money	(number I digit$^+$) (devise I symbol)

Comparing examples of the NUMEX NE category in TD with those of MSA, we notice that they are similar. Thus, in this case, we have to use word-to-word translation only in one category: measure NEs. The one exception is when the number is

زوز (zUz)(zUz) 'two'. For example, the TD measure NE زوز كتب (zUz ktub)(zUz ktub) 'two books' becomes a single word in MSA: كتابان(kitAbAni).

4   Proposed Method

Our proposed method is based on the linguistic approach. This approach consists of two principal steps, as shown in Fig. 1. Our TD corpus is analyzed by the morphological analyzer using dictionaries and morphological grammars. The first step provides recognized words. This analyzed corpus goes through the ANER and translation system. Thanks to bilingual dictionaries, gazetteers, and syntactic grammars, TD NEs are recognized and translated into MSA.

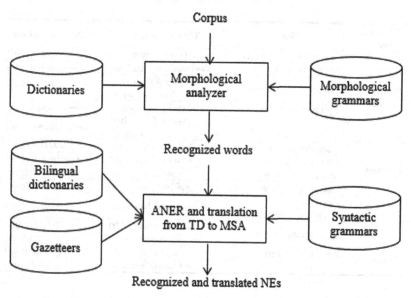

Fig. 1. Architecture of our ANER and translation system

Figure 1 describes the architecture of our ANER system. In the following subsections, we detail each step.

4.1   The Morphological Analyzer

The morphological analyzer [11, 12] enables us to analyze the TD corpus using finite-state technologies. Each recognized word possesses a set of information such as a part-of-speech tag (N, V, PREP), gender (f, m), number (s, p, d), syntactic information (Transitive), and semantic information (Month).

Thanks to large-coverage TD dictionaries and inflectional and morphological grammars which are a set of finite-state transducers, we resolve the agglutination phenomenon. Our morphological analyzer identifies the different parts of a word such as a definite article attached to a noun, such as the word الكولاج(*ilkUlAj*) 'the middle school', and also identifies a noun followed by a suffix, such as the word عمري('*umrI*) 'my age'. This linguistic phenomenon almost always appears in trigger words. Therefore, this step is very necessary for recognizing NEs.

4.2 The ANER and Translation System

Our ANER system needs trigger words and gazetteers to detect NEs. The trigger words precede the gazetteers. They are indicators that determine the types of NEs. In Table 6, we present lists and some examples of trigger words.

Table 6. Trigger word lists.

Trigger word	List	TD Example	MSA translation
Personal name	2 person name triggers	اسمي (*ismi*) 'my name'	اسمي (*ismI*)
	10 civility nouns	مدام (*madAm*) 'madam'	سيدة (*sayyidatun*)
	240 profession nouns	كوارجي (*kawArjI*) 'soccer player'	لاعب (*La'Ibun*)
	2 profession verbs	يخدم (*yikhdim*) 'work'	يشتغل (*yachtaghilu*)
	305 nationality nouns	فرنساوي (*fransAwi*) 'French'	فرنسي (*firansiyyun*)
Location	1 country trigger	بلاد (*blAd*) 'country'	بلاد (*bilAdun*)
	5 city triggers	مدينة (*mdIna*) 'city'	مدينة (*madInatun*)
	15 nature triggers	بحر (*bhar*) 'sea'	بحر (*bahrun*)
	4 address triggers	ثنية (*thniya*) 'road'	طريق (*tarIqun*)
Organization	23 public establishment triggers	ستاد (*stAd*) 'staduim'	ملعب (*mal'abun*)
	11 company trigger	مقاولات (*muqAwlAt*) 'contracting'	مقاولات (*muqA-wlAtun*)
Age	4 age trigger verbs	قفل (*qfal*) 'have'	بلغ (*balagha*)
	1 age trigger	عمري ('*umri*) 'my age'	سني (*sinnI*)

Gazetteers are the most important items in the NE. They are a special dictionary that contains names already known and classified into types of named entities with their translation. In Table 7, we present the lists and some examples of gazetteers.

Furthermore, we prepare the different written forms for all gazetteers of all NE types. For example, the day name ثلاث(*thlAth*) 'Tuesday', which is a temporal expression, can be written as تلاث(*tlAth*) and ثلاثاء(*thlAla'*). In addition, we provide some abbreviations for organization NEs. For example, the abbreviation ت ت)(*a ta ta*) presents والتلفزة التونسية الإذاعة(*alidhA'Ah wiltafzah iltunsiyah*) 'Tunisian radio and television'.

Our ANER and translation system needs to combine gazetteers and trigger words to recognize NEs. We establish a syntactic grammar which is a set of recursive transition networks and finite state transducers. This syntactic grammar allows to set trigger words, gazetteers, and other elements in a specific order to constitute the right structure rules so that they can correctly recognize NEs.

Table 7. Gazetteer lists.

Gazetteer	List	TD Example	MSA translation
Person name	407 first names	حبيب (hbib) 'Habib'	حبيب (habib)
	305 last names	الشعري (ilch'ri) 'Chaari'	الشعري (alch'ri)
Location	280 country names	فرانسا(frAnsA) 'France'	فرنسا(firansA)
	540 city names	صفاقس (sfaqis) 'Sfax'	صفاقس (safaqus)
	40 road names	سكرة (sukrah) 'Sokra'	سكرة (sukrah)
Organization	70 company name	كارفور (kArfUr) 'Carre-four'	كارفور (kArfUr)
Temporal expression	6 time units	عام ('Am) 'year'	سنة (sanatun)
	14 day names	خميس (khmIs) 'Thursday'	الخميس (alkha-mIs)
	4 part days	ليل (lIl) 'night'	مساء(massA')
	12 month names	مارس (mAris) 'Mars'	مارس (mAris)
	4 season names	شتا (chtA) 'winter'	شتاء (chitA')
Numerical expression	11 weight units	كيلو (kIlU) 'Kilo'	كيلو (kIlU)
	170 devises	دينار (dInAr) 'Dinar'	دينار (dInArun)

The main graph contains three subgraphs, which are ENAMEX, TIMEX, and NUMEX. For each of these subgraphs, we attribute an annotation to precisely identify the type of NE, as shown Fig. 2. For example, we attribute the annotation "<ENAMEX>" for ENAMEX NEs.

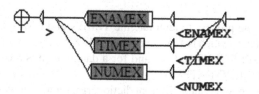

Fig. 2. The main graph

The ENAMEX subgraph also contains three other subgraphs, which are person, location, and organization, as shown in Fig. 3. Moreover, we attribute to each of them an additional annotation. For example, we attribute the annotation "+PERS" for person NEs. So from this graph, we obtain "<ENAMEX+PERS>".

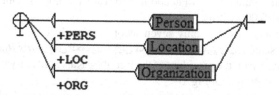

Fig. 3. The ENAMEX transducer

The Person subgraph also contains other subgraphs: name, profession, and nationality. Likewise, we add to each one an additional annotation. For example, we attribute the annotation "+NAT" for nationality NEs. As a final result, we obtain the annotation "<ENAMEX+PERS+NAT>".

In the Nationality subgraph, we establish a finite-state transducer corresponding to structure rule in Table 1 for this NE category. As presented in Fig. 4, this transducer contains the trigger word "<N+Nationality>" and two gazetteers "<N+FName>" for a first name and "<N+LName>" for a last name, which are stored in the NN1, NF1, and NL variables, respectively. The contents of these variables are translated into MSA thanks to $AR. Thus, this transducer enables us to recognize TD NEs for the nationality category and to translate them into MSA using word-to-word translation.

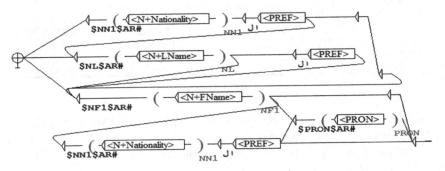

Fig. 4. The Nationality transducer

We apply the same process to annotate the TIMEX and ENAMEX subgraphs. For example, for percentage, which is a category of NUMEX NE, we obtain the specific annotation "<NUMEX+PERCENTAGE>" and for a date, which is a category of TIMEX NE, we obtain "<TIMEX+DATE>".

In conclusion, we have created different dictionaries for trigger words and gazetteers. In addition, we have developed a syntactic grammar that consists of thirty-one graphs and covers all different types of NEs.

5 Experimentation and Evaluation

All linguistic resources (dictionaries and morphological and syntactic grammars) were implemented and compiled into the NooJ linguistic platform. Our TD corpus was collected from social media such as Facebook and Tunisian novels. Our TD test corpus contained around 20,000 words.

The linguistic analysis took only seven seconds to analyze our TD test corpus. For example, the TD sentence رئيس الجمهورية قيس سعيّد غلب نبيل القروي(raIs iljumhUriyah qays s'yid ghlib nabil ilqarwI) 'the president of the Republic Kais Said has won Nabil Karoui.' was analyzed as mentioned in Fig. 5.

Figure 5 indicates that رئيس(raIs) 'president' is a profession noun. It also indicates that قيس(qays) 'Kais' and نبيل(nabil) 'Nabil' are first names. It also indicates that سعيّد(s'yid) 'Said' and قروي(qarwI) 'Karoui' are last names.

رَئِيسٌ, N+Prof+AR="رئيس"+Genre=m+Nombre=s

اِل, PREF

جُمْهُورِيَّة, N+Nombre=s+Genre=f+AR="جمهورية"+NRZ

قَيْسٌ, N+FName+Genre=m+AR="قيس"

سُعَيّد, N+LName+AR="سعيد"

غَلَبَ, V+Synt=Tr+AR="غلب"+Voix=A+
Temps=I+Pers=3+Genre=m+Nombre=s

نَبِيلٌ, N+FName+Genre=m+AR="نبيل"

قَرُوي, N+LName+AR="قروي"

Fig. 5. Morphological analysis of the first TD sentence

We present two other examples – ستاد 14 جانفي مسكر (stAd 14 jAnfI msakkar) 'The stadium is closed on 14 January' and خرجنا نهار 14 جانفي (khrajnA nhAr 14 jAnfI) 'we went out on 14 January'. Figure 6 shows that the word ستاد (stAd) 'stadium' is an establishment noun, the word نهار (nhAr) 'day' is a day indicator, and the word جانفي (jAnfI) 'January' is a month name.

سْتَا د, N+AR="ملعب"+Nombre=s+Genre=m

جَانفِي, N+Date+Mois+AR="جانفي"

مُسَكَّر, ADJ+AR="مغلق"+Genre=m+Nombre=s

خْرُجْنَا, V+InTr+AR="خرج"+Voix=A+Temps=I+Pers=1+Nombre=p

نَهَا رْ, N+PartDay+AR="يوم"+Nombre=s+Genre=m

Fig. 6. Morphological analysis of the second and third TD sentences

After applying the grammar of ANER and translation from TD into MSA on our test corpus, we obtained the results that are given in the NooJ concordance table. In Fig. 7, we present an extract of the results from our corpus, precisely, for the three sentences indicated above.

	Seq.
+PROF+PERS>	رئيس الجمهورية قيس سعيّد/ENAMEX>قيس سعيّد رئيس الجمهوريّة
+NAME+PERS>	نبيل القروي/ENAMEX>نبيل القروي
+ETAB+ORG>	ستاد 14 جانفي/ENAMEX>ملحب 14 جانفي
+DATE>	نهار 14 جانفي/TIMEX>يوم 14جانفي

Fig. 7. Extract of results of recognized and translated NEs

The concordance table exhibits the longest match and all matches that correspond to our syntactic grammar. Figure 7 shows the results of the sentences mentioned above.

The first NE رئيس الجمهورية قيس سعيّد (raIs iljumhUriyah qays s'yid) 'the president of the Republic Kais Said' is annotated as <ENAMEX+PERS+PROF> which mean is a profession NEs and it is translated into MSA رئيس الجمهورية قيس سعيّد (raIsu aljumhUriyati qays s'yid). The second NE, نبيل القروي(nabIl ilqarwI) 'Nabil Karoui', is annotated as <ENAMEX+PERS+NAME> which means that it is a person name, and it is translated into MSA as نبيل القروي(nabIl alqarwI). The third NE ستاد 14 جانفي(stAd 14 jAnfI) 'the stadium 14 January' is annotated as <ENAMEX+ORG+ETAB> which mean it is a public establishment and it is translated into MSA ملعب 14 جانفي(mal'abu 14 jAnfI). The fourth NE, نهار 14 جانفي(nhAr 14 jAnfI) '14 January', is annotated as <TIMEX+DATE> and it is translated into MSA as يوم 14 جانفي(yawma 14 jAnfI).

In Table 8, we present the obtained results by calculating the precision, recall, and f-measure metrics of the recognized NEs. This table shows the result of ENAMEX and its sub-categories, TIMEX and NUMEX.

Table 8. Obtained results

	Precision	Recall	F-measure
ENAMEX	91%	83%	86.81%
TIMEX	96%	**94%**	**94.98%**
NUMEX	**98%**	91%	94.37%

Table 8 shows that there are some problems that are not yet resolved. Some problems are related to the lack of standards for writing proper names. For example, the first name الصحبي(elsa7bi) 'Alsahbi' cannot be recognized. This problem produces silence. Other problems are related to TD. We can find a NE recognized as NUMEX, but it is not. One example is واحد صاحبي(wAhid sAhbI) 'My friend'. It is true that this starts with a number, but it is not an NE of measure. Such problems as these are rare, but they produce noise.

Thanks to different types of translation, we obtained finer results. Ninety-six percent of the NEs that our system supplies were well translated while respecting the specificities of MSA. The obtained results are ambitious, but they do show that there are some problems. These problems are related to the multiple translations attributed to homographs. For example, to the word مكتب(maktab) because it can be translated like مدرسة(madrassatun) 'school', or مكتب(maktabun) 'office'.

6 Conclusion

In this paper, we have developed an ANER and translation system from TD to MSA implemented in the NooJ platform and based on the linguistic approach. This system recognizes the different types of NEs. In addition, it is based on bilingual dictionaries and grammars. Thereby, the grammars are specified by a set of finite-state transducers and by adopting NooJ's new technologies. The evaluation is performed on a set of sentences belonging to a TD corpus. The obtained results are ambitious and show that our system can efficiently translate NEs into MSA despite the origins of words and the phenomenon of agglutination.

In the future, we will continue to extend the coverage of our designed bilingual dictionaries. In addition, we will improve the quality of our translation system.

References

1. Abdul-Hamid, A., Darwish, K.: Simplified feature set for Arabic named entity recognition. In: Proceedings of the 2010 Named Entities Workshop, pp. 110–115, July 2010
2. Benajiba, Y., Diab, M., Rosso, P.: Arabic named entity recognition using optimized feature sets. In: Proceedings of the 2008 Conference on Empirical Methods in Natural Language Processing, pp. 284–293, October 2008
3. Benajiba, Y., Rosso, P., Benedíruiz, J.: Anersys: an Arabic named entity recognition system based on maximum entropy. In: Gelbukh, A. (ed.) CICLing 2007. LNCS, vol. 4394, pp. 143–153. Springer, Heidelberg (2007). https://doi.org/10.1007/978-3-540-70939-8_13
4. Darwish, K., Gao, W.: Simple effective microblog named entity recognition: Arabic as an example. In: LREC, pp. 2513–2517, May 2014
5. Fehri, H., Haddar, K., Hamadou, A.B.: Recognition and translation of Arabic named entities with NooJ using a new representation model. In: Proceedings of the 9th International Workshop on Finite State Methods and Natural Language Processing, pp. 134–142, July 2011
6. Hkiri, E., Mallat, S., Zrigui, M.: Arabic-English text translation leveraging hybrid NER. In: Proceedings of the 31st Pacific Asia Conference on Language, Information and Computation, pp. 124–131, November 2017
7. El bazi, I., Laachfoubi, N.: Rena: a named entity recognition system for Arabic. In: Král, P., Matoušek, V. (eds.) TSD 2015. LNCS (LNAI), vol. 9302, pp. 396–404. Springer, Cham (2015). https://doi.org/10.1007/978-3-319-24033-6_45
8. Mesfar, S.: Named entity recognition for Arabic using syntactic grammars. In: Kedad, Z., Lammari, N., Métais, E., Meziane, F., Rezgui, Y. (eds.) NLDB 2007. LNCS, vol. 4592, pp. 305–316. Springer, Heidelberg (2007). https://doi.org/10.1007/978-3-540-73351-5_27
9. Shaalan, K., Oudah, M.: A hybrid approach to Arabic named entity recognition. J. Inf. Sci. **40**(1), 67–87 (2014)
10. Silberztein, M.: The Formalisation of Natural Languages: The NooJ Approach, 346 p. Wiley, Hoboken (2016)
11. Torjmen, R., Haddar, K.: Construction of morphological grammars for the Tunisian dialect. In: Mauro Mirto, I., Monteleone, M., Silberztein, M. (eds.) NooJ 2018. CCIS, vol. 987, pp. 62–74. Springer, Cham (2019). https://doi.org/10.1007/978-3-030-10868-7_6
12. Torjmen, R., Haddar, K.: Morphological aanalyzer for the Tunisian dialect. In: Sojka, P., Horák, A., Kopeček, I., Pala, K. (eds.) TSD 2018. LNCS (LNAI), vol. 11107, pp. 180–187. Springer, Cham (2018). https://doi.org/10.1007/978-3-030-00794-2_19
13. Zirikly, A., Diab, M..: Named entity recognition system for dialectal Arabic. In: Proceedings of the EMNLP 2014 Workshop on Arabic Natural Language Processing (ANLP), pp. 78–86, October 2014
14. Zirikly, A., Diab, M.: Named entity recognition for Arabic social media. In: Proceedings of the 1st Workshop on Vector Space Modeling for Natural Language Processing, pp. 176–185, June 2015

A Legal Question Answering Ontology-Based System

Ismahane Kourtin[1,2]([✉]), Samir Mbarki[2], and Abdelaaziz Mouloudi[2]

[1] ELLIADD Laboratory, Bourgogne-Franche-Comté University, Besançon, France
kourtin_ismahane.math@yahoo.fr
[2] MISC Laboratory, Faculty of Science, Ibn Tofail University, Kenitra, Morocco
mbarkisamir@hotmail.com, mouloudi_aziz@hotmail.com

Abstract. Question-answering systems (QASs) aim to provide a relevant and concise answer to questions asked in natural language by a user. In this article, we describe our method of developing a question-answering system, operating in the legal domain in Morocco, which mostly uses the French and Arabic languages, and sometimes English. Its purpose is to give relevant and concise answers to questions in the legal domain, stated in natural language by a user, without him having to go through the legal documents to find an answer to his question. The implementation of the proposed system is based on three processes: the first process consists of modeling the legal domain knowledge by an ontology, both (i) independent of the language, and (ii) capable of supporting several languages. The second process consists of extracting the RDF triplet components from the user's question. The third process consists of reformulating the question by a SPARQL query(s) with which we can query the ontology and thus retrieve the appropriate answer to the question asked by the user.

Keywords: Question-answering system · QAS · Information retrieval · Natural language processing · NLP · NooJ · Legal domain · Ontology · RDF · SPARQL

1 Introduction

The mass of information in the legal domain, which is constantly increasing, has generated a capital need to organize and structure the contents of available documents, and thus transform them into an intelligent guide capable of providing complete and immediate answers to natural language queries. Hence, question-answering systems (QASs) respond perfectly to this need by offering different mechanisms to provide adequate and precise answers to questions expressed in natural language.

Our objective is to set up a QAS operating in the legal domain in Morocco, which mostly uses the French and Arabic languages, and sometimes English. Its purpose is to give a relevant and concise answer to questions in the legal domain, stated in natural language by a user, without him having go through the legal documents to find an answer to his question. The implementation of the proposed system is based on three processes: the first process consists of modeling the legal domain knowledge by an ontology, both

© Springer Nature Switzerland AG 2021
B. Bekavac et al. (Eds.): NooJ 2020, CCIS 1389, pp. 218–229, 2021.
https://doi.org/10.1007/978-3-030-70629-6_19

(i) independent of the language, and (ii) capable of supporting several languages. The second process consists of extracting RDF triplet components from the user's question. The third process consists of reformulating the question by SPARQL query(s) with which we can query the ontology and thus retrieve the appropriate answer to the question asked by the user.

The rest of this paper is organized as follows: Sect. 2 presents related work on QASs, their criteria, and classifications, as well as the main motivations for our project. Section 3 describes the methodology proposed for the ontological modeling of the legal domain. Section 4 presents the principle and architecture of the proposed QAS. Section 5 describes the approach used in the question analysis, starting with the definition of the types of questions, followed by the categorization of the legal questions, then the development of patterns according to question category, and finally, the construction of grammars for extracting data from questions. Section 6 presents the SPARQL query generation corresponding to the question. Finally, we end this paper with the results of the experimentation of our system in Sect. 7 and conclude in Sect. 8.

2 Question Answering Systems

QASs are defined in [1]. They aim to give a relevant and concise answer to questions asked in natural language by a user. They claim to be a first step towards the realization of one of the fantasies of artificial intelligence, namely, the possibility for a human to communicate with a machine as if it were another human. From a more realistic point of view, QASs offer a very interesting alternative to keyword queries, whose expressiveness is limited, and formal query languages, whose complexity is unsuitable for end users. They have been the subject of active research since the late 1960s.

Based on the literature studied, we identify three main criteria that differentiate between the available QASs: (1) the application domains for which QASs are developed, (2) the types of data sources used in extracting responses, and (3) approaches used for the analysis of questions and source documents. Table 1 gives a brief description of each criterion and the classification of QASs based on each criterion with some examples.

No QAS has been developed for the legal domain in Morocco. Therefore, we have decided to develop a restricted domain QAS, operating in the legal domain in Morocco, which mostly uses French, Arabic, and sometimes English. We have chosen to use a legal domain ontology as a data source given the reliability of the answers that can be obtained thanks to structured data sources, such as ontologies, and their capacity to support several languages according to our ontological modeling method of the legal domain. For the analysis of users' questions, we opted for a pattern-based linguistic approach using the NooJ natural language processing platform. This platform allows the construction, testing, and managing of formal descriptions in several natural languages, in the form of electronic dictionaries and grammars.

3 Proposed Ontological Modeling of the Legal Domain

The first phase in the development of the proposed QAS consists of building an ontology of the legal domain.

Table 1. The main criteria of QASs and their classifications

Criterion	Explanation	Classifications	Examples
(1) Application domain	Users' questions are related to the application domain, which can be restricted or open Restricted domain QASs are suitable for domain expert users, as they need specialized answers, while open domain QASs are suitable for casual users who are very numerous	• Restricted domain QASs	• Start [2] • Webcoop [3] • Naluri [4]
		• Open domain QAS	• Webclopedia [5] • Mulder [6] • Answerbus [7]
(2) Types of data sources used in extracting responses	There are three types of data sources: structured data sources (relational databases or ontologies), semi-structured data sources (XML documents), and un-structured data sources (collections of documents or the web) The reliability of answers is higher in QASs that use structured data sources because the correct information is stored in the data source, but they are labor intensive to build	• Structured data sources	• NLIDB [8] • BASEBALL [9] • LUNAR [10]
		• Semi-structured data sources	• Start [2] • Webcoop [3] • Naluri [4] • Webclopedia [5]
		• Un-structured data sources	• Mulder [6] • Answerbus [7]
(3) Approaches used for question and source-document analysis	There are three types of approach: statistical approaches (using quantitative relationships), pattern-based linguistic approaches (using linguistic rules and human knowledge) and hybrid approaches (statistical and linguistic) Statistical approaches do not require any expert knowledge but do not take into account the semantics and context of words and sentences; linguistic approaches deal more effectively with questions but require expert or domain knowledge; and hybrid approaches minimize the limitations of statistical and linguistic approaches	• Statistical approach	
		• pattern-based linguistic approach	• Webclopedia [5] • Start [2] • Answerbus [7] • Webcoop [3] • Naluri [4]
		• Hybrid approach	• Mulder [6]

The knowledge representation community appropriated the term ontology during the 1990s to designate the object resulting from a knowledge modeling process. The most consensual definition of an ontology is that introduced by Gruber [11] and extended by Borst [12]: an ontology is an explicit formal specification of the shared conceptualization of a given domain. Studer [13] details this definition: formal refers to the fact that the specification must be machine readable; explicit means that the types of concepts and the constraints on their use are explicitly defined; conceptualization refers to an abstract model of a certain phenomenon of the world based on the identification of the relevant concepts of this phenomenon; and shared refers to the notion that an ontology captures consensual knowledge, which is not unique to an individual but validated by a group.

The ontology is based on the RDF model, which allows users to represent and exchange knowledge as triplets. The RDF model is a triplet model in which we describe resources by triplets: (subject, predicate, object). For example, modelling in RDF the statement: "Article 9 of the general tax code is entitled 'taxable products'", consists of breaking down this statement in a controlled language, into elementary units, which will each be able to be represented by a triplet.

- "article 9" has for field "the general tax code",
- "article 9" has for title "taxable products".

We thus obtain two triplets which both have as subject "article 9":

- (article 9, field, the general tax code)
- (article 9, title, taxable products).

We will now differentiate between what we will call a *concept* and a *term*. Indeed, there are several ways to call "article 9". For example, we can say "article 9" in French and English, and "المادة 9"in Arabic. But these two terms can refer to the same notion, the same concept that we would share between English, French, and Arabic speakers. We will therefore say here, for example, that there is a concept – let's call it concept **#TCARTICLE9** – which represents "article 9", and that we will attach to this concept the label "article 9" in French and English, and the label "المادة 9"in Arabic. In the same way, there is a concept – let's call it concept **#TC** – which represents "the general tax code", and that we will attach to this concept the label "le code général des impôts" in French, the label "the general tax code" in English, and the label "المدونة الـ عامة لـ ضرائب بـ"in Arabic (see Fig. 2). These identifiers, their organization, and the logical dependencies that exist between them, are what we will call a formal ontology. It is this knowledge in the logic of the legal domain that we will put into a machine so that the machine is able to simulate the inferences that we naturally make.

The legal domain is made up of a set of documents called "codes", each dealing with a specific subject. Therefore, we have opted for a modular construction, by code, of the legal domain. In this regard, we have decided to start with the general tax code. The first part of the constructed ontology includes the architecture and the decomposition of the general tax code into subdomains and articles. To represent this machine knowledge, we used the RDF language Turtle syntax, the RDFS and OWL vocabularies, as well as the two ontologies: SKOS, which allows us to represent thesauri, and the Dublin Core, which allows us to describe documents (Fig. 1).

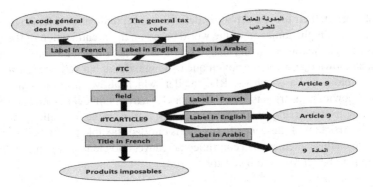

Fig. 1. Representation graph of ontology concepts and their labels

4   Proposed Question-Answering System

The ontology is based on the RDF model, which allows us to represent and exchange knowledge as triplets (subject, predicate, object). In addition, SPARQL is a query language that allows us to query RDF graphs. This means that, if we know at least one element of a triplet, then we can query the RDF graph through SPARQL queries to retrieve the rest of the data from the triplet. For example, in the triplet (article 9, title, taxable products), if we know the name of the subject, which is "article 9" and its desired property which is the "title", then we can recover through a SPARQL query, which will query the ontology, the value of this property which is "taxable products". This answers the question: What is the title of article 9 of the general tax code?

So our challenge is to analyze the user's question and extract the components of its RDF triplet(s). These RDF triplet components will be transformed into SPARQL queries which retrieve, from the ontology, the values of the unknowns of the triplets, which retrieves the answer to the user's question. Figure 2 illustrates the overall architecture of the proposed QAS.

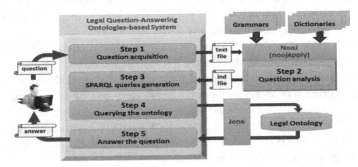

Fig. 2. The overall architecture of the proposed question-answering system

Step 1: Question acquisition. The QAS is developed by java programming language. It includes an interface allowing the user to select the input language, edit his question, select the response language (by default, the input language), and finally, send his question (see Fig. 3). The content of the entry, containing the user's question, and the input and answer languages, is saved in a text file.

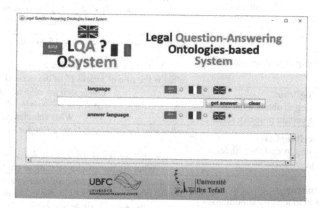

Fig. 3. The question-answering system interface

Step 2: Question analysis. The text file containing the question, and the input and answer languages, is transmitted to NooJ platform with noojapply, which allows, from a constructed grammar according to the input language, to extract the components of the RDF triplet(s) of the question. The result of the extraction is retrieved as an ".ind" file. The question analysis process and extraction grammars will be detailed in Sect. 5.

Step 3: SPARQL query generation. After having retrieved the file containing the RDF triplet components of the question, we extract these components from the file, and then we generate the appropriate SPARQL query specifying the language of the requested data depending on the response language chosen by the user.

Step 4: Querying the ontology. In this step we use the SPARQL query built into step 3, to query our legal ontology using jena API. This allows us to retrieve the unknown values of the RDF triplet(s) of the user's question in the language chosen by the user.

Step 5: Answer the question. Finally, the result obtained is displayed in the system interface, in the response language chosen by the user.

5   Question Analysis

5.1   Types of Questions

Whatever the domain and the used language, questions can be grouped into two types according to the expected answer: Boolean questions whose answer is either yes or no ("**AskQuestion**"); and questions that require a constructed answer ("**SelectQuestion**").

5.2   Categories of Legal Questions

Based on the study of the topics covered by the articles, six categories of legal questions were identified according to their objective (see Table 2).

Table 2. Categories of legal questions with examples

Category	Example
YesNoHavingProp: questions aiming to find out whether the value of a property corresponds or not	*Est-ce que les véhicules agricoles sont taxables?* ﻟ ﻟﻀﺮﻳ ﺑﺔ؟ ﺧﺎﺿﻌﺔ اﻟﺰراﻋ ﻳﺔ اﻟ ﺳ ﻴﺎرات ﻫﻰ Are agricultural vehicles taxable?
ValueOfProp: questions aiming to find out the value of a property	*Quel est l'intitulé de l'article 15 du code général des impôts?* ـ ﻟ ﻟﻀﺮاﺋ ب؟ اﻟ ﻌﺎﻣﺔ اﻟﻤﺪوﻧﺔ ﻣﻦ 15 اﻟﻤﺎدة ﻋ ﻨﻮان ﻫ و ﻣﺎ What is the title of article 15 of the general tax code?
EntitiesHavingProp: questions aiming to obtain a list of entities with a certain property value	*Quels sont les véhicules taxables?* ﻟ ﻟﻀﺮﻳ ﺑﺔ؟ اﻟ ﺧﺎﺿﻌﺔ اﻟﻤﺮﻛ ﺑﺎت ﻫﻲ ﻣﺎ What vehicles are taxable?
ArticlesPrescribingClass: questions aiming to find the articles relating to a given subject	*Quelles sont les articles relatifs à l'impôt sur les sociétés?* اﻟ ﺷﺮﻛﺎت؟ ﻋ ﻠﻰ ﺑ اﻟ ﺿﺮﻳ ﺑﺔ اﻟﻤ ﺘﻌﻠ ﻘﺔ اﻟﻤﻮاد ﻫﻲ ﻣﺎ What are the articles relating to corporate tax?
ConditionOnProp: questions used to identify conditions or contexts on a certain property value	*Dans quelles conditions les coopératives sont exonéré des impôts?* اﻟ ﺿﺮاﺋ ب؟ ﻣﻦ اﻟ ﺘﻌﺎوﻧ ﻴﺎت إﻋ ﻔﺎء ﺷﺮوط ﻫﻲ ﻣﺎ Under what conditions are cooperatives exempt from taxes?
TargetedEntities: questions aiming to identify the entities targeted by a given legal text	*Quels types de véhicules sont concernés par l'article 259 du code général des impôts?* اﻟﻤﺪوﻧﺔ ﻣﻦ 259 اﻟﻤﺎدة ﺗ ﻐﻄ ﻴﻬﺎ اﻟ ﺘﻲ اﻟﻤﺮﻛ ﺑﺎت أﻧ ﻮاع ﻫﻲ ﻣﺎ ﻟ ﻟﻀﺮاﺋ ب؟ اﻟ ﻌﺎﻣﺔ What types of vehicles are covered by article 259 of the general tax code?

5.3 Construction of Patterns and Extraction Grammars

For the question analysis and the extraction of their data, we used a linguistic approach based on patterns. The question data extraction process consists of looking for correspondences between the patterns and the question. Each category of question is represented by a pattern. The patterns are based on a formal language and will be described by grammars in the NooJ platform. Note that a question is a sequence of words that can be divided into three parts: the question type ("**QuestionType**"), which can be either "AskQuestion" or "SelectQuestion" (see Sect. 5.1 for details), the question body ("**QuestionBody**"), which is formed by one of the categories of questions mentioned in Subsect. 5.2, and finally, the question mark ("**QuestionMark**"), which is the symbol *?* in French and English, and the symbol ؟ in Arabic. Table 3 shows the lexical representation of the question type, Table 4 shows the lexical representation of the question body from the "ValueOfProp" category, Table 5 shows the lexical representation of the question mark, and Table 6 shows the decomposition of a question from the "ValueOfProp" category according to the established patterns.

Table 3. Lexical representation of the question type

French	QuestionType	= :SelectQuestion | :AskQuestion;
	SelectQuestion	= :Ws :BePredicate :Article;
	Ws	= Qui | Quel | Dans quel;
	BePredicate	= est | sont;
	Article	= le | la | l';
	AskQuestion	= Est-ce que;
Arab	QuestionType	= :SelectQuestion | :AskQuestion;
	SelectQuestion	= :Ws :BePredicate;
	Ws	= من | ما;
	BePredicate	= هو | هم | هي;
	AskQuestion	= هل;
English	QuestionType	= :SelectQuestion | :AskQuestion;
	SelectQuestion	= :Ws :BePredicate :Article;
	Ws	= What | Who;
	BePredicate	= is | are;
	Article	= the;
	AskQuestion	= is | are | does | did;

Table 4. Lexical representation of the question body from the "ValueOfProp" category

French	ValueOfProp	= :Property :Of :Subject (<E> | :OfRestriction :Restriction);
	Property	= <WF> <WF>*;
	Of	= de (l' | la) | du;
	Subject	= <WF> <WF>* (<E> | <NB>);
	OfRestriction	= du | (dans) (le | la | l') ;
	Restriction	= <WF> <WF>* (<E> | <NB>);
Arab	ValueOfProp	= :Property :Of :Subject (<E> | :OfRestriction :Restriction);
	Property	= <WF> <WF>*;
	Of	= ال | أل;
	Subject	= <WF> <WF>* (<E> | <NB>);
	OfRestriction	= في | من ;
	Restriction	= <WF> <WF>* (<E> | <NB>) ;
English	ValueOfProp	= :Property :Of :Subject (<E> | :OfRestriction :Restriction);
	Property	= <WF> <WF>*;
	Of	= of (<E> | the);
	Subject	= <WF> <WF>* (<E> | <NB>);
	OfRestriction	= of (<E> | the);
	Restriction	= <WF> <WF>* (<E> | <NB>);

Table 5. Lexical representation of the question mark

French	QuestionMark = ? ;
Arab	QuestionMark = ؟ ;
English	QuestionMark = ? ;

Table 6. The decomposition of a question from ValueOfProp category with established patterns

Language	Example
French	QuestionType Property Of Subject OfRestriction Restriction QuestionMark Quel est l' intitulé de l' article 15 du code général des impôts ?
Arab	QuestionMark Restriction OfRestriction Subject Of Property QuestionType ؟ المدونة العامة للضرائب من 15 مادة ال عنوان ما هو
English	QuestionType Property Of Subject OfRestriction Restriction QuestionMark What is the title of article 15 of the general tax code ?

5.4 Grammars for Extracting Data from Questions

We have built a grammar which extracts the RDF triplet components from questions from the "ValueOfProp" category, and this for each language integrated into the system, namely Arabic, French, and English. Below, we present the extraction grammar established for English.

Extraction Grammar for the English Language. The grammar in Fig. 4 describes the main components of the question. The grammar of Fig. 5 recognizes the RDF components of questions from the "ValueOfProp" category. Figure 6 shows the result of the extraction by the constructed grammar: the question category and RDF components.

Fig. 4. Grammar that recognizes the main components of the question in English

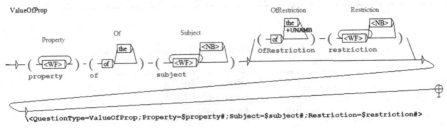

Fig. 5. Grammar that extracts RDF components from ValueOfProp category questions

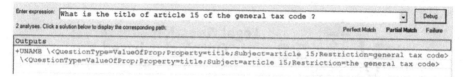

Fig. 6. Extraction result by the constructed grammar applied to a question in English

6 SPARQL Query Generation

Once the RDF components of the question in natural language are extracted, the last step is to build an equivalent SPARQL query. The following is a the SPARQL query corresponding to the question in English dealt with in Subsects. 5.3 and 5.4 (Fig. 7).

```
select DISTINCT ?value
where {
   ?x   a skos:Concept;
        skos:altLabel ?subject;
        skos:prefLabel ?value;
        skos:broaderTransitive ?y.
   ?y   a skos:Concept;
        skos:prefLabel   ?restriction.
   FILTER (regex(?subject, "^article 15$", "i")
           && langMatches(lang(?subject), "en") = true
           && regex(?restriction, "^the general tax code$", "i")
           && langMatches(lang(?restriction), "en") = true
           && langMatches(lang(?value), "en") = true)
   }
```

Fig. 7. Extract from the SPARQL query corresponding to the question analyzed in English

7 Experimentation and Evaluation

The developed system is able to answer questions about the architecture of the general tax code such as the title of a given article. Moreover, the system is able to answer questions in French, Arabic or English, such as:

- *Quel est l'intitulé de l'article 15 du code général des impôts ?*
- ؟بئارضلل ةماعلا ةنودملا نم 5ما هو عنوان المادة 1
- What is the title of article 15 of the general tax code?

Figure 7 shows the result obtained by the system in response to the question in English language: What is the title of article 15 of the general tax code? (Fig. 8).

Fig. 8. The system's response to a question in English

8 Conclusion

In this work we have developed the first version of a multilingual system operating in the legal domain based on ontologies. In the first phase of the development of the system, we modeled the legal domain knowledge with an ontology that is both independent of language and capable of supporting several languages; then, in the second phase, we typed and categorized the questions of the legal domain, and we established the patterns and constructed grammars for extracting the RDF triplet components from "ValueOfProp" category questions for Arabic, French, and English; and finally, in the third phase, we formulated the equivalent SPARQL query to the RDF triplet of the question, which we used to query the ontology in order to retrieve the unknown of the RDF triplet(s) of the question and thus answer the question of a user asked in natural language.

In the future, we will extend our ontological modeling work on the content of the general tax code before extending it to the other codes, and we will establish grammars for other categories of questions and formulate the equivalent SPARQL queries. We will also build a corpus of questions for the legal domain which will serve both to enrich the established categories of legal questions, and as a basis for testing the reliability of the system developed.

References

1. Hirschman, L., Gaizauskas, R.: Natural language question answering: the view from here. Nat. Lang. Eng. **7**(4), 275–300 (2001). https://dl.acm.org/citation.cfm?id=973891
2. Katz, B., et al.: Omnibase: uniform access to heterogeneous data for question answering. In: Andersson, B., Bergholtz, M., Johannesson, P. (eds.) NLDB 2002. LNCS, vol. 2553, pp. 230–234. Springer, Heidelberg (2002). https://doi.org/10.1007/3-540-36271-1_23

3. Farah, B.: Cooperative question answering in restricted domains: the WEBCOOP experiments. In: Workshop on Question Answering in Restricted Domains, 42nd Annual Meeting of the Association for Computational Linguistics, Barcelona, Spain, pp. 31–38 (2004)
4. Wong, W.: Practical approach to knowledge-based question answering with natural language understanding and advanced reasoning (M.Sc. thesis), Kolej Universiti Teknikal Kebangsaan Malaysia (2004)
5. Hovy, E., Gerber, L., Hermjacob, U., Junk, M., Lin, C.: Question answering in webclopedia. In: Ninth Text Retrieval Conference. NIST Special Publication, vol. 500–249, pp. 655–664. National Institute of Standards and Technology, Gaithersburg (2000)
6. Kwok, C., Etzioni, O., Weld, D.S.: Scaling question answering to the web. ACM Trans. Inf. Syst. (TOIS) 19(3), 242–262 (2001)
7. Zheng, Z.: The AnswerBus question answering system. In: Proceedings of Human Language Technology Conference HLT, San Diego, CA, 24–27, March (2002)
8. Androutsopoulos, I., Ritchie, G., Thanisch, P.: Natural language interfaces to databases–an introduction. J. Lang. Eng. 1(1), 29–81 (1995)
9. Green, B.F., Chomsky, C., Laughery, K.: BASEBALL: an automatic question answerer. In: Proceedings of the Western Joint Computer Conference, pp. 219–224. Institute of Radio Engineers, New York (1961)
10. Woods, W.: Progress in natural language understanding – an application to lunar geology. In: Proceedings of the American Federation of Information Processing Societies (AFIPS), vol. 42, pp. 441–450 (1973)
11. Gruber, T.R.: A translation approach to portable ontology specifications. Knowl. Acquisition 5(2), 199–220 (1993). https://secs.ceas.uc.edu/~mazlack/ECE.716.Sp2011/Semantic.Web.Ontology.Papers/Gruber.93a.pdf
12. Borst, W.N.: Construction of engineering ontologies for knowledge sharing and reuse. Universiteit Twente (1997). https://doc.utwente.nl/17864
13. Studer, R., Richard Benjamins, V., Fensel, D.: Knowledge engineering: principles and methods. Data Knowl. Eng. 25(1), 161–197 (1998). https://www.sciencedirect.com/science/article/pii/S0169023X97000566

A Bottom-Up Approach for Moroccan Legal Ontology Learning from Arabic Texts

Kaoutar Belhoucine[✉][ID], Mohammed Mourchid, Samir Mbarki,
and Abdelaaziz Mouloudi

Faculty of Science, MISC Laboratory, Ibn Tofail University, Kénitra, Morocco
kaoutar.belhoucine@gmail.com, mourchidm@hotmail.com,
mbarkisamir@hotmail.com, mouloudi_aziz@hotmail.com

Abstract. Ontologies constitute an exciting model for representing a domain of interest, since they enable information-sharing and reuse. Existing inference machines can also use them to reason about various contexts. However, ontology construction is a time-consuming and challenging task. The ontology learning field answers this problem by providing automatic or semi-automatic support to extract knowledge from various sources, such as databases and structured and unstructured documents. This paper reviews the ontology learning process from unstructured text and proposes a bottom-up approach to building legal domain-specific ontology from Arabic texts. In this work, the learning process is based on Natural Language Processing (NLP) techniques and includes three main tasks: corpus study, term acquisition, and conceptualization. Corpus study enriches the original corpus with valuable linguistic information. Term acquisition selects tagged lemmas sequences as potential term candidates, and conceptualization drives concepts and their relationships from the extracted terms. We used the NooJ platform to implement the required linguistic resources for each task. Further, we developed a Java module to enrich the ontology vocabulary from the Arabic WordNet (AWN) project.

The obtained results were essential but incomplete. The legal expert revised them manually, and then they were used to refine and expand a domain ontology for a Moroccan Legal Information Retrieval System (LIRS).

Keywords: Ontology learning · Taxonomies definition · Arabic WordNet · NooJ · Legal field · Arabic text

1 Introduction

Ontologies hold great importance for modern knowledge-based systems. They serve as explicit, conceptual knowledge models to share a common understanding of information in a domain and make that knowledge available to information systems [1]. However, the manual construction of ontologies is an expensive and time-consuming task because of the difficulty in capturing knowledge, an issue also known as the "knowledge acquisition bottleneck." A solution for this issue is providing automatic or at least semi-automatic support for ontology construction. This operation is usually referred to as Ontology Learning (OL) [2].

© Springer Nature Switzerland AG 2021
B. Bekavac et al. (Eds.): NooJ 2020, CCIS 1389, pp. 230–242, 2021.
https://doi.org/10.1007/978-3-030-70629-6_20

Cimiano [3] compares the tasks involved in OL to forming a layered cake. The cake is composed, in ascending order, of term acquisition, synonym acquisition, concept formation, taxonomy definition, relation definition, and finally, axiom definition (see Fig. 1). Several ontology-learning tools are proposed in the literature for accomplishing these tasks [4–6]. They differ according to input data types (format and language), output formats, and mainly the methods used in order to extract the ontological structures. Unfortunately, the Arabic language is still not supported by these tools, even though it is one of the most common languages spoken worldwide.

In this paper, we deal with ontology learning from Arabic legal texts. We use the NooJ linguistic platform to semi-automatically process the identified steps: corpus study, term acquisition, and conceptualization. Then we use the AWN project to accomplish the ontology enrichment. Section 2 presents the overall ontology learning process from text: input, output, existing approaches, and prominent ontology learning tools. Section 3 discusses related works in the legal domain. In Sect. 4, we describe the proposed learning process and its implementation in NooJ. Section 5 comments on the learning process and the obtained results. Finally, in Sect. 6, we present our conclusions and plans for future work.

2 Ontology Learning

The term ontology learning refers to the automatic or semi-automatic support for the construction of an ontology [7]. It aims at extracting ontological elements (conceptual knowledge) from a given input text with limited human exertion. Techniques from established fields, such as NLP, data mining, and information retrieval, have been fundamental in developing ontology learning methods [8]. This section presents the inputs used to learn ontologies, the ontology learning tasks, and outputs, existing approaches, and most prominent ontology learning tools.

2.1 Input

There are three different kinds of ontology learning input data [9]: structured (such as databases), semi-structured (e.g., XML), and unstructured (natural language text documents). Unstructured data is the most widely available format for ontology learning input and presents the most common sources for ontology extraction [10]. However, processing unstructured data is a tedious task; indeed, human language is mostly very implicit and allows different people to conceptualize it in different manners [11]. The legal domain is strictly dependent on its linguistic expression and therefore inherits all the challenging problems that this implies. McCarty overtly claimed, "one of the main obstacles to progress in the field of artificial intelligence and law is the natural language barrier" [12].

2.2 Tasks and Outputs

Ontology learning is primarily concerned with defining concepts, relations, and (optionally) axioms from texts. Although there is no standard regarding this development process, Cimiano [3] describes the tasks involved in ontology learning as forming a layer cake (see Fig. 1). These tasks aim at returning six main outputs: terms, sometimes synonyms, concepts, taxonomic relations, non-taxonomic relations, and finally, axioms.

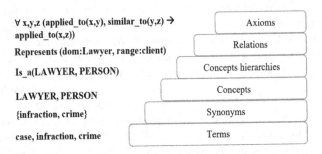

Fig. 1. Ontology Learning "Layer Cake" from [25].

Terms are the most basic building blocks of ontology learning [13]. They can be simple (i.e., single-word) or complex (i.e., multi-word), and are considered linguistic realizations of domain-specific concepts. There are many term extraction methods in the literature. Most of them are based on terminology and NLP research [14–16]; others, on information retrieval methods for term indexing [17].

Synonym discovery consists of finding words that denote the same concept [18]. The synonym layer addresses the acquisition of semantic term variants in and between languages. It is either based on sets, such as WordNet synsets [19] (after sense disambiguation), on clustering techniques [20–23], or on other similar methods, including Web-based knowledge acquisition.

Concepts can be abstract or concrete, real or fictitious. However, the consensus in this field is that concepts should include the following:

- Intension: a formal definition of the set of objects that this concept describes;
- Extension: a set of objects that the definition of this concept describes;
- Lexical realizations: a set of linguistic realizations, (multilingual) terms for this concept.

Most of the research in concept extraction addresses the question from a clustering perspective, regarding concepts as clusters of related terms [3]. This approach overlaps almost entirely with that of term and synonym extraction [24] and can be found in [25].

Concept hierarchies (generalization and specialization) or taxonomies are crucial for any knowledge-based system [24]. There are three main paradigms to induce concept hierarchies from texts:

- Lexico-syntactic patterns, as proposed in [26],
- Harris's distributional analysis using clustering algorithms [27],
- The document-based notion of term subsumption, as proposed in [28].

Relations refer to any relationship between concepts except taxonomical relations. This includes specific conceptual relationships such as synonymy, possession, attribute-of, and causality, as well as more general relationships referring to any labeled link between a source concept. In the literature, few approaches have addressed the issue of relations extraction from texts, such as the use of an association rules extraction algorithm [29] and the use of syntactic dependencies [30].

Lastly, axioms are propositions that are always taken as true. They act as a starting point for deducing other truths and verifying the correctness of existing ontological elements. The extraction of axioms from the text occurs at an early stage [31]. Initial blueprints of this task can be found in [32]. This work proposes an unsupervised method based on an extended version of Harris's distributional hypothesis in order to discover inference rules.

2.3 Approaches

Several approaches deal with ontology learning from textual resources in the literature. We briefly discuss the most relevant ones for our concerns. Aussenac-Gilles [33] proposed an ontology learning approach based on knowledge elicitation from technical documents. This approach enables the creation of a domain model by analyzing a given corpus using natural language processing (NLP) tools and linguistics techniques. It includes four main activities: corpus constitution, linguistic study, Normalization, and Formalization. Sabou [34] proposed a natural language processing approach that uses syntactic patterns to discover the dependency relations between words. This approach consists of four main steps: term extraction, conceptualization, and enrichment. Mazari [35] proposed an automatic construction approach that uses statistical techniques to extract elements of ontology from Arabic texts. The ontology learning tasks are carried out in three steps: preparing the corpus, extracting concepts, and discovering relations. In the legal domain, all ontology learning experiments mainly focus on concept extraction as the primary step in the ontology development process [36].

2.4 Tools

Ontology learning tools aim to reduce both the time and cost of the ontology development process. They differ in terms of input data types, output formats, and mainly the methods and algorithms used in order to extract the ontological structures. In this subsection, we present the most relevant ontology learning systems from unstructured textual resources.

TERMINAE [6] is a tool based on a methodology elaborated from practical experiments of ontology building. Its originality is to integrate linguistic and knowledge engineering tools. The linguistic engineering part allows term acquisition from textual resources. The knowledge engineering part provides knowledge-base management with an editor and browser for the ontology. This tool helps to represent a notion as a concept, which is called a terminological concept.

Text2Onto [7], is a framework for learning ontologies from textual resources. Text2Onto represents the learned knowledge into a meta-level model called a probabilistic ontology model (POM), which stores the learned primitives independently of a specific Knowledge Representation (KR) language. It calculates confidence about the correctness of the ontology elements and updates the learned knowledge each time the corpus is changed to avoid processing it from scratch.

Text-to-Knowledge (T2K) [8], is a generic computer platform for data and text mining. T2K extracts domain-specific information from texts by combining linguistic technologies and statistical techniques in three main phases: preprocess text and extract terms, form concepts, and relations or knowledge organization (Table 1).

Table 1. A summary of ontology learning tools.

Tools	Language	Elements extracted	Techniques
Terminae (2005)	French	Terms, synonyms, concepts, taxonomies, non-taxonomic relations	Linguistic and knowledge engineering
Text2Onto (2005)	English Spanish German	Terms, synonyms concepts, taxonomies, non-taxonomic relations, instances	Linguistic processing statistical text analysis, machine learning, association rules
T2K (2008)	Italien	Terms, concepts, taxonomies	Statistical text analysis and machine learning

Unfortunately, most of the existing ontology learning tools do not support Arabic language processing, while a few others lack support.

3 Related Work

Our proposed approach aims to use NLP techniques and tools in order to build a domain-specific ontology from Arabic textual resources. The most closely related works in the legal domain are Francesconi [37] and El Ghosh [10]. Francesconi [37] performed the term extraction task with two different acquisition tools: GATE for English texts and T2K for Italian.

The other tasks, such as evaluating terms, linking them to concepts, and defining relations, were processed under the supervision of ontology engineers and domain experts. For El Ghosh [10], the ontology extraction process has used Text2Onto and is composed of two main phases: linguistic preprocessing and extraction of modeling primitives (concepts, instances, taxonomies, general relations, and disjoint axioms). The resulting ontology is considered an inexpressive ontology and needs to be re-engineered.

Our work differs from previous work in the following aspects. First, we are processing Arabic, one of the most challenging natural languages in the NLP field. Second, we use the NooJ platform to implement the linguistic resources needed for term acquisition and conceptualization. Finally, we are developing a Java module to enrich the ontology vocabulary from the AWN project.

4 Our Work

After a comprehensive literature review, we can see that most of the approaches proposed for learning ontologies from text strongly depend on their specific environment, consisting of language, input, domain, and application. Thus, there is no standard regarding the ontology learning process and no guarantee that the (semi-) automatically generated ontology is sufficiently correct and precise to characterize the domain of interest [10].

For this reason, domain expert intervention throughout the learning process is highly necessary in order to control, complete, and validate the extracted elements. From this perspective, we defined a semi-automatically learning process that involves legal expert intervention and comprises mainly four tasks: corpus study, term acquisition, conceptualization, and enrichment. This section presents the corpus and the platform used to learn the ontology, introduces each learning task, and discusses the obtained results.

4.1 Corpus Definition

We constituted the corpus from the Moroccan family code (Fig. 2), which consists of Arabic natural language texts and includes seven main books composed of 400 articles of law, about 2,700 text units, and 18,000 different tokens.

Fig. 2. Moroccan family code Corpus excerpt.

4.2 Tool Selection

Arabic is a Semitic language that has a very complex morphology [38]; it is a highly inflected and agglutinative language; and, due to this complex morphology, it requires a set of preprocessing routines to be suitable for manipulation.

In the current project, we used NooJ [39] as a natural-language processing tool in order to formalize inflectional and derivational morphology, lexicon, regular grammars, and context-free grammars. NooJ uses an annotation mechanism (stored in each Text Annotation Structure, or TAS) that integrates every single piece of linguistic information, making it possible to combine morphological constraints in syntactic rules. NooJ is also a powerful corpus processor that supports sophisticated operations, such as information extraction, concordances, and statistical analyses.

4.3 Ontology Learning Process

Corpus Study. This step consists of a lexico-syntactic analysis of Moroccan legal texts. First, we built a legal domain-specific dictionary based on the family code dictionary available on the ADALA Morocco legal and judicial Portal [40]. The built dictionary comprises more than 1,000 entries, consisting of simple terms (nouns and adjectives), compound nouns, pronouns, prepositions, adverbs, and conjunctions. Furthermore, we added to the simple terms the required related inflectional and derivational forms. Below are some examples of the dictionary's entries (Table 2):

Table 2. Excerpt of dictionary entries.

ميراث,N+Juri+FLX=FlxM+DRV=Mawarit:Flx
هـدذ يـة حـالـ ة,N+UNAMB+Juri
شَرعِيّ,ADJ+Juri+FLX=FlxFM+DRV=DrvFM

Second, inspired by Mesfar [41], we modeled a set of morphological grammars that recognize the component morphemes of the agglutinative forms. For instance, the morphological grammar in Fig. 3 allows the identification of the agglutinative word, including various prefixes {[[definite article (the, الـ)], [prepositions (for, لـ), (by, بـ)], (conjunctions (and, و)]}, and the suffix [pronoun (her, ـه)], e.g.: (Her husband, زوجها), (By its expiration, بانتهائها).

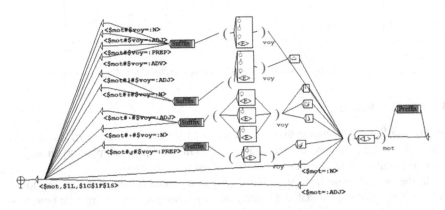

Fig. 3. A morphological grammar of tokenization.

Finally, to solve multi-word unit ambiguities, we modeled local grammars using the feature " + UNAMB". The local grammar in Fig. 4 recognizes as nouns both (Son, ابن) and (Son of son, ابن الإبن). The corpus was annotated with a lexical coverage rate of 81.83%, which we consider to be a very satisfactory result.

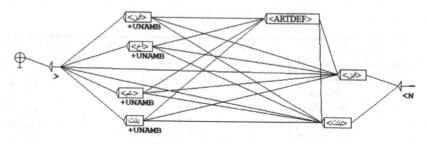

Fig. 4. A syntactic grammar for kinship relationship.

Term Acquisition. After preparing the corpus, we moved to extract the ontology elements. We identified manually, with the legal expert's help, about 13 patterns of nominal compositions that reference the potential candidate terms (see Table 3). We modeled these patterns using the NooJ local grammars and applied them to extract the corresponding sequences in the corpus. Finally, to keep only the relevant terms, we employed TF-IDF measures of the NooJ statistical module. As a result, we acquired 398 single and multi-word candidate terms.

Table 3. Patterns of the potential candidate terms.

1 unit Pattern	2 units Patterns	3 units Patterns
Noun	Noun_adjectif	Noun_noun_noun
	Adjectif_noun	Noun_noun_adjectif
	Noun_prep_noun	Noun_adjectif_noun
	Noun_prep_adjectif	Noun_noun_conj_noun
		Noun_noun_prep_noun
		Noun_adj_prep_noun

Conceptualization. In this step, concepts and their relations are derived from the extracted terms. We elaborated a cascade of local grammars that identifies the candidate terms sharing a large number of syntactic contexts, for instance, those sharing the same head or the same expansion (see Table 4.).

The legal expert used the obtained clusters to define the concepts, their properties, and semantic relationships between them – for instance, hyponymy, hypernymy, and synonymy. For example, the lexical units (daughter, بِنت), (wife, زوجة), and (father, أب) share the same syntactic context [(نفقة, expense), noun] and specialize the concept (Close relative, قريب). The lexical units (طلاق, divorce) and (زواج, marriage) share several syntactic contexts – [noun, (types, أنواع)], [noun, (date, تاريخ)] and [pre-pNoun, (registration of, بـ توثيق)] – and specialize the concept (Situation, حالة). Two hundred and thirty single and multiword concepts and 10 semantic relations were identified single and multiword, concepts were identified and 10 semantic relations.

Table 4. Excerpt of the clustered terms.

The terms sharing the expansion (طلاق, divorce)	The terms sharing the expansion (زواج, marriage)	The terms sharing the head (نفقة, expense)
الفسخ أوالطلاق	مستندات الزواج	نفقة القرابة
أسباب الطلاق	أهلية الزواج	نفقة المحضون
بتوثيق الطلاق	بتوثيق الزواج	نفقة نفسه
وثيقة الطلاق	رسم الزواج	نفقة الزوجة
أنواع الطلاق	ولي الزواج	نفقة الأقارب
عدة الطلاق	فترة الزواج	نفقة الأب
تاريخ الطلاق	انواع الزواج	نفقة البنت
عدة الطلاق	إثبات الزواج	نفقة الآباء
رسم الطلاق	تاريخ الزواج	

An excerpt can be seen in Fig. 5, below.

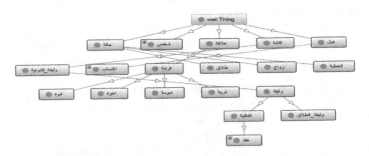

Fig. 5. Excerpt of the taxonomy identified.

Enrichment. At the end of the previous step, we added to the NooJ dictionary the semantic properties that referred to the concepts and their reference hypernym trees. In the current task, we identify the concept synonym sets from the AWN Project [42]. AWN is a lexical database for the Arabic language that groups words into clusters of synonyms called synsets that are linked by semantic relationships. Based on JAWS API [43], we developed a Java module that located for each simple word concept the corresponding synsets in AWN. If a concept had multiple senses, the module constructed an AWN hypernym tree for each and calculated their semantic similarity to the reference hypernym tree. Finally, the module adds the most similar sense's synonyms to the concept as semantic property in the NooJ dictionary. In following the structure of our lexicon:

Entry,GrammaticalCategory**+Concept+HypenymTree**=listOfString**+Synonyms**= istOfString

Example:

زَوْج,**N + Concept + HypernymTree** = شَخُص|قَريب|زَوْج+ **Synonyms** = زَوْج|قَرين|بَعْل|حَليل| شَّريك حَيَاة.

5 Discussion

This section briefly highlights the main issues and remarks identified throughout the learning process from Arabic legal texts. First, the Arabic language's complexity and lack of an ontology learning tool make the learning process from Arabic texts more complicated and challenging than learning from Romance languages. Second, the acquired pieces of information using lexical analysis and term extraction are essential but inexpressive. They need to be revised by a domain expert and re-engineered into the following ontological elements: concepts, concept properties, and relations. Third, analyzing a legal domain-specific corpus can identify relevant concepts and relationships relating to a regulated domain, which provides significant indications for building a legal domain ontology. Last, the NooJ platform offers all the linguistic tools required to implement the ontology learning methods proposed in the literature. Regrettably, it does not support knowledge engineering tools to model the ontological model.

6 Conclusion

In this article, we have presented an overview of ontology learning from text and proposed a bottom-up approach to building a legal domain-specific ontology from unstructured Arabic text. The learning process was identified. We used the linguistic platform NooJ as an NLP tool to extract the ontology elements (concepts and relations) and the AWN project to enrich the ontology vocabulary. The obtained results were validated and completed manually by the legal expert. Future work will focus on the formalization and implementation of the designed ontology. We will also focus on developing our LIRS according to available information in the ontology. We expect that using the ontology will help the results be more semantically related to the query than other related works.

References

1. Grimm, S., Abecker, A., Völker, J., Studer, R.: Ontologies and the semantic web. In: Domingue, J., Fensel, D., Hendler, J.A. (eds.) Handbook of Semantic Web Technologies, pp. 507–579. Springer, Heidelberg (2011). https://doi.org/10.1007/978-3-540-92913-0_13
2. Cimiano, P., Völker, J., Studer, R.: Ontologies on demand? - A description of the state-of-the-art, applications, challenges and trends for ontology learning from text. Inf. Wissenschaft und Praxis **57**(6–7), 315–320 (2006)

3. Cimiano, P.: Ontology Learning and Population from Text. Algorithms, Evaluation and Applications. Springer, New York (2006). https://doi.org/10.1007/978-0-387-39252-3. ISBN 978-0387-30632-2

4. Biébow, B., Szulman, S., Clément, A.J.B.: TERMINAE: a linguistics-based tool for the building of a domain ontology. In: Fensel, D., Studer, R. (eds.) EKAW 1999. LNCS (LNAI), vol. 1621, pp. 49–66. Springer, Heidelberg (1999). https://doi.org/10.1007/3-540-48775-1_4

5. Cimiano, P., Völker, J.: Text2Onto. In: Montoyo, A., Muñoz, R., Métais, E. (eds.) NLDB 2005. LNCS, vol. 3513, pp. 227–238. Springer, Heidelberg (2005). https://doi.org/10.1007/11428817_21

6. Dell'Orletta, F., Venturi, G., Cimiano, A., Montemagni, S.: T2K^2: a system for automatically extracting and organizing knowledge from texts. In: Proceeding of LREC, pp. 26–31, Iceland (2014)

7. Drumond, L., Girardi, R.: A survey of ontology learning procedures. Proceedings of the 3rd Workshop on Ontologies and their Applications, vol. 427 of CEUR Workshop Proceedings, Salvador, Bahia, Brazil (2008)

8. Wong, W., Liu, W., Bennamoun, M.: Ontology learning from text: a look back and into the future. ACM Comput. Surv. **44**, 1–36 (2011)

9. Benz, D.: Collaborative ontology learning. Master's thesis, University of Freiburg (2007)

10. El Ghosh, M., Naja, H., Abdulrab, H., Khalil, M.: Ontology learning process as a bottom-up strategy for building domain-specific ontology from legal texts. ICAART **2**, 473–480 (2017)

11. Rogger, M., Thaler, S.: Ontology Learning. Seminar paper, Applied Ontology Engineering, Leopold–Franzens–University Innsbruck (2010)

12. McCarty, L., T.: Deep semantic interpretations of legal texts. In: Proceeding of ICAIL, pp. 217–224 (2007)

13. Wong, W.Y.: Learning Lightweight Ontologies from Text across Different Domains using the Web as Background Knowledge. Ph.D. thesis, University of Western Australia, School of Computer Science and Software Engineering (2009)

14. Borigault, D., Jacquemin, C., L'Homme, M.C. (eds.): Recent Advances in Computational Terminology. Natural Language Processing Series, vol. 2, pp. 328–332 John Benjamins Publishing Company, Amsterdam (2001)

15. Frantzi, K., Ananiadou, S.: The C-value/NC-value domain independent method for multiword term extraction. J. Nat. Lang. Process. **6**, 145–179 (1999)

16. Pantel, P., Lin, D.: A statistical corpus-based term extractor. In: Stroulia, E., Matwin, S. (eds.) AI 2001. LNCS (LNAI), vol. 2056, pp. 36–46. Springer, Heidelberg (2001). https://doi.org/10.1007/3-540-45153-6_4

17. Salton, G., Buckley, C.: Term-weighting approaches in automatic text retrieval. Inf. Process. Manag. **24**(5), 515–523 (1988)

18. El Ghosh, M.: Automation of legal reasoning and decision based on ontologies. Ph.D. thesis, Web. Normandie Université (2018)

19. Miller, G., Beckwith, R., Fellbaum, C., Gross, D., Miller, K.: Introduction to WordNet: an on-line lexical database. Int. J. Lexicogr. **3**, 235–244 (1990)

20. Bourigault, D., Jacquemin, C.: Term extraction+ term clustering: an integrated platform for computer-aided terminology. In: Proceedings of the Ninth Conference on European Chapter of the Association for Computational Linguistics, pp. 15–22 (1999)

21. Faure, D., Nédellec, C.: Knowledge acquisition of predicate argument structures from technical texts using machine learning: the system ASIUM. In: Fensel, D., Studer, R. (eds.) EKAW 1999. LNCS (LNAI), vol. 1621, pp. 329–334. Springer, Heidelberg (1999). https://doi.org/10.1007/3-540-48775-1_22

22. Maedche, A., Staab, S.: The text-to-onto ontology learning environment. In: Software Demonstration at ICCS-2000-Eight International Conference on Conceptual Structures, August 2000
23. Drymonas, E., Zervanou, K., Petrakis, E.G.M.: Unsupervised ontology acquisition from plain texts: the OntoGain system. In: Hopfe, C.J., Rezgui, Y., Métais, E., Preece, A., Li, H. (eds.) NLDB 2010. LNCS, vol. 6177, pp. 277–287. Springer, Heidelberg (2010). https://doi.org/10.1007/978-3-642-13881-2_29
24. Buitelaar, P., Cimiano, P., Magnini, B.: Ontology Learning from Text: An Overview, Ontology Learning from Text: Methods, Evaluation and Applications. IOS Press, Amsterdam (2005)
25. Reinberger, M., Spyns, P.: Unsupervised Text Mining for the Learning of DOGMA-inspired Ontologies. Ontology Learning from Text. IOS Press, Amsterdam (2005)
26. Hearst, M.A.: Automatic acquisition of hyponyms from large text corpora. In: Proceedings of the 14th Conference on Computational Linguistics, vol. 2, pp. 539–545, Association for Computational Linguistic (1992)
27. Harris, Z.: Mathematical Structures of Language. Wiley, Hoboken (1968)
28. Sanderson, M., Croft, B.: Deriving concept hierarchies from text. In: Research and Development in Information Retrieval, pp. 206–213 (1999)
29. Maedche A., Staab, S.: Discovering conceptual relations from text. In: Horn, W. (ed.) Proceedings of the 14th European Conference on Artificial Intellignece (ECAI 2000), (2000)
30. Gamallo, P., Gonzalez, M., Agustini, A., Lopes, G., de Lim, V.S.: Mapping syntactic dependencies onto semantic relations. In: ECAI Workshop on Machine Learning and Natural Language Processing for Ontology Engineering (2002)
31. Lin, D., Pantel, P.: DIRT - Discovery of inference rules from text. In: Proceedings of the ACM SIGKDD Conference on Knowledge Discovery and Data Mining, pp. 323–328 (2001)
32. Lin, D., Pantel, P.: Induction of Semantic Classes from Natural Language Text. In: Proceedings of ACM SIGKDD Conference on Knowledge Discovery and Data Mining, pp. 317–322 (2001)
33. Aussenac-Gilles, N., Biébow, B., Szulman, S.: Revisiting ontology design: a method based on corpus analysis. In: Dieng, R., Corby, O. (eds.) EKAW 2000. LNCS (LNAI), vol. 1937, pp. 172–188. Springer, Heidelberg (2000). https://doi.org/10.1007/3-540-39967-4_13
34. Sabou, M.: Visual support for ontology learning: an experience report. In: Proceeding of IV 2005, London (2005)
35. Mazari, C., Aliane, H., Alimazighi, Z.: Automatic construction of ontology from Arabic texts. In: Proceeding of ICWIT, pp. 193–202 (2012)
36. Lenci, A., Montemagni, S., Pirrelli, V., Venturi, G.: Ontology learning from Italian legal texts. In: Breuker, J., et al. (eds.) Law, Ontologies and the Semantic Web – Channelling the Legal Information Flood, Frontiers in Artificial Intelligence and Applications, vol. 188, pp. 75–94. Springer
37. Francesconi, E., Montemagni, S., Peters, W., Tiscornia, D.: Integrating a bottom–up and top–down methodology for building semantic resources for the multilingual legal domain. In: Francesconi, E., Montemagni, S., Peters, W., Tiscornia, D. (eds.) Semantic Processing of Legal Texts. LNCS (LNAI), vol. 6036, pp. 95–121. Springer, Heidelberg (2010). https://doi.org/10.1007/978-3-642-12837-0_6
38. Gharib, T.F., Habib, M.B., Fayed, Z.T.: Arabic text classification using support vector machines. Int. J. Comput. Appl. 16(4), 192–199 (2009)
39. Silberztein, M.: Formalizing Natural Languages: The NooJ Approach. Wiley, Hoboken (2016)
40. ADALA Morocco legal and judicial Portal. https://adala.justice.gov.ma/FR/Home.aspx. Accessed 12 Sept 2020

41. Mesfar, S.: Named entity recognition for Arabic using syntactic grammars. In: Kedad, Z., Lammari, N., Métais, E., Meziane, F., Rezgui, Y. (eds.) NLDB 2007. LNCS, vol. 4592, pp. 305–316. Springer, Heidelberg (2007). https://doi.org/10.1007/978-3-540-73351-5_27
42. Black, W.: Introducing the Arabic WordNet project. In: Sojka, Choi, Fellbaum, Vossen (eds.) Proceedings of the third International WordNet Conference (2006)
43. JAWS. https://github.com/jaytaylor/jaws. Accessed 12 Sept 2020

Author Index

Printed in the United States
By Bookmasters